ARTS OF BEING YORÙBÁ

GW01018365

To Sarah

Merry Christmas and happy new year
I hope you enjoy reading this book
love from
Beatrice

AFRICAN EXPRESSIVE CULTURES

Patrick McNaughton, editor

Associate editors
Catherine M. Cole
Barbara G. Hoffman
Eileen Julien
Kassim Koné
D. A. Masolo
Elisha Renne
Z. S. Strother

ARTS OF
BEING YORÙBÁ

Divination, Allegory, Tragedy,

Proverb, Panegyric

Adélékè Adéẹ̀kọ́

Indiana University Press

Bloomington and Indianapolis

This book is a publication of

Indiana University Press
Office of Scholarly Publishing
Herman B Wells Library 350
1320 East 10th Street
Bloomington, Indiana 47405 USA

iupress.indiana.edu

© 2017 by Adélékè Adéèkó

All rights reserved

No part of this book may be reproduced or utilized in any form or
by any means, electronic or mechanical, including photocopying
and recording, or by any information storage and retrieval system,
without permission in writing from the publisher. The Association
of American University Presses' Resolution on Permissions constitutes the only exception to this prohibition.

The paper used in this publication meets the minimum
requirements of the American National Standard for Information
Sciences—Permanence of Paper for Printed Library Materials,
ANSI Z39.48-1992.

Manufactured in the United States of America

Cataloging information is available from the Library of Congress.

1 2 3 4 5 22 21 20 19 18 17

for

Táíwò Francisca Abísóyè Ògúnkọ̀yà Adéẹ̀kọ́
Catholic, Ìbàdàn, Ìjẹ̀bú, Nigerian, American;
An Eminently Practical Yorùbá

Contents

Acknowledgments

I WAS INTRODUCED to Kúnlé Ajíbádé—executive editor of *The News* (Lagos) and, now, collaborator and very good friend—when Tẹjú Ọláníyan intervened on my behalf as I sought contacts in Lagos for leads on the sections of the book that deal with the praise magazine (see chapter 6) and book launch (see the Conclusion). That contact and subsequent friendship introduced me to Bùnmi Ajíbádé and also gave me the chance to meet Kúnlé Bákàrè and Délé Mọmọdù, owners and editors of the *Encomium* and *Ovation* stable of publications, who both granted me interviews and gave me access to back issues of their magazines. Michael Effiong, editor of one of Mọmọdù's publications, responded generously to my e-mail enquiries. The highly esteemed Mọlará Ògúndípẹ̀ took me around in her car in Accra, Ghana, looking for Délé Mọmọdù in August 2008. Before I went to Ghana, Ato Quayson and Kwasi Ampene instructed me about how to navigate Accra. Sam Omatseye, a longtime friend, acclaimed columnist, and editorial director at Nigeria's *Nation*, constantly updated me regarding book-launching ceremonies in and around Lagos in 2012. Reuben Abati, then editorial page editor at the *Guardian*, rendered similar help in 2008.

Members of the Adéẹ̀kọ́ family in Lagos and Ìjẹbú-Imuṣin made my trips to Nigeria easier and far less costly. I must thank my brother Ṣèsan, my sister-in-law Bọ́sẹ̀, and my nieces Tárá, Tèmiladé, and Títí, for housing and feeding me, and for never making me think for a second that I might have overstayed my welcome in their home. Two of my other brothers, Rẹ̀mí and Kúnlé, drove me around on different occasions, sometimes as far as Ilé-Ifẹ̀. Kíkẹ́ and Mosún, my other sisters-in-law, were unfailingly hospitable. At Imuṣin, my brother Sunday and my sister-in-law Ṣọlá, and my cousin Gbayì Adébánjọ and his wife Yẹmí, pointed me in many useful directions and, along with Kẹ́hìndé Àtúnwá and Mrs. J. A. Ògúnkòyá (my mother-in-law), took extraordinary measures to protect me. I once had to drag Ọpẹ́, my nephew, from his campus dormitory to the newspaper archives at the Hezekiah Oluwasanmi Library in Ifẹ̀ for two days. At Ifẹ̀, a few calls made by my cousin and immediate past Dean of Engineering, Kẹ́hìndé Táíwò, were a trip saver. What of Ṣeun and Buki Anífowóṣe! Unfortunately, Ṣeun passed away in February 2015 and will not read this book. Apart from other unforgettable graces, I remember Ṣeun instructing his driver to get me, safely and on time, notwithstanding the chaotic Lagos roads, to a book launching. In taking this dear nephew of mine at the time it did, death has been very, very unkind to my family.

Many colleagues helped me along. Miriam Conteh-Morgan gave consistently valuable interlibrary loan information when she was the Africana Librarian at Ohio State University. Ohio State's Center for African Studies, then directed by Kelechi Kalu, gave me the opportunity to test some of the ideas in the Introduction when I was invited to give the first Owomoyela Lecture on Yorùbá Studies, sponsored by Yoruba Club 21 of Columbus, Ohio. The appearance of Yoruba Club 21 members at the lecture decked fully in white agbádá in solidarity with me, the lecturer who is also one of their own, gave a practical demonstration of one way of being Yorùbá. (Till today, Yoruba Club 21 members grace the Owomoyela Lecture in white attire. In a case of absolute coincidence, the guest speaker in 2015, Lorand J. Matory of Duke University, and professor in the history and anthropology of gender transformations in Ọ̀yọ́ spheres of influence, wore a full white agbádá suit for his talk.)

Other forums at which I have shared ideas in the book include the Sawyer Seminar at the University of Michigan and the Baraza Lecture Series at the University of Florida, for which I thank Túndé and Ìkẹ́ Akínyẹmí, and Hunt Davis Jr. for the pleasure of returning to Gainesville after twenty-one years. Niyi Okunoye invited me to address the Ifẹ̀ Humanities Group at Obafemi Awolowo University. The Ifẹ̀ visit, a homecoming of sorts, enabled me to reconnect with Moji Fabusuyi. I have to thank Tẹjú Ọláníyan—again—for inviting me twice to participate in the African Studies Lecture series at the University of Wisconsin, Madison. Mojí Ọláníyan welcomed me generously both times. The book would probably have ended with another publisher were it not for Tẹjú's intervention and calm counsel. Jacob Olúpọ̀nà invited me to give a paper at the conference he hosted on Ifá discourses in 2008 at Harvard University. Fẹ́mi Táíwò, Kúnlé George, Anthonia Kalu, Kwaku Korang, Táyọ̀ Àlàbí, Túnjí Ọ̀ṣínúbi, Rowland Abíọ́dún, Níyì Afọlábí, Rónkẹ́ Òyéwùmí, Bíọ́dún Jeyifo, and Akin Adéṣọ̀kàn responded to parts of this book, either formally in writing or informally during conversations. I hope Mallam Táíwò would be satisfied with what his philosopher's unstinting criticism has done to my understanding of *ìwà* (being). Tóyìn Fálọlá introduced me to Jídé Owóèyẹ, chair of the Governing Council of Lead City University, Ibadan, who gave me free room and board at the second TOFAC conference, hosted on his campus in 2013. Adémọ́lá DaSylva, Túndé Babáwálé, and Doyin Aguoru welcomed me with open arms at the TOFAC conference held in Lagos in 2012. I cannot forget Akin Àlàó for sending me a pristine copy of Adébóyè Babalọlá's *Àwọn Oríkì Bọ̀rọ̀kìnní* after he read my plea that this book is not listed in any online library catalog in the United States. I reserve my deepest gratitude for one of a rare breed of artist-scholars, Moyọ̀ Òkédìjí, Professor of Art and Art History at the University of Texas, Austin, whose work, given free of charge, adorns the front cover of this book. John-Michael Rivera, Frederick Luis Aldama, Cheryl Higashida, Dan Kim, and the late Vincent

Woodard gave me collegial support in the early days of the project when we were all teaching at the English Department of the University of Colorado, Boulder.

It is certain that my folks in Cincinnati, Chicago, and Columbus, Táyé, Bólájí, Diméjì, and Táyọ̀, are tired of my unsolicited musings about the ungraspable ways of being Yorúbá, thoughts that I usually interject into discussions of apparently unrelated conversations with "as they say in Ìjẹ̀bú" or "as they do in Ọ̀yọ́." This is to thank them for being my ideal audience. They all saw through, and still accommodated, the poorly disguised disalienation ambition that is condensed in my formulaic phrasing and, perhaps, this book project.

Parts of chapter 1 and a section of chapter 6 have appeared in *Oral Tradition* 25, no. 2 (2010) and *Critical Inquiry* 38, no. 2 (2012). I thank the editors and the anonymous reviewers who evaluated the articles. For including an earlier version of chapter 2 in *Yoruba Fiction, Orature, and Culture: Oyekan Owomoyela and African Literature and the Yoruba Experience* (2011), I thank Toyin Falola and Adebayo Oyebade. The publishers of *Ovation* magazine kindly granted permission to reproduce in this book—and earlier in *Critical Inquiry*—pictures originally printed in the magazine.

Introduction

In this book, I conceive of culturally significant ideas, objects, and motions in two ways. The first concerns the gestures that people who self-identify as Yorùbá construe and circulate to articulate their proclamations to others, both in ordinary circumstances and at critical life passages such as birth, death, and marriage. The second principle of cultural being that I deploy requires that those who identify as non-Yorùbá concede as intelligible, tacitly or implicitly through various means of reciprocation and participation, those gestures that the Yorùbá present as theirs. In the grounding assumptions of this book, two individuals can be acting as Yorùbá while haggling over the price of a packet of spaghetti in English language at a market in Ilé-Ifẹ̀, Nigeria, every time a bargain seeker, even if non-Yorùbá, appeals to the seller with the name of the Yorùbá divinity of commerce, saying "ajé," and the Yorùbá seller tries to maintain her price position by pleading, even in English, "You are my first customer today" to convince the buyer into believing that he or she is the embodiment of his or her good fortune for the day. In the interpretation presented here, the non-Yorùbá person who says "ajé" to the seller acknowledges as Yorùbá the intelligence of those who use the word to call down the spirit of trade to adjudicate benevolently in a commercial interchange. The self-avowed Yorùbá seller who quotes, albeit in English, the Yorùbá verbal formula regarding good fortune and timeliness presumes his or her customer's acquiescence to the logic. As lived today, being Yorùbá entails administering several registers of mutual recognition and exchange at different degrees of self-awareness.

I assume that the type of clothing worn, the manner of greetings exchanged, and the sense of order considered acceptable can make a person Yorùbá while holidaying in Dubai, or getting married in Tbilisi, or celebrating a daughter's first Holy Communion in Broomfield, Colorado. Even if the implicit meaning of the trappings of appearing as Yorùbá in these circumstances is not obvious to the immediate sociopolitical environment, that the individuals are left alone to indulge in them validates the projected desire to be so construed. When a non-Yorùbá appears at a Yorùbá wedding engagement in a manner that indicates the individual concerned is making an effort to be like those who call themselves Yorùbá—say, a fellow looking anxious in flowing agbádá or a woman whose body language suggests awkwardness while wearing a skirt made of Swiss lace in the middle of winter in Dublin, Ireland, or at the peak of harmattan in Maiduguri—the obvious act of reciprocation acknowledges the cultural certitudes that the outfit represents for those who claim it as theirs. The momentary appearances of the non-Yorùbá at these occasions endorse Yorùbá self-understanding. As in the expressions analyzed in the chapters that follow, the hypothetical illustrations given above stage cultural self-constitution as circulating as, in, and with the repeatable material gestures and intangible forms and styles that members of a self-identifying cultural community depend on to broker recognition.

Some of the being-Yorùbá practices that I discuss in this book are very old; others are very new. Among the largely inherited practices are naming traditions, physical gestures that accompany verbal greeting utterances, divination counseling, and praise poetry. The book launch, like the celebrity magazine, is an emergent institution. In contemporary Yorùbá societies, naming ceremonies are more likely to be supervised by imams and pastors rather than by the oldest blood relative present at the occasion; even outside the urban communities, skilled praise poets will not be found in many of the typical locations at which modern Yorùbá people congregate. In this book, I argue that being Yorùbá entails embedding elements of the old (or things presented as such), many times imperceptibly, in motions and gestures mostly of recent, diverse provenance, fit for addressing the present. Unlike other books about Yorùbá culture, territoriality is not the organizing principle here. Hence there is no discussion of where Yorùbá people live, be it in the homeland or in the diaspora. For this book, everywhere is Yorùbá-land; "Ilẹ̀ gbogbo ntòrìṣà" (All the earth belongs to òrìṣà), Hubert Ogunde once sang passionately. Denoting, as late as the end of the twentieth century, some areas on the map as Yorùbá-land contradicts the fluid and acutely self-aware cultural reality of the people such demarcations seek to characterize and restrict. To risk a little exaggeration for the purposes of making a point, there is no land on earth where some people, no matter how few in number, do not strive to be Yorùbá. This book is also not devoted to what Yorùbá people living within the areas scholars characterize as Yorùbá-land do differently. No cultural rule precludes the self-consciously non-Yorùbá living in Ìjẹ̀bu-Òde, Òǹdó, Sabe, Ìbàdàn, or even Lagos, to seek divination counsel and enjoy performances of praise songs.

Positivists might ask what exactly is Yorùbá about this notion of cultural self-conception and self-presentation. The texts and artifacts that I analyze as Yorùbá in this book qualify to be so characterized because they serve, through articulation, the worldly being of groups of individuals that identify as Yorùbá and which others, through participation, allow them to portray as such. By implication, the makers and consumers of the texts that I analyze realize the plastic character of the cultural affirmations they manifest. (D. O. Fágúnwà's novels, for example, have been assimilated through translations into Francophone and Anglophone cultural spheres just as the novels themselves assimilated influences from many other traditions.) By following internal textual leads, *Arts of Being*

Yorùbá characterizes cultural being as art; that is, as instituted selections and combinations held together strategically to facilitate pleasing worldly intercourse within and among self-identifying social formations. Within the system of understanding I follow in this book, whatever practices are favored as culturally conforming (àṣà) by a people can be shared with others and are constituted with items taken from many sources. Ifá divination practice is retailed in Chicago and Miami by ordinarily non-Yorùbá people. Christianity and Islam are now the majority beliefs in regions of Nigeria that physical and cultural geographers conventionally depict as Yorùbá. In this book, self-identifying individuals are Yorùbá in whichever ways allow them to achieve their aspirations in the manners they find most amenable to the particular conditions they find themselves. Except in monotheistic communities—and even there things are not straightforward—cultural fundamentalism and unanimism have no great chance of survival within Yorùbá notions of being. It should also be clarified that in this book no entity is completely Yorùbá at all times. The caveats summarized in this paragraph are meant to mark the differences between this book's intent and the sensibility inherent to those— for example, A. B. Ellis's *The Yoruba-Speaking Peoples of the Slave Coast of West Africa*, J. S. Eades's *The Yoruba Today*, and even Margaret Drewal's *Yorùbá Ritual*, despite the nuanced attention it gives to textuation and diversity of processes—that seek to account for the discrete terms and features that define the Yorùbá as essentially Yorùbá. This book refers to those elements of social organization traditionally thought of as distinct features of culture as inscriptions: Ifá divination, oríkì praise poetry, proverbial wisdom, and ìtàn olówe allegorical stories. Going beyond standard accounts of cultural being, this book argues that it is in the ever-changing expressions of desires, or commentary making, that constitute historical life that durable inscriptions and iterable forms assume cultural significance. This is where written divination signs exist as practical, negotiated instructions for the counseled, where oríkì infiltrates photography in celebrity publications and book-launching spectacles, where inventoried proverbs merge with speech pragmatics, and where allegorical novels and tragic drama institute gender inequities.

Thus in this book I analyze the complex entanglements of some of the many ways Yorùbá cultural forms are always in flux, shape shifting across media. In chapter 1, " 'Writing' and 'Reference' in Ifá Divination Chants," I analyze the foundational function of inscriptions in Ifá, the most privileged of Yorùbá divination practices. Whether the diviner uses palm nuts (ikin) or the chain (ọ̀pẹ̀lẹ̀), producing a readable autograph is the goal of the initial step in Ifá divination. In either method the priest must first identify which one of the 256 units of Ifá graphemes (odù ifá) has appeared on the divination tray. The unit presented by the cast nuts or chain clues the diviner as to which stories to tell to illustrate the problems revealed by the divination God and to decipher what ritual sacrifices or behavioral changes to prescribe. The casting, imprinting, and narrating processes typically start after the client has whispered his or her purpose into some tokens mixed up with the divination objects. The sign revealed and the illustrative stories told must bear some allegorical semblance to the problems the client wants to solve.

To the ordinary observer, the link between palm nut manipulation (or chain casting) and readable, visible imprints is thoroughly occultic. In chapter 1, I argue that the credit for Ifá's decoding the client's mind, and its canonical status among divination practices, goes largely to the discourse's association of consistently named, visibly embodied signs with prognostic narrations. Diviners gain respect and command attention because they operate as disinterested agents of a knowledge disclosure apparatus anchored by an inscription sign system whose production is outwardly indifferent to the "writer's" time- and space-bound will. The notation system, in theory and in perception, removes the individual priest's influence and will from the intercourse between the client and the witness to creation, the divination God himself, who inspirits its knowledge in the presentation of the material divination instrument. The notation system, not the human diviner, arbitrates the most important steps in discovery and disclosure. The stable inscription system frees diviners to incorporate any and all historical developments into Ifá narratives and thereby expand infinitely the capacity of divination clients to remain Yorùbá, even as their conditions change in all material respects.

In chapter 2, "Culture, Meaning, Proverbs (For Oyekan Owomoyela, in Memoriam)," I address the pragmatics of proverb usage. According to Oyekan Owomoyela, the proverb is "a speech form that likens, or compares, one thing or situation to another, highlighting the essential similarities that the two share. In Yorùbá usage it is always at least one *complete* sentence" (*Yorùbá Proverbs*, 3). In response to the heavy emphasis on difference—and its entailments—in Yorùbá terms for text and meaning, Owomoyela represents the proverb as a tool for synthesizing meaningful deictics out of temporally unconnected concepts and ideas. In Yorùbá, the proverb (òwe), comparison or simile (àfiwé), riddle (àló), narrative (ìtàn), and interpretation or translation (ìtúmò) all imply folding, entwinement, unwrapping, or unfolding. Placed within this terminological relay, it is assumed that the proverb user quotes from a linguistically and culturally delimited body of anonymously authored texts to make both evaluative and argumentative judgments about a topic without having to start from scratch. Thus, on the one hand, proverbs represent material preservations of vetted meanings that live on in conspicuous language; they persist through mature speakers who hand them down from generation to generation and perpetuate traces of each tradition's cultural consensus. From this point of view, the proverb is a willing agent of culture, thought, and tradition. On the other hand, proverbs survive only in the contingent, fleeting—I hesitate to say flippant—moments of recall and usage; that is, they subject traditional thought and culture to contextual wiles. Within this perspective, the proverb resembles the messenger that cannot not choose its message. Comprehending the proverb without assessing the value of its cultural rootedness sounds unthinkable; neglecting the untethered "face value" of its terms, prevarications and all, is no less grim. The proverb's typically prominent mechanics of tangibility, including compelling imageries and arresting logic, valorizes appearance. Under usage conventions, however, the facade has to be peeled back (if not peeled off) to reveal the layers of meaning behind it. The extensive analysis of Yorùbá metaproverbs I undertake in chapter 5 reveals that proverbs work because they enable their users to cross continuity to contingency productively.

In the next two chapters, I focus on the cultural embodiment functions of writing processes in the works of D. O. Fágúnwà, the dean of modern Yorùbá fiction. In chapter 3, "Reading, Writing, and Epistemic Instability in Fágúnwà's Novels," I argue that moments of uncertain reading and writing in Fágúnwà's novels allegorize the intellectual instabilities that preoccupied the most advanced sectors of a Yorùbá society trying to reconcile itself with changes it has come to view as inexorable. The chapter presents the crucial seeds of generating stories in Fágúnwà's adventure tales—an older man afraid of being lost to history narrates biographical stories to a younger male editor who is co-opted into creating a project to preserve the memory of a time when rulers of city-states seeking development and peace risked the lives of highly accomplished men such as the older narrator by sending them on rewarding discovery trips to strange lands—as reflections on significant disruptions in the construction of normative means and manners of relating to the world in the novelist's environment. The textual exchanges between representatives of the society's gradually expiring present and its unfolding future that start Fágúnwà's novels, I argue, speak to epistemic instabilities in a changing world that is not yet quite fully understood, but to whose inevitability the community has reconciled itself. The knowledge-seeking brotherhoods, among whom the main storyteller in each adventure is a leader, allegorizes the advance guard of an emergent cohort that is not yet well positioned to take over the society but threatens, nonetheless, the prevailing order. Fágúnwà's novels consist of the stylized, self-revealing, and self-justifying stories that these men, who resemble no traditional tricksters or avatars of any known legendary figures, and whose progeny is not deeper than three generations, like to present as evidence of their entitlement to prominent leadership despite their odd social and cultural positions. The societies that these men aim to lead share few common myths, have no common pantheon, neither polytheism nor monotheism holds steady there, and their theological bearing is eclectic. In chapter 3, I describe the novels' depiction of shifts in cultural self-awareness by analyzing, first, the terms of the exchanges between the self-conscious and self-appointed representatives of the passing generation and their younger amanuenses. I follow this by discussing how Fágúnwà's understanding of the basis of modernized cultural enlightenment (ọ̀làjú) shapes the dominant internal movement of characters and plotting in the novels.

In chapter 4, "Sex, Gender, and Plot in Fágúnwà's Adventures," I shift attention to the most prominent narrative mechanisms of managing gender dynamics in the novels. From Àkàrà-ògùn to Àdììtú, love drives all the leading men in Fágúnwà's five novels. They put themselves in harm's way for the love of their homelands. They travel from one end of the earth to another to share their love of storytelling with young writers. Their love for fellow adventurers knows no bounds. Among the cardinal lessons they learn during their life-sustaining and storytelling journeys, none surpasses their repeatedly professed discovery of the supreme advantages of monogamous, heterosexual love. In this chapter, I go beyond the men's manifest proclamations on love to examine the reasons why those beloved (and the not so beloved) female partners of the storytelling male adventurers do not accompany them on the journeys of self discovery and community improvement that structure each novel. I analyze how critical changes in the many heroic, self-direction plots that define Fágúnwà's fiction typically occur at the expense of women. I argue that the central adventures that drive narrative progression in the forest tales pursue a male-pattern view of the world that is not fully supported by other story elements. The character focalization strategy that tightly restricts reading to an overwhelmingly male-determined ethics of gender relationships effectively conceals and naturalizes ongoing fluctuations in how to be men and women.

My main claim in chapter 5, "Akínwùmí Ìsọ̀lá's *Efúnsetán Aníwúrà* and Yorùbá Woman-Being," is that discourses of gender practices in Yorùbá life and culture are yet to consider fully how translations of categories from the language of discovery, particularly English, shape current intellectual classifications and explanations of observed social phenomena. My primary evidence will be the many ways in which known facts about the life of Ìyálóde Ẹfúnsetán Aníwúrà (ca. 1825–1874), a high-ranking female chief in nineteenth-century Ìbàdàn, are deployed in accounts of the evolution of woman-being in southwestern Nigeria. I focus on the linguistic, cultural, and philosophical ramifications of the depiction of gender matters in Akínwùmí Ìsọ̀lá's Yorùbá play, *Ẹfúnsetán Aníwúrà: Ìyálóde Ìbàdàn*, its two English translations, and its most recent film adaptation. The attention this series of texts has attracted from literary critics and feminist historians is so deeply enmeshed in gender terminologies that an ideal, "human," "Yorùbá" portrayal of Ẹfúnsetán Aníwúrà is impossible today. Issues highlighted in Ìsọ̀lá's translations of *Ẹfúnsetán Aníwúrà* raise historical and sociological questions whose significance impacts far beyond the scanty biographical certainties about her. Besides the difficulties of rendering bits of texts in one language in another, translation problems addressed in the chapter include textual considerations that affect the intermedial translations that Ìṣọ́lá must have faced while scripting the original play from sources in oral traditions and from written, typically Christian, nationalist histories. I also examine the unavoidable problems of translating the historical significance of events across different time periods, regardless of language and medium. Contrary to nationalist imaginations of cultural seamlessness, mid-nineteenth-century Ìbàdàn, a then imperial city-state, was not exactly like Ìbàdàn in 1966, when Ìṣọ́lá first wrote the play. Within the century-long historical span, the city-state lost its independence after it was subdued late in the nineteenth century by the British and regained in 1960 a different kind of independence as a regional capital within Nigeria, a country created by the colonizers. The intervening years also brought vast changes that irreversibly reconfigured the social, political, and economic life of Ìbàdàn such that rendering a pristine account of Ẹfúnṣetán Aníwúrà's life is nearly impossible. Even if the facts are somehow magically recovered, I conclude, our inescapable use of technologies of representation that Ẹfúnṣetán never had the advantage of using to shape her life will intervene decisively in the form that the resultant product will take. The gender components of Ẹfúnṣetán Aníwúrà's self-conception in extant historiographic, theatrical texts could not in any shape be pristinely Yorùbá as they are often represented.

In chapter 6, "Photography and the Panegyric in Contemporary Yorùbá Culture," I turn to an unmistakably contemporary institution, the celebrity magazine culture, specifically those devoted almost exclusively to publishing flattering pictures to depict signs of eminence. My central contentions in this chapter are that the southwestern Nigerian magazine audience has embraced this journalistic genre because it translates into photography the panegyric tendency that pervades popular, self-projection arts in the Yorùbá cultural environment of southwestern Nigeria and that the subgenre of Yorùbá panegyric transformed in the magazine is oríkì bọ̀rọ̀kìnní (chants in praise of the eminent).

Arts of Being Yorùbá tests the limits of the analytical possibility outlined in Olabiyi Yai's "In Praise of Metonymy." Working from Yorùbá metadiscursive terms regarding culture and aesthetics, Yai noticed that the freedom to separate, branch off, differ, and, when necessary, reassemble, dominates references to creativity. In the arts, he observes that there "is an invitation to infinite metonymy, difference, and departure" (35). At the level of culture generally, the ability to select (ṣà; ya; yà) and recombine preferences into new formations (àṣà; ẹya; ẹ̀yà) dominate terms of reference. Yai argues that "That which has not been the result of deliberate choice (ṣà) based on discernment and awareness of historical practices and processes (ìtàn) by individual or collective orí cannot qualify as àṣà [tradition or culture]. And since choice presides over the birth of an àṣà (tradition), the latter is permanently liable to metamorphosis" (35). Working with Helen Verran's findings about the cognition of numbers among schoolchildren in southwestern Nigeria and Australia, Andrew Apter, in a discussion aimed at settling debates about conceptions of descent in self-consciously Yorùbá communities, reached a conclusion similar to Yai's: "The child is not 'born into' a house or lineage, but is born out of it, coming to manifest the lineage through the ritual mode of naming itself, as in the proverb: 'Ilé ni à ń wò k'á tó s'ọmọ l'orúkọ' ('It is to the house that we look before we name the child')" ("Yoruba Ethnogenesis," 364). Unlike Apter, however, the delineations of selected late twentieth and early twenty-first-century systems of selections and combinations that are termed Yorùbá in this book are not arranged around a geographical center against which their authenticity or well-formedness could be accurately discerned. In divination practices, Ifá priests select and combine elements of their ostensibly narrative illustrations from many sources. In Fágúnwà's forest adventures only those culture leaders who select life paths with great discernment return home with vastly expanded knowledge of being in the world. At the end of their journeys, they pluck from stories they hear from wizened sages nuggets of wisdom they then urge their localities of departure to deploy for social advancement. In photographic and other panegyric practices I analyze, the most useful self-presentation strategies are those crafted on the basis of a history of relational entanglements. In this book, trajectories of cultural being are not dissimilar to those of artistic being or, in Karin Barber's terms, textuation ("Quotation"). Motions, gestures, objects, practices, and ideas selected and combined to embody traditions spread in genre, media, and forms that become cultural when they are institutionalized. My arguments about being Yorùbá in this book turn around principles derivable from processes and uses of inscriptions, mediating practices "constituted to have object-like properties, that is, to attain a certain solidity, a susceptibility to comment, and a partial detachment from the immediate context of utterance" (Barber, "Quotation," 18). *Arts of Being Yorùbá* speaks of cultural inscriptions in the extended sense of media and modes that are tangible, are bound by convention, and broker desire, including spoken forms, written texts, and photography.

When a highly educated Yorùbá-Russian bilingual person draws the attention of her colleagues to the egúngún (ancestral masque) beauty of the speaker of the formal regalia of the Speaker of the British House of Commons, that person, in the analytical path followed here, affirms the centrality of institutionalized, material constructions to cultural identification. Denoting the official outfit of the head of the British parliament as egúngún establishes difference and similarity simultaneously, worlding the egúngún cult and sacralizing the British parliament as a grove (ìgbàlè), although the two institutions serve different functions. In order that we do not mistake the association of egúngún and official outfits in the British parliament as an intercultural awareness that is possible only after intercontinental travels, we may consider the popular Yorùbá saying that insists that Fátìmá (a name borne by female Muslims) belongs to the family of Ifá divination signs, "Lára Ifá ni Fátìmá wà." The saying caused me some consternation when I was a choirboy in my Yorùbá hometown, because its logic sounded patently incoherent: Ifá and Fátìmà belong to different belief systems, one monotheistic, the other not; one is the gender-neutral name of a prognostication system, the other a woman's name in Islam. The analytical line that I follow in this book views the equation of the phoneme "fá" in *Fátìmá* and I*fá* to be a revealing indication of the core role of the fungible material sign, here a phonetic and phonological construct, in cultural being. The combination of letters and sound that turns "fá" (literally, "to scrape up") into a "puncept"—a thought held together by "similar signifiers rather than similar signifieds" (Ulmer, "The Puncept in Grammatology," 164)—and will ordinarily be called a verbal play draws attention, in effect, to the material component of cultural conception, although fundamentalists of either Ifá or Islam may repudiate it as unfunny and illogical. This saying, which reveres neither Ifá nor Islam, unabashedly valorizes the transformative influence that one material sign can exercise over the substantive entanglements of other material signs. Ifá relates to Fátìmà (and vice versa) only under the auspices of the spoken sound and the written letter and not from within the theological apparatus of either belief and worship system.[1] Ifá and Fátìmà are both Yorùbá because each system of relating the world seeks to "scrape up" (fá) and fit into one explanatory apparatus every element of life. As will be seen in the opening section of chapter 1, a similar tendency regarding the privileged position of the durable material in processes of Yorùbá divinatory prognosis is evident in the words that Bishop Phillips wrote about the relationship of divination narratives and biblical scriptures in his preface to the pioneering Ifá studies that Rev. E. M. Lijadu conducted at the end of the nineteenth century. The contents of the stories are not of great importance to the bishop; indeed, he considered them to be powerful mind-control weapons operated by a harmful guild against which Christian teachers must protect the unaware population. Yet Bishop Phillips mandated literate Christian missionaries to approach the study of Ifá oral narratives as they would the study of written books because the narratives constitute material forms amenable to recoding while serving as cultural self-assurance to Yorùbá converts.

Other canonical Yorùbá expressions reinforce the priority of fungible material forms and structures in cultural self-presentations. One common proverbial lore proclaims that the leaf used to wrap the soap will later itself be indistinguishable from its contents (Béwé bá pẹ́ lára ọṣẹ yóó dọṣẹ). While we know that in reality it is the soap's chemistry that transforms the organic leaf, the reference point of this saying is not just the chemistry of carbon-based matter but the predisposition, perhaps necessity, of one substance to turn, over time, into (and toward) an originally other, foreign substance with which it interacts. As the softened leaf is mashed with the soap during daily use, praise singing, we will see in this book, leaks in analogical fashions into praise photography, the contemporary academic festschrift in southwestern Nigeria absorbs the essence of praise poetry, and the novel assimilates the allegorical folktale. Another idiomatic expression about the tenacity of material signification came my way in the verbal response that Professor Rowland Abíọ́dún, a notable historian and theoretician of Yorùbá plastic arts, gave to a presentation I made at the 2004 African Studies Association conference in New Orleans. He said that the word (ọ̀rọ̀), spoken or written, is described in some Yorùbá speech and cultural communities as the entity that consumes red palm oil and is not soiled by it: "ajepo-má-pọ̀n-ọ́n" (that-which-eats-palm-oil-and-does-not-turn-red). In this book's understanding of Abíọ́dún, language is not a thief of substantive contents. Rather, speech (ọ̀rọ̀) performs its instituted tasks without concern for the nature of the substance to which it refers. Unlike the soap and leaf transmutation discussed above regarding the time-modulated mutability of signifying substances, the latter saying privileges synchrony; that is, the word, even in the face of time-bound constraints, names (consumes) things without deferring to the contents they sustain. A cheeky, contemporary observation, "'Dì Ẹ̀ndì' lòpin sinimá" ("The End" is the end of a cinema show), reiterates how material inscriptions establish boundaries and limits, independent of organic relations. The thought condensed here is that the conventional inscription, "The End" ("Dì Ẹ̀ndì") distinguishes the projection duration of a film show from the story's narrative closure.

The materialist imagination of the Yorùbá saying that insists that behind the ancestral masque is a living person ("Ènìyàn ló ńbẹ nínú egúngún") does not simply demystify the ancestral egúngún cult; it affirms the masque's subsistence on the masking conventions that constitute it, among which living human machinations (ènìyàn) are a critical component. It requires no Jacques Derrida—although he could be very helpful—to assert that this verbal quip embeds the specter's appearance in the spectacle of its masque; the departed ancestor cannot appear as itself, since it has ceased to be human, except through the masque worn and instituted by, in, and as sociocultural traditions; the "real" subject of representation in the multimodal, eclectic resources of the egúngún (the masque) simply cannot be found as itself. Revelers knowingly hail the masque as the ancestor because that is the object the society has instituted for direct apprehension. The saying, it ought to be noted, is probably a mocking jab at the other worldly essence that the egúngún secret cult is reputed to control—just as the Fátìmá saying might have been an Ifá partisan's indictment of agbigba, a competing divination system inspired by Islam. That motive does not vitiate the relevance of the observation being made here about the centrality of material, external, humanoid, artifacts to cultural recognition.

We can shift sideways from oral, popular phrases about material inscriptions and embodiments of culture to written texts and ordinary social practices. In *Àdììtú Olódùmarè*, the last novel published by D. O. Fágúnwà, one of the egúngún maskers hired by Iyùnadé to entertain guests at a birthday party for Àdììtú, her unrequited lover, was being fed palm wine through his visor when asked "'Ará ọrun kìnkin, ẹ ńmu ẹmu lọrun dan?'" (Ancestral one, so you guys drink palm-wine in the other world?), and the masquerade answered in plain Yorùbá that they do: "'A ńmu ú dáadáa'" (We jolly well do). This exchange literalizes the metacritical proverb that says inside the ancestral mask dwells a living human. But things quickly become less certain when the inquisitive guest probes further, "'Ṣé àńjọnnú ní ńdá ẹmu fún yín?'" (Do genies procure the wine for you?) This time, the human inside the mask rejects the implication that the costume has transfigured him into an ancestor and curses at his interlocutor: "'Àńjọnnú ni yóò dá ẹmu fún orí rẹ mu'" (It is for you that a genie will fetch palm-wine) (75). Without denying the other worldly affiliations of the egúngún, that the individual carrying the mask is not an ancestor is more than a whispered topic in this exchange. The conversation illustrates how irritating, laughable, and childish it is to seek to reach for the literal referent of what the egúngún mask makes present. The tenor of this exchange provides more evidence that the instituted masks and the contentious significations that follow them constitute the only certainty in lived culture, even in canonical, sacralized discourses. Those masks and the contentions around them are the bearers of cultural being.

One widespread instance of the loving, caressing embrace of the material cultural sign within Yorùbá societies is the trend among Evangelicals and Pentecostalists of replacing references to traditionally non-Christian deities in their family name prefixes with ostensibly godlier terms. Because they believe that being "born again" has transformed them in all essential ways, contemporary Yorùbá Christians whose family name used to be Ògúnsanwó (The metallurgy God paid the indemnity) or Fákúnlé (The divination deity enlarges the household) routinely substitute Jéésù (Jesus) and Olú (an abbreviation of Olúwa, the Lord Almighty, and also the generic term for edible mushrooms), and rename themselves as Jéésùsanwó, Olúsanwó, or Olúkunle. It is no longer uncommon to see Christian, self-identifying Yorùbá parents name their twin children "Goodness" and "Mercy" instead of the traditional Táíwò (first to arrive) and Kẹ́hìndé (latter arrival). The new names still acknowledge the pre-Christian belief that twins are a sign of extraordinary favor. With the direct reference to the dual blessings prayed for by the Psalmist, however, the explicit credit now goes to the biblical God (Psalms 23:6). Obviously, the parents of "Goodness" and "Mercy"—and other contemporary Christians—have convinced themselves that the extended family's historical allegiance to either the God of iron or the divination deity misrepresents their prevailing conceptions of being in the world. Traditional cultural identitarians lament this practice as un-Yorùbá. Ògúndáre Fóyánmu, a neotraditional poet in the ìjálá chanting mode associated with the hunters guild, a professional group devoted to the God of iron, once mocked the development by accusing the new generation of Yorùbá Christians of witlessly turning themselves into termites when they all adopt "Olú" as their patron deity; he sang, "Àwọn onígbàgbọ́ dòkìtì ọ̀gán, gbogbo wọn ńhu olú" (Behold Christians making themselves into ant-hill colonies, all sprouting mushrooms). Perhaps as a reaction to Ògúndáre's kind of criticism, many name-changing Christians now adopt the full form "Olúwa" (Lord Almighty); for example, Olúwasanwó.

In contrast to the meaning driven traditionalism that frowns at the contemporary naming practice, the analytical path that I follow in this book presumes that the Christians' focus on the exterior specifics of their names demonstrates their being Yorùbá in the most conventional Yorùbá way. Every self-aware Yorùbá—that is a figure of speech—knows that even raging lunatics care about their name. The form of contention I prefer is that while the irony of structurally equating Ògún and Jéésù (Jesus Christ) or Ifá and Olú Ọ̀run (Heavenly supremacy) might be completely lost to champions of the new Yorùbá, evangelical Christian onomastics—the underlying approach to showing one's presence in the world by bearing names that one believes represent one's earthbound circumstances, desires, and spiritual aspirations—could not be more Yorùbá. Jéésù or Olúwa might have replaced Ifá, but the expressive function of these divine entities in naming practices is not as radically dissimilar as Christians wish to signal. The paradigmatic substitutions made by modern Yorùbá Christians to testify to their departure from inherited beliefs do not alter the basic syntax of the Yorùbá naming strategy; Jesus, Ògún, or God Almighty each restate the common attitude toward the malleable, prognostic possibilities that names are meant to bear in Yorùbá. Today's evangelical descendants of the Ifátáyọ̀ family, who rename themselves Olúwatáyọ̀, announce, like their ancestors, how their devotion to a specific deity, to the exclusion of others, has been rewarded. Self-identifying Yorùbá in Lagos, Kano, Seattle, and London proclaim blatantly that an individual named Olúwatóyìn (The Lord Almighty is praiseworthy) has earned the right to become Olúwatóni (The Lord of Tony) at the moment that person moves to a new land because all immigrants should bear the name they fancy ("Orúkọ tó bá wu ni là á jẹ́ lẹ́yìn odi, Olúwatóyìn dé Amẹ́ríkà, ó di Olúwatóni"). Here, as with the Christian practice, malleable naming holds cultural self-conception and identification in place. "Tóyìn" becomes "Tóni" by deleting, with little regard for semantic coherence, the verb "yìn" (praise) and by splicing what remains to the prefix "Olúwa" (The Lord Almighty) and the systematized chain of words, and not essential meaning, materialize identities.

At the center of all the practices that I analyze in this book is the contention between, on the one hand, inherited systems of inscription that are supposedly construed to remain unchanging across time and space—for example, divination writing, inventory of proverbs, the allegorical tale, and praise poetry—and, on the other hand, commentary-making motivations that drive daily life. In *Arts of Being Yorùbá*, I argue that inherited inscriptions do not independently determine significations of cultural being, and that they owe their sustenance to commentary making—the space in which new referents are created, historical developments are updated, and cultural seamlessness is perpetuated.

Note

1. That possibility cannot be ruled out without further inquiry. Ifá partisans, for example, incorporate Islam's founding in ostensibly primordial divination narratives (see, for example, Yai's "Wútùwútù Yáákí").

ARTS OF BEING YORÙBÁ

1 "Writing" and "Reference" in Ifá Divination Chants

In july 1897, Bishop Charles Phillips, a leading member of the Yorùbá-speaking clergy of the Anglican Church in Nigeria, wrote a preface to the book of Ifá divination stories collected and annotated by Rev. E. M. Lijadu, a pioneering missionary in the Òǹdó region of southwestern Nigeria. Phillips especially praised Lijadu's commentaries on the theological ramifications of the stories as a bold first step toward understanding why the church had enjoyed so little success in evangelizing the Yorùbá people. Thinking of conversion work in warfare terms, Bishop Phillips likened Lijadu's collection and commentary to a brilliant reconnaissance:

> Bí a kò bá rí ìdí ibi tí agbára ọ̀tá gbé wà, a kò lè ṣẹgun wọn. Bí àwa Kristian kò bá mọ ìdí ìsìn àwọn Kèfèrí àti àwọn Ìmàle, a kì yóò lè gbé ìhìnrere Kristi síwájú wọn lí ọ̀nà tí yóò fi ká wọn lára. (Lijadu, *Ifá*, 4) (If we do not locate the source of our enemies' strength, we cannot defeat them. If we Christians do not fathom the foundation of pagan and Islamic devotion, we will not be able to present Christ's gospel in the most appealing form.)[1]

The bishop decried the unfortunate attitude that had led Christian mission-aries in Yorùbá-speaking societies to forget how mastery of pre-Christian prac-tices had helped conversion in biblical places and times.[2] He rebuked fellow church workers for their intellectual arrogance and for having not acted early enough to understand the thought institutions of pre-Christian Yorùbá religions, judging as unconscionable their believing that they could preach effectively and convert sufficiently without understanding the foundations of action among the people they were charged to persuade about the Gospel:

> Ṣùgbọ́n àwa ńja ogun àti-fi ìhìnrere Kristi múlẹ̀ ni ilẹ̀ wa láì wá ìdí ìsìn àtọwọ́dọ́wọ́ àwọn bàbá wa tí ó ní agbára tóbẹ̀ẹ̀ lórí àwọn Kèfèrí. Nítorí náà ni iwàásù wa kò ní agbára tó bẹ̀ẹ̀ lórí wọn. Òmíràn nínú wọn rò pé àìmọ̀ ni ó jẹ́ kí àwa máa sọ ìsọkúsọ sí ìsìn wọn. (Lijadu, *Ifá*, 4) (We strive to plant Christ's gospel in our country without researching the very strong, albeit pagan, an-cient beliefs of our fathers. Our preaching produces little impact for that rea-son. Unknown numbers among them think that we deride their religions because we know nothing about them.)

Perhaps the most important observation Bishop Phillips made in that short preface concerns the effect he believed publishing Ifá divination stories in book form would have on unbelievers:

> Nígbà tí àwọn tí ó ńkọ́ Ifá sórí bá mọ̀ pé wọ́n lè ka Odù Ifá nínú ìwé, mo rò pé yóò ṣí wọn lórí láti kọ́ ìwé kíkà, àti láti fi ọ̀rọ̀ inú Bíbélì wé ti Odù Ifá. Wọn yóò sì rí èyí tí ó sàn jù fún ara wọn. (Lijadu, *Ifá*, 4) (I believe that when rote learners of Ifá stories discover that they can read Ifá's words in a book, they will seek literacy eagerly, gain the capacity to compare the Bible to Ifá stories, and discover on their own the merit of the superior text.)

By casting Ifá stories in the comparatively permanent medium of writing, Christians would be creating for the literate unbeliever a self-reflection apparatus with which to critically examine thought spheres hitherto controlled by the guild of divination priests, the babaláwo. Taking divination stories to be Ifá's main tool of mind control, Bishop Phillips recommended print dissemination of these narratives as a means of freeing up the critical faculty of non-Christians against the shroud of secrecy (awo) with which Ifá priests had misled Yorùbá people through the ages. Print technology, he thought, would separate mystery (awo) from its curators (babaláwo). For Bishop Phillips, the core of Yorùbá idolatry lay not in sculptured icons but in the system. The theological errors of the Yorùbá religion, assuming that Christianity is not Yorùbá, could be easily pointed out if the stories were converted into portable packages comparable to the Bible, the only book authored by the true God. In a palpable, scripted shape, indigenous religious thought could be quoted and disputed, and its false teaching exposed.

Within Bishop Phillips's manifest desire to accelerate conversion through a literacy campaign sits a noticeable "nationalist" displeasure at the condescension of fellow missionaries who mistook the historical lack of printed scriptures among the Yorùbá as a sign of backwardness:

> Àwá fi ojú kékeré wo àwọn kèfèrí ilẹ̀ wa nítorí pé wọn kò ní ìwé. Bẹ́ẹ̀ ni àwa mọ̀ pé ó ní iye ẹ̀kọ́ tí ènìyàn ńkọ́ kí a tó gbàá bí babaláwo. Èdè Ifá jinlẹ̀ gidigidi. (Lijadu, *Ifá*, 4) (We belittle the intelligence of the pagans of our country because they do not have written scriptures, when the situation shows that babaláwo training truly involves extended and rigorous training. Ifá discourse is very profound.)

Bishop Phillips seems to be insinuating that if the situation were to be considered without prejudice, the unbelievers of "our land" have authored "books" waiting to be transcribed and analyzed. Although this book stops short of saying that Ifá stories constitute one book, this chapter's characterizing Ifá discourse as revolving around writing shares Bishop Phillips's representation of the storytelling elements of Ifá divination infrastructure as an instituted, durable signification system.[3] To convert Yorùbá people to Christianity, an understanding of their divination system, which I argue below turns on a system of written inscriptions, should be the beginning point.

Bishop Phillips isolated two questions that persist still in academic studies of Ifá: (1) Does the divination system, especially the contents of the stories, elaborate a unified Yorùbá theological or philosophical viewpoint? And (2) Are Ifá divination stories literal, oracular truths or fancy-driven poetic inventions? From the inside, professional custodians of Ifá divination, leaning heavily on the stories' assertions, claim divine origins for the narratives on which they base their authority to proclaim on the nature of all things and ideas—including ideas and thoughts about things and ideas—across time and space. From the outside, the radical polytheism of religious identification in Yorùbá traditional societies encourages skeptics to suspect Ifá's arrogation of theological centrality to itself.

As Karin Barber ("Discursive Strategies") implies, scholars make Ifá the central divinity in Yorùbá religion because they accept too easily Ifá's elaborate self-justifications, particularly its stories about itself. Scholars and divination practitioners speak as if the illustrative stories used in Ifá consultations are patently guileless and their divine authorship therefore ascertained. Wándé Abímbọ́lá's plain reporting of his informants' views that the firsthand knowledge that the divination God, Ọ̀rúnmìlà, gained exclusively by virtue of his presence at creation is the source of the disclosure system he supervises during divination (*Ifá Divination Poetry*, 1) illustrates Barber's point very well. In Abímbọ́lá's account, Ifá divination procedures are retrieval mechanisms for accessing the corpus of Yorùbá primordial knowledge stored in and as divination stories: "Ifá was put in charge of divination because of his great wisdom which he acquired as a result of his presence by the side of the Almighty when the latter created the universe. Ifá therefore knew all the hidden secrets of the universe. Hence, his praise-name Akéréfinúṣọgbọ́n (the small one who is full of wisdom)" (1).

Although he does not trust the truth claims of Ifá's self-justifying narratives, Lijadu, like Abímbọ́lá, does not question Ifá's centrality, even in the largely antagonistic first volume of his studies. Lijadu contests the theological basis of many stories, but accepts Ọ̀rúnmìlà's place next to the Almighty:

> Àwọn bàbá wa mọ̀, wọ́n sí ní ìmọ̀ náà lí èrò nígbà gbogbo, wọn kò sì ṣe tàbítàbí kí wọ́n tó jẹ́wọ́ ìmọ̀ yìí pé Eni kan ṁbẹ tí í ṣe Ẹlẹ́dàà ohun gbogbo, tí í ṣe Olúwa ohun gbogbo, tí ó sì ní ipa, ọlá àti agbára gbogbo, Olúwa rẹ̀ náà ni wọ́n ṁpe lí Ọlọ́run Olódùmarè tàbí Ọba ọrun . . . Olódùmarè ti fi Eni kan ṣe ibìkejì ara Rẹ̀, Òun à sì máa pe Olúwa rẹ̀ sí ìmọ̀ nínú ohun gbogbo, Òun á sì máa fi ohun gbogbo hàn án, Òun sì fí i ṣe ẹlẹ́rìí ara Rẹ̀ ninu ohun gbogbo, tóbẹ́ẹ̀ tí kò sí

ohun tí Olódùmarè mọ̀ tí Olúwa rẹ̀ náà kò mọ̀, kò sì sí ohun tí Olódùmarè rí tí Òun kò rí. Ẹni náà ni wọ́n ńpè ní "Ọ̀rúnmìlà, Ẹlẹ́rìí ìpín, ibìkejì Olódùmarè." Lọ́dọ̀ ẹni yìí nìkan ni wọ́n sì gbàgbọ́ pé ènìyàn lè gbọ́ òdodo ohùn ẹnu àti ìfẹ́ inú Olódùmarè. (Lijadu, *Ifá*, 17–18) (Our forefathers knew, always had the knowledge in them, and did not waiver in witnessing that there is a being by whom all things were made, the Lord whose might, glory, and power surpasses all. That being they named as God Almighty or Heavenly King . . . God has by his side a second entity to whom he discloses the knowledge of all things and in whom he reposes all confidence such that everything the Almighty knows this person knows, and everything the Almighty sees, he too sees. This person is the one called "Ọ̀rúnmìlà, the witness to the allotment of destiny, second to the Almighty." This person is the only true source of Almighty God's plans.)

Although understandable professional interests could have caused the preferment of Abímbọ́lá's informants, the admiration of indigenous Christian missionaries like Phillips and Lijadu for the promise Ifá stories hold for systematizing Yorùbá theology suggests that goals other than selfish ones are involved in the way Ifá is thought about.[4]

For Ifá priests and scholars—and their Christian antagonists, many of whom are Yorùbá—evidence of Ifá's supremacy in understanding Ifá comes from Ifá itself, a privilege that no other institution of rationality enjoys. Indeed, all other institutions seek validity in Ifá. It is easy to sympathize with Karin Barber's materialist, text-oriented critique of the incorporation mechanisms with which Ifá discourse presents its operations as unquestionably pantheistic. In this chapter I propose that Ifá divination discourse holds its position as the central repository of the essential bases of Yorùbá being and thought across time and space because it foregrounds an objective, graphematic approach to how it constitutes intellectual problems, the methods of analyzing them, and the means of teasing out solutions. I begin by briefly explicating the divination processes, their underlying reasoning, and the general problems of inquiry the system raises. I analyze the relationship of the storytelling part of Ifá divination to the inscription gestures that precede it and use this to argue that a referential gap separates the two and that the space between inscription and storytelling is the location from which practitioners derive their authority for creating narrative motifs and commentary making. That space is where new referents are constantly created, historical developments updated, and cultural seamlessness sustained. I conclude with a discussion of how the referential space between writing and storytelling in Ifá enables a view of time that allows divination clients to manage a coherent relationship to the past, the ostensible source of the solutions to their contemporary problems.

Writing in Ifá

The foundation of analysis in Ifá is the systematized, graphic translation of the results of the random presentation of the divination objects, among which the chain (òpèlè) and palm nuts (ikin) are the most prestigious. To divine with palm nuts, the priest encloses sixteen ritually sanctified nuts in his or her palms, shakes them well, and takes out a bunch with the right hand. If two nuts remain in the left palm, the diviner makes one short vertical fingertip imprint on the fine sand spread on the divination tray. If one nut remains, two imprints are made. A remainder of no nuts or more than two nuts does not yield any imprint. When the chain, which consists of eight hollowed half divination nutshells, attached four each to two sides of a string, is the preferred instrument, divination is a little different. The diviner holds up the string and then drops it on the small divination space in front of him or her. The presentation of each throw is transcribed on the tray. A nutshell that falls with its "concave inner surface upward" indicates two imprints; one that falls with its convex side up indicates one imprint. Producing readable inscriptions is obviously faster in the chain method. Either way, the priest reads the imprints, top down, right side first, to identify which of the 256 possible units of Ifá graphemes (odù ifá) is presented. The presented unit clues the diviner to which stories to tell to illustrate the problems revealed by the divination God and to decipher what ritual sacrifices or behavioral changes to prescribe. The casting, imprinting, and narrating process typically starts after the client has whispered his or her purpose into some tokens, which could be money, mixed up with the divination objects. The sign revealed and the illustrative stories told must bear some allegorical resemblance to the condition for which the client is seeking counsel.

Virtually all Ifá scholars agree on the names, appearance, and order of the characters that comprise the basic notation system (the graphemes), with Ogbè in the first position, Òyèkú in the second, and Òfún in the sixteenth. In practical counseling, the basic units must double to produce a diagnosis or prognosis, or both. A pattern that signals Òyèkú on the right and Ogbè on the left will be named Òyèkúlógbè—if the other way round, it will be Ogbèyèkú—and one that shows Òfún on both sides will be Òfún Méjì (Doubled Òfún).[5] The inscriptions issue from a grid structured so systematically that naming errors can be fixed with little ease.[6]

The foundational role of the inscription system in Ifá distinguishes Ifá as a "literate," learned means of inquiry—Ifá is commonly called alákòwé (the scribe or literate one)—and not a seance or other kind of intuitive, magical, or "gifted" fortune-telling. Its practitioners' rigorous and lengthy training further enhances Ifá's image as an honest dedication and discipline. References to the profession in everyday speech extol honesty and straightforwardness. The saying "A kìí sawo ká purọ̀" (The person sworn to the divination profession cannot lie) attests axiomatically to the diviner's commitment to truthfulness. Of course, professional practices and rituals lend the inscription system an air of mystery, if not mysticism. To the untrained observer, the link between palm-nut manipulation (or string casting) and readable, visible imprints is thoroughly occultic. The credit for the aura, I will argue, goes largely to the discourse's consistent association of named, visibly embodied signs with oracular revelations. Diviners gain respect and command attention because they operate as disinterested agents of a disclosure apparatus anchored by an inscription sign system whose production is outwardly indifferent to the "writer's" time- and space-bound will. The mute sign's lack of passion, one way or another, about the case presented and its theoretical ability to repeat consistently the same signification for all clients cannot but induce trust. The notation system, in theory and in perception, removes the individual priest's influence and will from the intercourse between the client and the witness to creation, Ọ̀rúnmìlà, who inspirits its knowledge in the presentation of the material divination instrument. The notation system, not the human diviner, arbitrates the most important steps in discovery and disclosure. When the most accomplished diviners attribute their acumen for making correct findings to Ifá—"Ifá ló wí bẹ́ẹ̀" (Ifá renders it thus) is the formula—I do not believe humility motivates them; they tout the superiority of their instruments of discovery.

Lijadu offers evidence of the importance of written inscriptions to Ifá's prestige. Although his Christian calling demands that he should reject Ifá as idolatry—and he does—he continued his studies nonetheless because of the need to decipher the intellectual intricacies that diviners use to tie Ifá's large body of etiological stories to the divinely revealed inscription system that is presumed to produce them . In Ifá discourse, the genealogy of human problems traces back to the Almighty, after passing through only the divination God and the system of honest inscriptions instituted in his name. In the second chapter of *Ifá*, Lijadu asks the main intellectual question, "Kínni a lè pè ní Ìfihàn-Ọ̀rọ̀ Ọlọ́run? Kí sì ni ẹ̀rí tí a lè fi mọ̀ ọ́ yàtọ̀ sí ọ̀rọ̀ míràn?" (What is a divine revelation? And what proof distinguishes it from others?). He answers the question thus:

> Ọ̀rọ̀ Ọlọ́run ni èyí tí a bá lè jẹ́rìí pé Ọlọ́run tìkára rẹ̀ li ó sọ ọ́ fún gbígbọ́ tàbí tí ó kọ ọ́ sílẹ̀ fún kíkà àwa ènìyàn. Lẹ́hìn èyí,—Ọ̀rọ̀ Ọlọ́run ni èyí tí ẹnikẹ́ni sọ, tàbí tí ó kọ sílẹ̀, ìbá à ṣe nípa àṣẹ tàbí nípa ìmísí Ọlọ́run tìkárarè. (*Ifá*, 30)
> (God's genuine revelations are the ones for which we can truly testify that he either spoke directly to us or wrote down for us to read. God's genuine revelations could also be those spoken out or written down by those directly ordered or inspired by the Almighty to do so.)

The Godhead is the original writer and speaker, who directly delivers his wishes in either spoken or inscribed words. He can speak to favored listeners or dictate to chosen scribes, who send the words forth. Either way, the message's medium—words, writing surfaces, or the inspired individual—must have been touched directly by God for the message to be valid.

The writing protocols in Ifá are the closest an "oral" society could devise to fulfill the basis of genuinely divine writing and speaking as the Christian Lijadu conceived it. Òrúnmìlà was present with the Almighty at the beginning of things. Skilled in inscriptions, he reduced to 256 symbols everything the Almighty had done. Òrúnmìlà did not create things; he only transcribed the Almighty's creations and designs. People trained to access Òrúnmìlà's writing and speech portray him as capable of correcting ill-fated life directions ("atórí ẹni tí kò sunwọn ṣe") not because he has an independent power to invent but because his exclusive knowledge of the transcriptions of the Godhead's intentions can offer clues to the right path. I would like to speculate that Lijadu's very close study of Ifá as a specimen of pre-Christian Yorùbá theology is based on the prominent role of direct writing in the disclosure system. Lijadu does not condemn Ifá as a system of direct divine revelation, probably because of its close ties to a minimally mediated writing system. He rejects Ifá because its stories—and not the graphic signs—about God's true nature, true worship, true human nature, and God's relationship to humans do not quite agree with biblical tenets. Lijadu is dissatisfied that Ifá teachings regarding divine truth, the love of God and of fellow men and women, holiness, and disinterested search for divine grace are too lax and, therefore, unmeritorious in comparison to Christianity.

Reference in Ifá

Divination continues when the priest, after transcribing the revealed sign, recites—following the set structure of the Ifá story unit (ẹsẹ)—a narrative whose central motif addresses a situation similar in some respect to the client's predicament. All the stories told for the purpose of interpreting revealed divination inscriptions pose at least one main problem that confronts a protagonist, who is believed to have been the original client for whom the inscription and the now retold story were first devised. The stories also construct at least one antagonist, a set of resolutions or an escalation, and the reaction of the entity that first experienced the problem.[7] Death (ikú), disease (àrùn), loss (òfò), malediction (èpè), paralysis (ègbà), general misfortune (òràn), incarceration (èwọn), accident (èṣe), and witchcraft (àjẹ́ and oṣó) are the most common antagonists. These problems can afflict a person at will. Enemies could also cause them through some diabolical machinations. Opposed to the antagonists are the dearly sought general blessings (ire gbogbo) of wealth (owó), childbearing (ọmọ), good health (àlàáfíà), and longevity (àìkú). The antagonists represent forces of illness, the protagonists those of wellness. The two groups fight for control of the client's body or social existence, or both. The story unit has no independently verifiable embodiment, in that it does not attach directly to one graphematic sign. In effect, the divined inscriptions generate stories, not phonemes. In this regard, Ifá writing is clearly mythographic, not phonocentric. To use the words of Jacques Derrida, the foremost late twentieth-century theorist of writing, Ifá inscription "spells its symbols pluri-dimensionally," and its referents are "not subject to successivity, to the order of a logical time, or to the irreversible temporality of sound" (Derrida, *Of Grammatology*, 85).

T. M. Ilesanmi's schematic analysis of Ifá inscriptions and narratives reveals a deep-seated binarism—"agbára méjì tó so ayé ró" (the two poles on which existence subtends) (*Yorùbá Orature and Literature*, 132)—that Ifá diviners use to manage the "pluridimensional" significations of their writing method. According to Ilesanmi, Ifá priests ascribe positive, or ire (good, desirable, well sought), values to some elements and negative, or aburú (bad, undesirable, abhorred), values to others.[8] They tie these values to the order of ordinal appearance: the first to appear in the divination process is the most positive and the next one less so; one notation is positive and two infer negative. The sixteen primary figures of the odù are valued according to how the imprinted signs (ones and twos) and the ordinal rank of the presented odù (first, second, etc.) add up. Thus Ogbè, signed with all ones and no two is totally positive (bẹ́ẹ ni), and Òfún, all twos and no ones, is completely negative (bẹ́ẹ kọ́). Although these two signs are ranked first and second in the ordinal system, they are actually polar opposites in the ideational scheme:

> Àwọn odù méjì yìí ló ta ko ara wọn jù nínú àbùdá oníbejì bẹ́ẹ-ni-bẹ́ẹ̀-kọ́. Ọkan kò ní bẹ́ẹ̀-kọ́ rárá; èkejì kò sì ní bẹ́ẹ-ni olóòkan. Kò sí ìgbà tí àwọn méjèèjì jọ wí ohun kan náà. Gbogbo àwọn odù yòókù ló ní bẹ́ẹ-ni díẹ̀, bẹ́ẹ̀-kọ́ díẹ̀ nínú. Nínú ọkan, ire le pọ̀ ju ibi lọ, nínú òmíràn, ibi le pọ̀ ju ire lọ. Wàyí o, ipò tí ibi àti ire wà ta ko ara wọn. Iye ire àti ibi kan náà ni Èdí àti Ìwòrì ní ṣùgbọ́n wọ́n fi ipò ta ko ara wọn. (*Yorùbá Orature and Literature*, 134–135) (These two odù are polar opposites in the positive and negative binary structure. One has no negative at all; the other has not one positive. At no point do the two odù express the same attributes. All the other odù signs express a little of positive and negative values. In some, positives outnumber negatives; in others, negatives outnumber positives. The positioning of the attributes might oppose each other. Èdí and Ìwòrì express an equal number of positives and negatives but in different positions.)

Ilesanmi constructs two very useful charts of the signs, the first of which, reproduced in table 1.1, depicts the ordinal sequence. In this table, "+" represents a positive value and "−" stands for a negative. Ọṣẹ́ (15) and Ọ̀fún (16) have the same number of positive and negative attributes but are placed in opposite positions. Ọṣẹ́ opens with a negative, behind which it lines positive, negative, positive in that order. Ọ̀fún unfolds in the opposite direction.

Table 1.1 Odù Ifá Ordinal Sequence

++++	Ogbè	1
– – – –	Ọ̀yẹ̀kú	2
– + + –	Ìwòrì	3
+ – – +	Èdí	4
– – – +	Ọ̀bàrà	5
+ – – –	Ọ̀kànràn	6
– – + +	Ìrosùn	7
+ + – –	Ọ̀wọ́nrín	8
– + + +	Ògúndá	9
+ + + –	Ọ̀sá	10
+ – + +	Ìrẹtẹ̀	11
+ + – +	Òtúrá	12
– + – –	Òtúrúpọ̀n	13
– – + –	Ìká	14
– + – +	Ọ̀sẹ́	15
+ – + –	Ọ̀fún	16

Source: Based on Ilesanmi, *Yorùbá Orature and Literature*, 135.

Ilesanmi argues that the assignment of values operates the referencing system in the odù inscriptions. He represents the "inner" oppositions of the odù system thus in table 1.2.

Ilesanmi does not speculate why the public, outer, ordinal ranking differs from the inner order. He also does not say why Ifá priests hide from public knowledge the underlying binary with which they operate their system. The language of his conclusion suggests, however, that they might be protecting their guild's secret: "Méjì, méjì ni Ifá ṣe ìgbékalẹ̀ èrò rẹ̀ lórí ayé; tibi-tire ló jọ ńrìn pọ̀ nínú ètò Ifá. Ìmọ̀ àbùdá oníbejì ló lè ṣí aṣọ lójú eégun Ifá" (Ifá's central structure rests on a binary design in which positives and negatives walk hand in gloves. Only the knowledge of how binary structures work can unmask Ifá) (*Yorùbá Orature and Literature*, 146).

We should not forget that even the outer order that the priests present to the uninitiated is not universal. William Bascom recorded ten variations in Nigeria alone, eight each in Benin and Togo, and two in Cuba. Moreover, the primary odù units do not carry any readable significance in practical, problem-solving divination until doubled or paired with another. This means that each consultation would involve ordering and decoding a minimum of thirty-two negative and positive values. A doubled Ọ̀fún, for example, would have to be arranged in

Table 1.2 Odù Ifá Value Sequence

++++	Ogbè	1
−+++	Ògúndá	3
+−++	Ìrẹtẹ̀	5
++−+	Òtúrá	7
−−++	Ìrosùn	9
−+−+	Ọ̀sẹ́	11
+−−+	Èdí	13
−−−+	Ọ̀bàrà	15
+++−	Ọ̀sá	16
−++−	Ìwòrì	14
+−+−	Ọ̀fún	12
++−−	Ọ̀wọ́nrín	10
−−+−	Ìká	8
−+−−	Òtúrúpọ̀n	6
+−−−	Ọ̀kànràn	4
−−−−	Ọ̀yẹ̀kú	2

Source: Based on Ilesanmi, *Yorùbá Orature and Literature*, 136.

the priest's mind as in table 1.3 (to the client, only the ordinal appearance—the two columns of ones and twos—is visible).

Ilesanmi's sketch of the foundation of reference in Ifá's mythography stimulates and absorbs, but there is no evidence that the temporal order implied in the sequence of positives and negatives is repeated in the narrative plots of the ẹsẹ. That is, the imprinted signs do not appear to govern the story units. In order for Ilesanmi's "revelations" to work for practical criticism, we need to have an idea of how the binary values affect narrative sequence (the relation of plot details to the ordering of values).

The only evidence I have seen that thematic coordination on the basis of imprinted signs is possible for the stories occurs in the Epega and Niemark collection (*The Sacred Ifa Oracle*). Stories in this book demonstrate an inscription-governed thematic unity that one does not find in earlier published collections like Bascom's *Ifa Divination* or Abímbọ́lá's *Ìjìnlẹ̀ Ohùn Ẹnu Ifá, Apá Kejì* and *Ifá Divination Poetry*. Stories gathered under the Ògúndá sign, for example, show judicious adjudication to be Ògún's forte. In the narratives, Ògún, the God of iron, creates (dá) the path to being (ọ̀nà ìwà) and acts as the guarantor of biological reproduction (ìṣẹ̀dá). In the same manner, the resolution of Ọ̀sá stories

Table 1.3 Ọ̀fún Méjì (Doubled Ọ̀fún)

Ordinal Appearance Based on Ones and Twos		Inner Attributes Based on Negative and Positive Values	
I (+)	I (+)	+ − + −	+ − + −
II (−)	II (−)	+ − + −	+ − + −
I (+)	I (+)	+ − + −	+ − + −
II (−)	II (−)	+ − + −	+ − + −

generally upholds the literal glossing of the root word, sá, as having to do with flee-
ing for refuge. Similarly, Ìká narratives support the etymology of ká, in multiple
references to encircling, circumscription, circumspection, reaping, bending, limit-
ing, and so forth. It is not clear whether the thematic unity of the Epega–Niemark
stories reflects regional (Ìjẹ̀bú) variations that might have influenced Epega—
Niemark's informant—or whether the coordination is a result of editorial selections
guided by a more "literary" sensibility.

While future studies might reveal a closer relationship between the inscription details and the illustrative stories, such discovery will not diminish the importance of inscription in Ifá, because it is the act of arriving at the right sign that
opens up channels of story and meaning generation to diviners and clients. The
client's whispering his or her desires and concerns into the divination object
brings, in theory, his or her past to the presence of the priest (who does not hear
what is whispered) and the attention of the divination God's representative, the
kernel or the chain. The inscriptions revealed by the objects cast in the divination point to traces of the emblematic primordial events to which the divination
God was witness. The signs also instigate deliberations on what actions the client
should take. In this order of events, the generated inscriptions regulate the relation of the past, the present, and the future, without much regard for the diviner's personal will or desire. The client's concerns and problems belong in the
present; the divination God's archetypal knowledge, in the past; the priest's verbal articulation of such knowledge, in the present; the realization of the agreed-
upon solutions derivable from the present interpretation of the divine codes, in
the future. The sample solutions modeled in the narrative have the chance to
work if the client's disposition helps it. Actionable reference, as the story unit or
as the directive resulting from it, comes after the inscription; it belongs in the
future of the inscription, the "letter." Things could not be otherwise, because
the past (the "historical" referent) of the entity I am calling the letter, in other
words, the imprinted sign, belongs in the experience of the deity who witnessed

creation at a moment that now lies permanently outside of immediate cognition. Ọrúnmìlà—the original writer and the inventor of both the inscription and the storytelling systems—never reads his text verbally; the transcribing diviner (the deity's "writes-person"), who can verbalize the contents of the inscriptions, does not "write" according to his or her own will but can create stories that illustrate the significations in ways that are meaningful for the client. Even so, the specifically present diviner does not claim authorship.

I contend that the space and time left empty by the discontinuity between the systematic notations and the free-floating themes they generate in stories breed commentary that the diviner fills with narrative illustrations. In that location, "implicit significations" of the written inscriptions are teased out, "silent determinations" are made, and "obscured contents" are rendered manifest (Foucault, "What Is an Author?," 145). Culture subsists here at the level of lived history. The considerable time and intellectual expense that pioneer Yorùbá Christian missionaries devoted to that location is instructive. Believing, on the grounds discussed earlier, that Ifá stories are theological, Lijadu found evidence in the narratives of admirable Godliness comparable to Christianity but was exasperated by the sheer humanity of the Godhead—an entity who would not command a simple kola nut at will for his personal use and who fails to detect that one presented to him by a sacrifice carrier was picked up from a crossroads offering. Lijadu exclaims, "Ẹléyà ni gbogbo ìtàn yìí" (These stories are utterly contemptuous) (*Ifá*, 32) because the Almighty they portray is not that mighty. "Irú Olódùmarè wo ni eyi ẹ jàrè?" (What a puny God this is?), he declaims. Karin Barber, a contemporary scholar, finds, for nontheological reasons, something untoward in how "Westernized members of the Yorùbá elite"—a group that, in my view, includes Lijadu—monumentalized Ifá by collecting, transcribing, and annotating the narratives recited by chosen priests and then misrepresented the texts, perhaps unwittingly, "as a fixed body of knowledge" ("Discursive Strategies," 197). According to Barber, the elite allow themselves to be seduced by the built-in incorporation strategies of the Ifá discourse that cast its priest as someone who espouses a storied "body of wisdom conceived of as anterior and external to his own existence" (202), independent of his or her will. The only divination element that either Lijadu (the Christian, elite monument maker) or Barber comments on critically is the Ifá story's relationship to the inscription it supports. Neither the written notation's anteriority to the priest's will, nor the client's wishes, nor the story structure, are ever questioned. Both Lijadu's project and Barber's critique, I argue, are possible because the site of commentary making is deliberately constructed and preserved in Ifá discourse so that the initiated and the uninitiated can interact over the meaning of the fundamental inscriptions of being. Left to Lijadu, what ought to be refashioned is not the Godhead but the characterization details of that Godhead. If it had been reconstituted from the perspective of

Christian scriptures, Christianity would thus have become compatible with a historically updated sense of Yorùbá being.

We can step aside from comparative theology and look at the four Ifá stories that William Bascom grouped as "parodies" on the last three pages of *Ifá Divination.* Two of the stories are about the coming of the railroad. The first, in contemporary orthography, reads:

Ọ̀nà tọ̀ tààrà má yà
A dá fún rélùweè
Níjọ́ tí ńṣawo rodò
Tí ńlọ bóyìnbó ṣòwò
Wọ́n ní gbogbo ẹrù òyìnbó
Rélùweè ni yóò ní i
Wọ́n ní kí ó rúbọ
Wọ́n ní àti òyìnbó
Àti akọ̀wé
Rélùweè ni yóò ni ẹrù wọn
Rélùweè kọ̀, kò rúbọ
Láti ìgbà náà
Bí gbogbo ènìyàn bá kó ẹrù sínú rélùweè
Nígbà tí wọ́n bá sọ̀
Wọ́n á sì kó ẹrù wọn kúrò nínú rẹ̀
Ifá ní ẹnì kan ńlọ sí ẹ̀hìn odi kan
Wọ́n ní kí ó rúbọ kí olè má ba gba ẹrù rẹ̀ ní ọwọ́ rẹ̀

Road be straight without turn
It was divined for railways
Out to trade with the whites
When he embarked on a river borne trip
'Twas said that all goods belonging to the whites
Shall belong to the railways
Was told to make ritual sacrifices
Was told that be it the white
Or the clerical worker
Transporting their goods shall be the railways' lot
Railways refused to make ritual sacrifices
Since that time
When passengers load their goods on a train
At their point of disembarkation
They leave with all their goods
Ifá warns that someone is going on a journey
Let that person make ritual sacrifices to prevent loss of goods to thieves
    (560; Bascom's translation modified)

Bascom does not tell the reader the odù inscription that produced this narrative. This is not surprising, because the 256 signs are not open to poetic fancy or inventions of any sort. But as Bascom notes, the first line comes unchanged from another story narrated under Ọ̀yẹ̀kú-(È)dí inscription regarding a groom who fails, like "Railways" here, to make a prescribed ritual sacrifice and ends up unable to consummate his nuptial with his new bride. If, as I am suggesting, the story about the origin of the "failure" of "Railways" is probably produced by Ọ̀yẹ̀kú-(È)dí, the point about the inscripted sign not carrying a direct relationship to the contents of the narrative that illustrates it is confirmed. Another story about the railroad goes thus:

Ọ̀nà tọ̀ tààrà má yà
Ló dífá fún rélùweè
Níjọ́ tí ńsọkún àìlẹ́ni
Wọ́n ní kó rúbọ
Àkùkọ mẹ́ta, ẹgbàafà, àt'aṣọ ara rẹ̀
Rélùweè rú ẹgbàafà àt'aṣọ ara rẹ̀
Ṣùgbọ́n kò rú àkùkọ mẹ́ta
Òun làwọn ènìyàn kìí fi bá a kalẹ́
Rélùweè bẹ̀rẹ̀ síí di ẹlẹ́ni
Bí gbogbo ènìyàn bá wọ inú rélùweè
Bó ba dalẹ́ wọn a kúrò nínú rẹ̀
Oníkálukú a sì lọ sí ilé e rẹ̀

Road be straight without turn
Divined for railways
At the time loneliness wracked its soul
Sacrifices were prescribed for it
Three roosters, 1,200 cowries, and the clothes on its body
Railways sacrificed money and the clothes on its body
But did not sacrifice three roosters
Hence all passengers desert it at sunset
Railways surely gained multitudes
But when crowds gather in trains
They all abandon it at dusk
All and sundry return home (560; Bascom's translation modified)

Whereas the first narrative speaks about the railroad to alert a client facing an imminent loss and how to prevent it and therefore avoid the immitigable dispossession fate that disobedience brought the railway service, the second story speaks completely about the etiology of impersonal scheduling in railway services. Many verbal quips warn about the dire consequences of turning away affines, who in ordinary Yorùbá speech are likened to fabrics that cover the body's nakedness and protect it against the elements. Railroads sacrificed the warm, personal, human touch as if it was of the same order as mere roosters. Through simple personification, the two commentary-making stories assimilate a modern means of communication into the longue durée structure of divination. The second story implies that impersonal scheduling is a loss of sorts for railroads but is not completely elegiac, in that passengers still troop willingly to use its services.

A Story of Origin

Because it calls attention to itself as an account of its own devices, one of the stories that Wándé Abímbọ́lá's informants associated with Ìwòrì Méjì (the sign that balances ones and twos on each side of the readable inscriptions) discloses much about how Ifá manages the movement of futurity and cultural development (*Ìjìnlẹ̀ Ohun Ẹnu Ifa, Apá Kejì*, 34–40). The story begins with the names of the four priests who coordinated the original divination consultation, two of which are "Apá Níí Gbókoó Tan Iná Oṣó" (Apá is the tree that takes to the bush to kindle its wizard red fire) and "Orúrù Níí Wẹ̀wù Ẹ̀jẹ̀ Kalẹ̀" (Orúrù tree is the one that dons the blood red garment from top to bottom). The third is "Ilẹ́ Ni Mo Tẹ̀ Tẹ̀ẹ̀ Tẹ̀ Kí Ntóó Tọpọ́n" (For a long while did I cut ordinary earth before I began to cut divination tray sand); the fourth, "Ọ̀pẹ̀ Tẹ́ẹ́rẹ́ Erékè Níí Yà sí Ya Búkà Mẹ́rìndínlógún" (The slender uphill palm tree divides into sixteen branches). To reflect the tonal counterpoint principles that governed the poetic performance, Abímbọ́lá breaks the names of the third and fourth diviners into two lines each:

> Ilẹ́ ni mo tẹ̀ tẹ̀ẹ̀ tẹ̀
> Kí ntóó tọpọ́n;
> Ọ̀pẹ̀ tẹ́ẹ́rẹ́ erékè
> Níí yà sí ya búkà mẹ́rìndínlógún.

> I cut the earth for a long while
> Before cutting the divination tray sand;
> The uphill slender palm tree
> The one that divides into sixteen branches.

The four diviners cast their objects and disclosed to Ọ̀rúnmìlà that he will be barren. But their findings were mocked.

The ensuing narrative does not specify the odú inscription that produced it, and the only authority we have that this is a story fitted for Ìwòrì is the priest who narrated it to the scholar. Abímbọ́lá does not identify which of Pópóọlá Àyìnlá (of Ìkòyì, near Ògbómọ̀ṣọ́), Oyèédélé Ìṣọ̀lá (of Bẹẹ̀sin compound, Pààkòyí quarters, Ọ̀yọ́), and Adéjàre (of Pààkòyí quarters, Ọ̀yọ́) recited the story. But this cannot delay analysis.

The story of the original diviners is not a simple one. According to Abímbọ́lá, the named diviners led the first consultation recounted in the text. He also adds that the names are either fragments of praise epithets (oríkì) or pseudonyms (*Ifá Divination Poetry*, 19). Conventional wisdom presumes that these names belong to real individuals and that the events actually happened.[9] From a more realistic viewpoint, the diviners' names recited formulaically at the beginning of Ifá divination stories are tale specific and are rarely repeated even when the motif of events addressed in one story appears in another. Most often, the names summarize the topic of the events in the consultation scenario presented. Even Abímbọ́lá, a practitioner-scholar of Ifá, admits that the names could be personifications of animals or plants, or both, devised for creating narrative unity. This implies that the names are a story element, more precisely a characterization strategy, and that they do not identify people whose lineage chants a listener can recite, or whose compound or hometown one can always locate precisely. From the beginning of the narrative, the names hold together the activities of the coordinator(s) of an Ifá consultation and serve as a textual resource for brokering attribution. Invoking antecedence with the original priest's names helps place the contemporary performer in a discursive line of descent.

The motif of the importance of patience to overcoming barrenness, the central theme of the narrative under discussion here, inhabits every facet of the story, including the names of the original diviners. The first diviner's name implies a paradox: although the blossoming of the hardy mahogany tree (apá) is beautiful, it draws the attention of malevolent forces. And although the tough apá wood is useful for building, its hardiness also attracts witches and wizards, who gather round it for their nightly deliberations (see Abraham's *Dictionary of Modern Yoruba*). Ifá priests also use apá seeds as active ingredients in protective amulets. To name the second diviner, Abímbọ́lá's informant pairs the scarlet flowers of the formidably tall orúrù (African Tulip) tree with that of the apá to juxtapose threat and ultimate victory. The witches' malevolence has no effect on the trees' florescence. The victory theme is also present in the colorless but forbearing nature of the other diviners. In time, it seems, the person who begins cutting divination signs on coarse soil will graduate to professional-grade fine sand on the divination tray; given time, the slender palm tree in the tough uphill landscape will grow into sixteen full branches.

Events narrated in the next section of the story, lines 11–34, contradict the four wise diviners' prognostication, a development that shows divination's fallibility. Ọ̀rúnmìlà, contrary to predictions, had children—Alárá, Ajerò, Ọlọ́yẹ́, Oǹtagi, and Ọlọ́wọ̀—who became rulers all over, mainly in the provinces. Alákégi and Ẹ̀léjẹ̀lúmọ̀pẹ́ each assumed the throne of a territory not identifiable on a contemporary map. Ọwáràngún became the leader of a diviners' guild. Further analysis of these names reveals more about the circumstances of their birth and the feelings of the parent who named them: Alárá (Companionship) colloquially translates as "I would make a companion of my child"; Ajerò (Communality) translates as "Children's causes warrant collective deliberations"; Ọlọ́yẹ́ (Harmattan) implies that having a child weathers the body. Others are identified by their father's professional activity at the time of the child's birth: woodcutting, wood selling, and dye making. The older children (Alárá and Ajerò) represent the parents' ambition of youth, the middle four (Ọlọ́yẹmoyin, Alákégi, Oṅtagi, and Ẹléjèlúmọ̀pé) denote phases of material strivings for the sustenance of life, and the youngest two—Ọwáràngún and Ọlọ́wọ̀—commemorate the accomplishments of old age. The children's names signify the different stages of the life cycle, from the search for companionship to respectful regard. Reproduction involves more than procreation; it entails companionship, bracing the elements, physical work, participation in the exchange of goods and services, and rest.

The next section, consisting of thirty-five lines, further expands the meaning of reproduction to include the need for creating instruments for managing contacts and sustaining relationships. These lines describe how the father of the far-flung rulers and master professionals manages his extended family under a central influence by instituting an annual pilgrimage to Ifẹ̀ during the Ifá festival. On one such occasion, Ọlọ́wọ̀, the child imagined at birth as the symbol of respectful regard, shows up determined to publicly topple the father's authority. Ọlọ́wọ̀ dresses up in a replica of the official outfit of Ifẹ̀'s chief diviner—then Òrúnmìlà—and refuses to pay proper homage. When asked to pay due respect, Ọlọ́wọ̀ remains adamant. The confrontation is dramatized thus:

Ó ní òun ò lè pábọrúbọyè bọ ṣíṣẹ.
Òrúnmìlà ní èé ti jẹ́
Ọlọ́wọ̀ ní ìwọ Òrúnmìlà sọ̀dùn kọ́, o sòdùn kọ́;
Òun Ọlọ́wọ̀ naa sọ̀dùn kọ́, òun sòdùn kọ́
Ìwọ Òrúnmìlà fòsùn idẹ lọ́wọ́
Òun Ọlọ́wọ̀ náà fòsùn idẹ lọ́wọ́
Ìwọ Òrúnmìlà bọ sálúbàtà idẹ
Òun Ọlọ́wọ̀ náà bọ sálúbàtà idẹ
Ìwọ Òrúnmìlà dádé,
Òun Ọlọ́wọ̀ náà dádé.
Bẹ́ẹ̀ ni wọ́n sì ní
Ẹ̀nìkan kìí forí adé balẹ̀ fẹ́nìkan.

He said he cannot wish him good tidings.
Òrúnmìlà asked why?
Ọlọ́wọ̀ said you, Òrúnmìlà, are in raffia garments;
He the Ọlọ́wọ̀ too dons raffia garments
You Òrúnmìlà carry a brass staff of office

He the Olọ́wọ̀ too carries a brass staff of office
You Ọ̀rúnmìlà wear brass slippers
He Olọ́wọ wears brass slippers
You Ọ̀rúnmìlà wear a crown,
He Olọ́wọ̀ has a crown on.
And it is known that
One crowned head does not prostrate to another.

A rival chief diviner exists now, the determined Olọ́wọ̀ wants to say. The angry father, probably realizing the redundancy of his presence in the reflection mounted in Olọ́wọ̀'s appearance, exiles himself into a tall, sixteen-branch palm tree.

It looks like Ọ̀rúnmìlà holds the key to some reproduction essentials because all motion on the cycle of life stopped after his departure: the pregnant could not deliver, the barren continued fruitless, the infirm remained bedridden, semen dried up in men, women ceased to menstruate, yams refused to grow, peas did not flower, chickens pecked at the few raindrops that fell, and goats mistook sharpened blades for yam peels and munched on them. The community sought help from unnamed diviners, who prescribed for them what sacrifices to make and counseled them to assemble at the foot of the palm tree into which Ọ̀rún-mìlà had disappeared. The people gathered around the tree as instructed and chanted the self-exiled priest's praise epithets, believing that they could coax him to return "home." But Ọ̀rúnmìlà stayed in exile and offered sixteen palm nuts as his proxy:

Ọ̀rúnmìlà ní òun ò tún relé mọ́
Ó ní kí wọn ó tẹ́wọ́,
Ó wáá fún wọn ní ikin mẹ́rìndínlógún.
Ó ní bẹ́ ẹ bá délé,
Bẹ́ ẹ bá fówóó ní,
Ẹni tẹ́ẹ́ mọọ bi nù un.
Bẹ́ ẹ bá délé
Bẹ́ ẹ bá fáyaá ní,
Ẹni tẹ́ẹ́ mọọ bi nù un.
Bẹ́ ẹ bá délé
Bẹ́ ẹ bá fọ́mọọ́ bí
Ẹni tẹ́ẹ́ mọọ bi nù un.
Ilé lẹ bá fẹ́ẹ́ kọ́ láyé,
Aṣọ lẹ bá fẹ́ẹ́ ní láyé,
Ẹni tẹ́ẹ́ mọọ bi nù un.
Ire gbogbo tẹ́ ẹ bá fẹ́ẹ́ ní láyé,
Ẹni tẹ́ẹ́ mọọ bi nù un.
Ìgbà tí wọ́n délé,

Gbogbo ire náà ni wọ́n ńrí.
Ọrúnmìlà afèdèfẹ̀yọ̀,
Ẹ̀lààsòdè
Ifá relé Olókun kò dé mọ́.
Ó lẹ́ni tẹ́ ẹ bá rí,
Ẹ ṣá mọọ pè ni baba.

Ọrúnmìlà says he will never return home
He asked them to open their palms,
And handed to them sixteen palm nuts.
He said, when you get home,
If you desire wealth,
That is the person to ask.
When you get home
If you desire a wife,
That is the person to ask.
When you get home
If you desire children
That is the person to ask.
Should you want to build a home,
In case you want clothes,
That is the person to ask.
Any other comfort you might seek,
That is the person to ask.
When they got home,
All the blessings became theirs.
Ọrúnmìlà, the polyglot,
The redeeming deity of Ìsòdè
Ifá left for Olókun's abode.
He said whoever you see,
That is the one to call upon.

The presentation of one divination as a function of an antecedent divination in this story reveals a characteristic of Ifá processes to which scholars do not usually pay attention: Ifá divinations are a consultation of a consultation. The first divination in the origin of divination story summarized above concerns Ọrúnmìlà's engagement with the four diviners and the details of the client's success despite contrary oracular predictions. The second divination describes the Ifẹ̀ people's failed attempt to bring back Ọrúnmìlà, who had been exiled because he had been unable to manage his children. The third story, the one that presents the first two, is told by Abímbọ́lá's informants, probably as it was handed down to them from other diviners. It supplements the first two, one of which involves the birth of the discursive practice that governs all the stories. All divination sessions involve the use of at least the first and the third types of stories, but only the first type is marked as a story because the diviner in charge of the present moment has to efface the importance of his or her own active material input. The individual diviner, babaláwo, as it were, has to spirit away his or her own presence by not marking the story of his storytelling.[10]

Ethnographic studies of Ifá will not suffice for analyzing this narrative of presence, absence, doubling, writing, conjuring, and responsiveness. The story describes the irremediably "occultic" nature of signification: bare meaning, unmediated, Ọ̀rúnmìlà's knowledge of the details of the allotment of destiny, has disappeared permanently. Ọ̀rúnmìlà is never coming home with us! However, life will continue in the exchange of traces of the instituted codes that bear fragments of Ọ̀rúnmìlà's record. The search for recovery launched by Ifẹ̀ people left behind in the material world shows that continued existence revolves around the anxiety of what is yet to happen. According to this narrative, the structure of meaning production named for Ọ̀rúnmìlà construes being as the continuous coaxing from tokens of the unrecoverable past useful means of approaching the present, which is in the future of that past.

Significantly, the story categorizes the reference of divination writing as material well-being in all its aspects (ire gbogbo) and more concretely as money (owó), spouse (aya), childbearing (ọmọ), shelter (ilé), and clothing (aṣọ). The authority (or spirit) that controls the knowledge of the distribution, use, and acquisition of these blessings—none other than the eyewitness to creation—cannot be accessed directly, but can be accessed through its culturally occulted proxies, which in practice exist as a structure of appellation, a system of calling into being; "Ẹni tẹ́ mọọ bi nù un" (That is the person to ask), the oracle instructs. The permanently absent Ọ̀rúnmìlà offers the palm nuts (and the inscriptions generated through them) as his principle of "being-there." Culturally situated operators of the divination infrastructure make the best efforts to ensure that the palm nuts accurately transmit the spirit's reply to their labors of enquiry.

In the calculus of material existence worked out in this story, Ifá's animating spirit is in permanent exile. This spirit's irreversible alienation, as well as the trace forms in which it partially appears when properly invoked (a good part of which is the story unit), is essential for the creation of life in general. The palm nuts, the remainders, constitute the "masque" of the spirit that has become unpresent-able.[11] The spirit mitigates the effect of its absence with the mute palm nuts that are signs of its absent-presence. The written signs transcribe patterns of the knowledge Ọ̀rúnmìlà gained as a result of his one-time presence at the time of destiny. The divination narrative connects and translates the significance of the traced-out presence (which is a sign of an irremediable absence) as stories to be interpreted for the present moment, with the collaboration of the client who is seeking insights into a fragment of general existential difficulty.

In theory, reference in Ifá discourse approximates what Ọ̀rúnmìlà witnessed at the distribution of destiny.[12] Divination therefore involves probing the inner reaches of essential occultation (awo) for the main purpose of making it yield fundamental knowledge (ìmọ̀) about life. Divination hermeneutics as instituted in Ifá practices requires efforts to draw plain, cultural knowledge from the occulted. Stories are used to translate inscripted codes of Ọ̀rúnmìlà because the record of the events witnessed at the distribution of destiny can no longer travel as events. Those events happened only once; even if Ọ̀rúnmìlà did not disappear into the palm tree, he can only relate narrativized versions of what he witnessed. Events survive beyond happenstance only in stories, or ìtàn.

The Ìwòrì Méjì story shows that several translations occur between the priest's transcription of the signs indicated by the palm nuts and the client's response to counseling. Ọ̀rúnmìlà's four priests probably recited a narrative whose contents Abímbọ́lá's informants summarized in one line about barrenness. Ọ̀rúnmìlà's curt reaction to the diviners' conclusion indicates that while clients can follow their own will, priests are not free to do as they wish and must be guided by the inscription story. After interpretation, priests can conclude their brief and depart, while the clients begin to exercise their intelligence and will. Ọ̀rúnmìlà laughs off his counselors and ends up inside a palm tree!

The Past and Present in Ifá Writing

Early Yorùbá Christian clergymen believed that divination priests led an "oracular cult" that, according to Peel, made "hegemonic claims to a special relationship with the Supreme Being, with a key theme—the powerful precedent—which presents a highly refracted memory of the vanished greatness of its sacred centre" ("The Pastor and the Babalawo," 344). The clergymen invested much interest in the diviners, I observed earlier, because the former held sway over the non-Christian population mainly through the mystique of their graphematic practice. Befriending and converting powerful local divination priests netted for the Christians not an individual pagan but a "truth regime" leader, as it were. Converting a divination priest brings the pagan mythography under the authority of a phoneticized and allegedly more democratic writing system. At least, that is what Bishop Phillips believed. The missionaries did not attack the mythography, but they exploited the commentary-making space, the space between inscription and action—the place where cultural continuity and discontinuity is established— to discredit the divination priests as selfish charlatans who use the mystical basis of their technique to do as they wished and mislead their clients. According to Lijadu:

> Lára jíjẹ àti mímu ni olórí aájò àwọn babaláwo kulẹ̀ sí; níbẹ̀ kan náà ni ti àwọn olùsìn tìkárawọn náà mọ pẹ̀lú. Síbẹ̀síbẹ̀ a wá ọ̀pọ̀lọpọ̀ ìtàn asán jọ láti já àwọn

ọ̀gbẹ̀rì lí àyà tàbí láti yá wọn lórí, tàbí láti fo àwọn adéjàá lí ẹyẹ, kí wọ́n má ṣe lè ṣe ọrùn líle, ṣùgbọ́n kí wọ́n fi ohùn sí ibi tí àwọn babalawó bá fí i sí. (*Ifa*, 66) (Subsistence interest is the be-all and end-all of divination priests; the same goes for their followers. Jejune tales are gathered to either scare or enthuse the uninitiated or to mislead the inquisitive so that they will cease asking questions and agree with the priests' self-serving conclusions.).

Lijadu addresses more than theological facts here; he construes the use of narratives in Ifá divination as a barefaced "presentism," that is, as a system by which divination priests construct the past to suit only today's needs. After all, the divination priest's claims for the past cannot be verified.

Karin Barber also focuses on the post-inscription elements of the divination protocols for her analysis of Ifá discourse's incorporation of multiple others to position itself strategically as the governor of the Yorùbá intellectual universe. As noted above, Barber too does not question the consistency of the inscriptions. Her concern is how the priests' stories use verifiable "techniques of argument" to place Ifá above all else. The strategies include "narrative positioning," by which the unrestrained thematic range of divination stories authorizes diviners to appropriate tales from all sources, from all domains, and about any topic, consign them to the past, and then retrieve the same as ideas activated by the revealed imprinted sign. Barber caricatures Ifá's "narrative positioning" in words similar to Lijadu's: "The 'moral' is always the same, whatever the origin of the story: 'Ifá knows best. . . . Do what Ifá tells you and you will prosper; disobey Ifá and disaster will ensue'" ("Discursive Strategies," 208). Another incorporation strategy Ifá uses is "preempting time": the problems addressed in each story report an event as having taken place in the distant past, and the diviner comments on the events as if Ọ̀rúnmìlà constructed and handed down a model of future action from patterns observed in the past. The cleverest part of the presentation of Ifá's all-encompassing model, Barber says, is that the divination God himself appears as a bewildered client in many of the stories: "Ifá the deity himself appeals to a body of wisdom, encoded in precedents, which must be seen as outside his consciousness and antecedent to him. Nothing can go behind this paradox: the argument of the precedent is arrested at that point in a permanent and unresolvable deadlock. This has the effect of enhancing the authority both of Ifá as system and as spiritual being" (209). Ifá's third main discourse-making technique is "lexical layering," or the invention "of strange names" for familiar acts and objects. For example, Ifá stories frequently refer to the mouth as "olúbọ́bọ́tiribọ́ baba ẹbọ" (the insatiable devourer of all sacrificial offerings).

Barber evaluates Ifá stories in the way we currently think of histories: as reports of past events in proportions narratively scaled to reflect how persons interacted among themselves and with their environment in verifiable spaces and time. But this model of the past would apply to Ifá divination stories only if the graphic notation stage of the divination process is treated as an extraneous element with no significance at all. To refer back to the reading proposed above, Barber neglects the significance of the mythographic inscriptions that stand for the permanent barrier to our capturing past events in their "true" proportions. The commentary space in Ifá divination protocols would also have to be completely disregarded in order for the "presentism" criticism to be fully accepted. But we cannot speak about Ifá discourse or extract significance from its practices without considering "writing" and "commentary." The central axiom of Ifá practice that enjoins critical listening and acting on the client was recorded by Lijadu himself: "Bí o bá tẹ'fá tań, kí o tún 'yè rẹ tẹ̀" (When you're done consulting Ifá, be sure to reconsult your gumption) (*Ifá*, 37). A person counseled in Ifá is duty bound to then counsel him- or herself and decide to what extent instructions and prescriptions would be followed—Ọrúnmìlà mocked his diviners in the story discussed above. The injunction to counsel oneself means that while every story unit gives an allegorical account of how things were in the past and how similar they might be in the present, although not in mimetic proportions, the priest's retelling must, to the extent permitted by prevailing cultural practices, generate a directive, evince a pledge, articulate a feeling, or change the status quo (see Searle, *Expression and Meaning*), all gestures of àtúntẹ̀ (re-imprinting, re-counseling). In other words, the divination client is expected to *not* make the past present as it was. Even Ọrúnmìlà could not perform such a feat. As records of divination sessions show, the priest and the client, voluble readers of Ifá's mute signs in the commentary space, are not absolved of the responsibility of contemplation and self-reflection. Although the solutions to the problems presented by Ifá divination clients might have been "authored" by precedence, stories told to articulate antecedent transactions are not therefore exempted from answering to genuinely new responsibilities.

Ifá narratives are not like simple, constative, or descriptive charters whose primary referential relationship is to an event, a moral goal, or the performers' other vested interests. In the divination story, bound by convention as it is, the narrator-priest, in theory, is obliged to *not* pursue a detectable personal interest—except that of proving to be a competent, honest broker of the revelations of destiny—in the problem addressed by the story. This is why, I suggest, the referent of the Ifá story is the inscription and not the event of the story, something that, in theory, only the disappeared Ọrúnmìlà experienced. The "letters" that signify the story proceed not from the priest's will but from the divination instrument, that is, from the palm nuts or the chain. Ifá clients do not just seek a reading; they are best served only when the "writing" is done correctly.

How does Ifá practice actualize a theory of time and history and elaborate how the past influences (or does not influence) the present and the future? In *Ifá*

Divination Poetry, Abímbọ́lá asserts that the divination story "is a type of 'historical' poetry" (20); that is, the divination stories are historical references that illustrate virtually all possible combinations and patterns of social action. A more nuanced explanation that could liberate divination clients from the tyranny of the past as construed in Abímbọ́lá's mysticism could be achieved with J. D. Y. Peel's thoughts on the workings of a flexible presentism, one in which although "present practice is governed by the model of past practice," fundamental conceptions of antecedence will not be so sacrosanct that they could not be revised to accommodate genuinely new developments ("The Past in the Ijesha Present," 113).

The expectation that the client should act willfully on the reports of the events presented by the diviner demonstrates that the stories that diviners tell in the present constitute—and do not just report—the events. The stories, in other words, construct the past. The client can forestall the portentous past from repeating itself or allow it to fulfill its propitious potential. In Ifá, the past is not fully available for the living client, who must still make the labor of sacrifice in the present, within cultural constraints. That past sacrifices and offertories (ẹbọ) do not protect against present and future peril is clear evidence of how the past differs from the present. Living clients are responsible for their ẹbọ, made not to the past but in the present for the smoothing of paths yet to be trodden. Were Ifá stories merely constatives of past events, history, in theory, would have ended with Ọ̀rúnmìlà's disappearance, and no new narratives would be formed. But Ifá stories recount the basis of belief in Islam, explain the peculiarities of Christian beliefs, and divine the etiology of the structure of railroad schedules, all of which are historical developments that came about after Ọ̀rúnmìlà's disappearance into the palm tree. That is why we have to conclude that in Ifá practice the inscription system physically marks what Peel calls the "otherness of the past" and authorizes the relative autonomy of commentary in the form of storytelling. The inscription is the name of the self-consciously contentless, guileless referent of culture-making and culture-sustaining stories.

Notes

1. Rev. Fr. Placide Tempels would, three decades later, speak about the necessity of Bantu philosophy in nearly identical terms: "If one has not penetrated into the depths of the personality as such, if one does not know on what basis their acts come about, it is not possible to understand the Bantu. One is entering into no spiritual contact with them. One cannot make oneself intelligible to them, especially in dealing with the great spiritual realities" (*Bantu Philosophy*, 17).

2. His examples include Paul's learning Jewish traditions under Gamaliel and his studying Greek idolatry at Tarsus. Bishop Phillips also attributes Moses's success in the book of Exodus to his intimate knowledge of Egyptian religions.

3. Those are the terms Jacques Derrida uses to describe general writing in *Of Grammatology*; see p. 46.

4. Rev. James Johnson declares Ifá to be "the great Oracle of the Yorùbá country" (*Yoruba Heathenism*, 19).

5. For details of the inscription process, see Bascom, *Ifá Divination*, 3–12 and 49–59; Abímbọ́lá, *Ifá Divination Poetry*, 9–11. Epega lists by name and visual illustrations all the 256 possible units in the system, from Ejiogbé to Ofúnṣèé (*Ifá*, 7–38).

6. For example, an obvious typographic mistake in Abímbọ́lá records similar graphic marks for both Ìròsùn (the fifth basic unit) and Ọ̀bàrà (the seventh). An attentive reader, without being a trained babaláwo, can correct the mistake simply by following the order of twos and ones. See also Bascom's "Odu Ifa" for a discussion of the principles that can be used to place variations in the grid.

7. See Abímbọ́lá, *Ifá*, 43–62; Bascom, *Ifá Divination*, 120–137; Olatunji, *Features of Yorùbá Oral Poetry*, 127–134.

8. Ilesanmi, a Catholic priest, was for a long time professor of Yorùbá at the Obafemi Awolowo University, Ilé-Ifẹ̀. He follows the tradition established by three pioneering indigenous Ifá scholars cited earlier, Phillips, Lijadu, and Johnson, all Anglican priests.

9. Bascom (*Ifa Divination*) says that the only autochthonous sections of divination stories are the names of the diviners. Other parts could be sourced from folktales, myths, legends, and so forth.

10. Ọ̀rúnmìlà here institutes a system of iteration: "the possibility for every mark to be repeated and still to function as a meaning mark in new contexts that are cut off entirely from the original context, the 'intention to communicate' of the original maker of the mark. That originator may be absent or dead, but the mark still functions, just as goes on functioning after the death of its intended recipient" (J. Hillis Miller, *Speech Acts in Literature* 78).

11. It should not be forgotten that the "odù" writing practice is literally operated by remainders; in the palm-nut divination system, for example, only remainders express portentous inscription. I have borrowed the idea of the spectral relationship of "masque" to "spirit" from Derrida's *Specters of Marx*.

12. Ìpín (literally "allotment" or "destiny" in colloquial Yorùbá) is what Ọ̀rúnmìlà reveals through (and in) the divination process. But in practical divination terms, ìpín is what recurs in narrativity. The divination story contains what has happened at least once in the past.

2 Culture, Meaning, Proverbs

(For Oyekan Owomoyela, in Memoriam)

From the most banal banter to the highly stylized, ritual texts, proverbs are the most frequently invoked art form of asserting cultural being. In film, storytelling, drama, comedy, and tragedy, proverbs are cited straightforwardly as if they are inscriptions of cultural wisdom, usually prefaced with the formulaic introduction "The Yorùbá concluded thusly" (Àwọn Yorùbá bọ̀) or with the one that pleads, "As the elders say in proverb" (Gẹ́gẹ́ bí àwọn àgbà ti ń pa á lówe). Canonical forms of popular sayings are also commonly distorted either to evince easy laughter about deviations from cultural conventions or to argue against the folly of nonsensical insistence on received wisdom. Earnest quotations of proverbs rest on the axiomatic belief that the sayings permanently encode a store of cultural meaning and wisdom whose injunctions should be followed; ironic quotations usually revise received wisdom in light of newer, historical developments rather than contradict tradition's heft. I argue in this chapter that evidence in proverbs about proverbs—metaproverbs, as it were—suggests a complicated relationship among the verbal text, cultural wisdom, and historical (conversational) meaning. In Yorùbá proverb pragmatics, texts in the proverb inventory, like divination inscriptions, communicate wisdom and meaning not as settled cultural terms but as subjects of constantly shifting, instituted interests.

The proverb has incurred the greatest scrutiny from the most diverse tribes of scholars, philosophers, literary and cultural critics, ethnographers, anthropologists, and language pragmatists, each aiming, unsuccessfully, to finalize its character in one explanation. The more closely scholars examine the proverb, the less we know about its essential nature; the more pronouncements are hazarded about its nature, the less assured the reader becomes. The proverb is always about something else and hardly ever about itself. When it is not serving tradition, the proverb is found to be leasing itself free of compensation to numberless communications that cannot voice their will or intention without its help. Any time the Yorùbá divination priest is asked, "Kínni Ifá wí?" (What does the divination God say?), the formulaic response always declares, "Òwe n'Ifá ńpa" (Ifá speaks in proverbs). That is, the oracle speaks in still more figurative language; the form of the inventoried proverb is the spokes-figure, as it were, of a disclosure and counseling protocol that speaks for the Gods.

A Yorùbá proverb recommends that a gourmand should work his or her way into the center of a wrap of delicious steamed bean mush from the flat end (Ibi pẹlẹbẹ ni a ti ńmú ọ̀lẹ̀ jẹ). That is why I want to start with three proverb definitions and use Oyekan Owomoyela's Yorùbá-based account of the nature of the proverb as the flattest end of the serving. According to Owomoyela, the proverb is "a speech form that likens, or compares, one thing or situation to another, highlighting the essential similarities that the two share. In Yorùbá usage it is always at least one *complete* sentence" (*Yoruba Proverbs*, 3). In response to the heavy emphasis on difference and its entailments in Yorùbá terms for text and meaning, Owomoyela generalizes that the proverb is a tool for synthesizing meaningful deictics out of ordinarily disparate concepts and ideas.[1] Relying on materials from the Haya language in Tanzania, Peter Seitel describes the proverb's distinctive features as "explicit and/or implicit reasoning, distinctively stylized language, forceful thematic statement, a characteristic kind of contextualization combining reference to the vivid present and the wider horizon, and different forms of embeddedness in the syntactic and interactional structures of speech" (*The Powers of Genre*, 36). In Haya and Yorùbá, proverbs hinge ordinary utterances to much larger universes of preceding cultural intentions. Neal Norrick deduces the following definition from English proverbs: "a ready-made utterance with a standard ideational meaning and perhaps a standard textual and/or interactional meaning as well, [with which] the speaker avoids the necessity of formulating an original utterance of his own" (*How Proverbs Mean*, 25). In other words, the proverb user quotes from a linguistically and culturally delimited body of anonymously authored texts to make both evaluative and argumentative judgments without having to start from scratch. These definitions agree on four points:

1. In the ideal, fully formed state, proverbs are semantically complete texts.
2. Prior to use, the dictionary meanings of a proverb's lexis add up to a literal statement.
3. During use, a proverb's lexical items enter fields of meaning wider than can be entered in dictionaries and anthologies.
4. Being full utterances, proverbs relieve speakers of the need to author new articulations.

In these definitions, proverbs preserve vetted meanings in conspicuous language. The sayings persist in mature speakers, who hand them down from generation to generation, thereby perpetuating traces of each tradition's cultural consensus. From this angle, the proverb is a willing agent of culture, thought, and tradition. From another viewpoint, the definitions reveal that proverbs make practical sense only in the contingent, fleeting moments of recall and use, at which point they subject traditional thought and culture to contextual interests. Within this perspective, the proverb resembles the proverbial messenger that cannot not deliver a message that is not inherited. Thus it seems unthinkable that the proverb can be understood without valuing its rootedness in culture; neglecting the untethered "face value" of its terms is no less grim. The proverb's typically prominent verbal mechanics, including compelling imageries and arresting logic, valorizes appearance. Under usage conventions, however, the facade has to be peeled back (if not peeled off) to reveal the meaning behind it. In this chapter, I argue that although verbal formulas claim that proverbs preserve antecedent, vetted wisdom, quoted sayings, like divination inscriptions, do not exercise unquestioned cultural validity over the new, contingent contests and interests they are deployed to help sort. A successful proverb usage results from how well the speaker manages the centrifugal tug that stretches the quoted statement between the contingent, lexical face value, and deeper cultural meaning. Proverbs work not because they follow cultural consensus—many times, a proverb's use indicates disagreements over a cultural practice—but because they help speakers of a language cross continuity to contingency. To use the idiom of ordinary language semantics, proverbs are performative utterances that weld syntax and conventions to create (and not just to reflect) desires.

Proverbs on Proverbs: Message or Messenger

A number of European and Mediterranean traditions speak of proverbs as ornaments of well-wrought and carefully sorted propositions. The Arabic proverb, for example, is not real food but the spice added to the main dish (A proverb is to speech what salt is to food), and in Hebrew, proverbs, like garden flowers, exist to induce emotional pleasure (What flowers are to gardens, spices to food, gems to a garment, and stars to heaven, such are proverbs interwoven in speech). Many African traditions think of proverbs as facilitators of conversations and as materials for plumbing the inner landscape of discourse strategies: a digestive herb or soothing vegetable oil in Igbo, a bowl of soup in Birom, flesh to skeleton in Zulu (Ojoade, "African Proverbs on Proverbs," 20). Syntactically, sayings that represent proverbs as decorators of speech and thought, or as agents of other pleasures, usually take on the form of "A is B" or "A is like B," where "A" is the proverb and "B" is either the cultural theme the proverb expresses or some remark on the proverb's appearance. The proliferation of "A is B" sentences in proverbs about proverbs encourages the dominant view in cultural studies that proverbs are metaphors by other means. Proverb-as-metaphor explanations do not worry that their naming one figure of speech as another figure of speech is itself figurative and not literal or "natural."

The Yorùbá metaproverb "Òwe lẹsin ọrọ̀; bí ọrọ̀ bá sọnù, òwe la fi ńwá a" is often translated into English as "The proverb is the horse of the word; when the word is lost, it is the proverb that we use to look for it." This phrasing in English

imposes an "A is B" syntax that does not quite reflect the more open-ended order in the original wording; the underlying proverb-as-metaphor of analytical
paradigm, far more than a folk, Yorùbá "A is B" theory of figuration, I contend,
drives the English translation. Ojoade's rendering of the Yorùbá saying as "A
proverb is the horse of conversation; (thus) when the conversation droops, a
proverb revives it" in the study from which I have taken all the flower-of-speech
sayings mentioned above overtranslates the original to emphasize the discourse
agent theme that has ruled academic studies of proverbs since the Greeks. A
closer look would affirm that the "A is B" introit of the original (The proverb is
the horse of words) does not carry over to the other part, and that ebbing and
resurgence—discourse pragmatic features not mentioned in the original—are
added to make the whole saying cohere around the "A is B" formulation. Ojoade
adds the English-language duration linker "thus" to construct a happy-ending
allegory that illustrates how proverb use approximates conversation reclama-
tion.[2] This translation reconfigures the open-ended original into a discourse
elixir in order to produce a transcultural communication helper theory of the
proverb that works alike in Birom, Idoma, Igbo, Arabic, Hebrew, Ovambo, and
Latin.

One need not be an apostle of radical difference in cultural matters to
conclude that the conceptual uniformity sought in Ojoade's translation derives
more from the "A is B" framework than from a common thread in his informing
texts. Some sayings, according to Ojoade, remark on the national peculiarities of
proverb functions: "Proverbs are the affairs of the nation" (Kikongo); "As the country, so the proverb" (German). Other proverbs Ojoade cites about proverb use do
not support the transcultural thesis. The sayings, typically lacking the "is" pred-
icate, are longer and more difficult to attach to an overriding figure of speech,
and their controlling imageries vary widely. Jarawa speakers use the proverb to
"sell" their less discerning opponents and to "end long talks." The discourse closure
function of proverbs in Krobo carries a more bellicose tone; it is not unlike "spear-
ing animals with a pointed raffia midrib." The Hausa, too, speak of proverb use as
verbal dueling.

I want to further illustrate how the proverb-is-metaphor viewpoint drives
English-language translations of the Yorùbá "Word's Horse" proverb, particularly of its key term, the word or lexis (ọ̀rọ̀). The saying is often translated into
English because the opening part positions proverbs as word substitutes; that
is, the proverb is the word's horse in the manner that the Latin "pro-verbo" works
in the word's behalf. In their 1973 book, Lindfors and Owomoyela render the
saying thus: "Proverbs are the horses of speech; if communication is lost, we use
proverbs to retrieve it" (*Yorùbá Proverbs*, 1). They translate "ọ̀rọ̀" (the word) as
"speech" in one part and "communication" in the other to fit the theoretical assumption that insists proverbs, in their true form, facilitate conversations, or

"speech," one of the several terms in the semantic range of the Yorùbá "ọ̀rọ̀." To avoid repeating the same term in the other part of the proverb, Owomoyela and Lindfors substitute the synonym "communication," another translation still in the meaning orbit of "ọ̀rọ̀." In the book published in 2005, Owomoyela translates the "Word's Horse" proverb in two ways. The body of the anthology says "Proverbs are the horses of communication; if communication is lost, proverbs are what one uses to find it" and glosses the saying as "Effective discourse is impossible without resort to proverbs" (*Yoruba Proverbs*, 497). This version straightens out the earlier book and represents "ọ̀rọ̀" consistently as "communication." The implication remains, however, that the word (ọ̀rọ̀) cannot be permanently lost. Proverb use, the translations imply, counteracts the threat of miscarried lexis and helps manage the successful delivery of intentions. Owomoyela thus constructs the proverb as something communicators ride toward securing the integrity of message delivery channels.

The long, theoretical overview of Owomoyela's 2005 book introduces still another translation: "The proverb is the horse of speech / When speech is lost, the proverb is the means we use to hunt for it" (*Yoruba Proverbs*, 12). The saying is now interpreted to mean a way of insisting "that bereft of proverbs, speech flounders and falls short of its mark, whereas aided by them communication is fleet and unerring" (12). Proverbs perform these functions because they "are held to express unexceptionable truths, albeit with some qualification, [and] their use is tantamount to an appeal to established authority" (12).

Owomoyela's three translations render "ọ̀rọ̀" as "speech" or "communication," or both, but never as "word." The variations are symptomatic not just because Owomoyela is a dominant figure in modern proverb studies but also because his writings on African thought and expressive cultures always put his unparalleled command of English and Yorùbá to the service of the endogenous African view of things. This is why it is remarkable that in the examples above, Owomoyela analyzes the nature of the proverb with information from Yorùbá sources without quite following the lead of the source language with regard to the central term of the all-important "Word's Horse" proverb, "ọ̀rọ̀." His translations follow the *Oxford English Dictionary* route, where communication means "the imparting, conveying, or exchange of ideas, knowledge, information, etc. (whether by speech, writing, or signs)." Of course, "communication" could be a synonym of "ọ̀rọ̀" when considered in the context of expressions generally. The most surprising and revealing part of Owomoyela's translations is that they place the proverb outside of communication, as if proverbs were not speech but merely delivery agents. Although he declares, rather stringently, that "a proverb that has no truth value, however inventive or striking its imagery, is of no value" (*Yoruba Proverbs*, 16), Owomoyela refrains from advancing the entrenched understanding within proverb studies that the proverb is essentially a *speech* or *communication* proxy.[3]

To further explore the possible reasons for Owomoyela's handling of "ọ̀rọ̀," I look into how he treats the same term in another proverb about "ọ̀rọ̀": "Ẹyin lọ̀rọ̀; bí ó bá balẹ̀, fífọ́ ló ńfọ́" (The word is an egg; once it falls, it cracks).[4] Lindfors and Owomoyela's 1973 translation reads, "Words are like eggs; when they drop, they scatter" and glosses the proverb to imply cautioning "a person to carefully consider his words before uttering them," the reason being that "words, once said, cannot be unsaid, just as a broken egg cannot be put together again" (*Yorùbá Proverbs*, 35). This translation changes a metaphor (The word is an egg) into a simile (Words are like eggs).[5] Unlike the situation in the "Word's Horse" proverb, "ọ̀rọ̀" is rendered literally as the "word," and its bare materiality as an occurrence is reflected. Eleven years later, however, Owomoyela develops another translation: "Speech is an egg; when dropped it shatters" ("Proverbs," 11). The metaphor of the original is retained, but "ọ̀rọ̀" is now "speech." Furthermore, the 1973 translation is in the active voice, with the proverbial word hitting the ground and breaking of its own volition. In the later version, the passive construction adopted elides the dropper. The suggested meaning also expands in Owomoyela's newer translation: "The message is that once speech is uttered, it cannot be recalled; it might be retracted, corrected, regretted, or repudiated, but the state of never-having-been-uttered can never be re-achieved" ("Proverbs," 11). Owomoyela's new interpretation includes discourse reception management strategies—retraction, correction, repudiation—that are not in the original.[6] Owomoyela's 2005 collection translates the saying as: "Words are eggs; when they drop on the floor, they shatter into pieces." Like the original, the translation contains metaphor-making syntax and is constructed in the active voice; "ọ̀rọ̀" is translated literally; and the discourse management extrapolations of earlier versions are excluded. The new meaning now reads, "Words are delicate things; once spoken, they cannot be retrieved" (*Yoruba Proverbs*, 168).

The clue to Owomoyela's preferring "speech" and "communication" over the literal "word" is to be found in the 1984 essay where, analyzing evidence from Yorùbá sayings about speech etiquette, he proposes that the one work that the proverb does well is to preserve the African "philosophy of communication" ("Proverbs," 3).[7] He deduces that the tendency of traditional African societies toward "ephemerality" or impermanence in issues affecting the archiving of words is not an accident but a well-considered approach to disseminating thought. Most African communities did not develop popular technologies of engraving sounds, probably because they saw no wisdom in permanently recording speech. Contrary to accepted wisdom, Owomoyela argues that the predominance of orality in African societies did not result from a lack of technical know-how. Yorùbá societies, for example, carry over their deep distrust of "permanence" to the era of widespread literacy in the proverb, "Òyìnbó tó ṣe lẹ́ẹ̀dì ló ṣè résà" (The white man who made the lead pencil also made the eraser). This saying, Owomoyela suggests, demonstrates that "the Yorùbá regard the invention of the eraser as a necessary and desirable corollary to the invention of writing" (7). Yorùbá speech is governed by contingent calculations, acute self-awareness, swift response, and a readiness to ride the horse of conversation in whichever direction things develop. Yorùbá societies favor "proverbial overt explicit communication" and "oral ephemerality over literal permanence." The cold indifference inherent in the materials of preserving words in permanent forms lacks the "softness, delicacy and wispiness" (8) of warm, ephemeral speech.[8]

In a radical move that has mostly gone unnoticed, Owomoyela opposes orality to literality and figurality to literacy and recommends the first item in each binary as underlying drivers of African thought on communication. He says that "societies with a writing tradition" are literal in their communication practice; they prefer "directness and precision in communication." In contrast, "those with an oral tradition favor circuitousness and opacity" ("Proverbs," 8). The advantages of figuration's nimbleness and suppleness, attributes inherent to discourses governed by proverbs, seem to have inspired Owomoyela's portrayal of "ọ̀rọ̀" as "speech" and "communication." For Owomoyela, "speech" and "communication" endow words with intention and free them from the word's cold literality (or materiality). It makes practical sense, he therefore argues, that the "Word's Horse" proverb should construct the proverbial "word" in the form of a horse that speakers ride to deliver messages. Owomoyela's ideal Yorùbá speaker is not interested in the fate of words as words but in how they can be used to deliver messages.

A significant irony attends Owomoyela's thinking on proverbs: Although he argues for ephemerality, he discounts the "face value" meaning of the keyword, "ọ̀rọ̀," in the "Word's Horse" proverb. Also, the "White Man and the Eraser" proverb, which is said to embody ephemerality, suggests a permanent philosophy. In both instances, the proverb means more than its literal terms. Nonetheless, reaching beyond the literal—beyond the cold "word"—to the communicated is far from easy; indeed, I am not sure we can prove that the ephemeral cover of proverbial words carries a full, obvious meaning independent of all extended possibilities. Even when we focus exclusively on extended meanings, assuming for a moment that it is possible to do so, the face value of the cold, material saying is still implicated. Hence the "White Man and the Eraser" proverb loses its virtuous meaning when it absolves perjury or justifies corrupt alterations of written records.

Text contra Context in Proverbs

Mining the face-value meaning of proverbs allows Mineke Schipper to confront women's unfavorable place in tradition's deep structure: "When authors talk about the general consensus on proverbs and their objectivity as a source of information, they often idealize, nostalgically and romantically, their eternal truth, indestructible roots and indispensable wisdom, as guards of social harmony and good conduct. For the time being, it seems justified to ask some questions on the speaker's (gender) perspective and interests before taking the general consensus for granted" (*Source of All Evil*, 5). Her study of face-value signification shows that many phrases in proverbs are depositories of prejudices, perhaps outright misogyny, and that they put women at a significant cultural and political disadvantage. When it is insisted in Shona that "One who applies proverbs gets what s/he wants," it is undeniable that sayings that denigrate women grant "authoritative validity" to men seeking to manipulate the world against women's interests. Syntactically, the Lingala saying "Woman is like the earth: everyone sits down on her" (24) operates as if the claims were natural facts. The declarative form of the first part of the Fulani proverb from Senegal that says "Woman is fire. If you have to, take a little" presents a prejudice as a scientific claim. Each of these sayings plies its users' cultural ethos and directs men to mistreat women.[9]

I will not examine the merit of Schipper's claims about women's status, but I will comment on her face-value theory of proverbs, which focuses on how the palpable shape of the material signifier directly involves itself in the process of making meaning.[10] The proverb's literal signification, in itself, ought to count for something, Schipper implies; after all, a proverb's being accepted into the cultural inventory implies that that proverb expresses some important idea, including thoughts on patterns of gender relations. In Yorùbá, they say "Ẹ̀ṣẹ́ kìí ṣẹ́ lásán" (The fist does not fist on account of nothing). The commonsensical appeal of the face-value contents of proverbs is the reason we quote them, as I have just done above, in cultural analysis. But this very important and popular view of proverbial meaning—that the proverb means what it says—needs further emendation because even the material sign means something only if it carries traces of differences and similarities with other signs. The Yorùbá proverb "Àwárí lobìnrin ńwá nǹkan ọbẹ̀" (A woman who wants something for her stew will not give up looking until she finds it) (*Source of All Evil*, 74) clearly ties domestic chores to sex roles. However, because anatomical sex does not equate with either discursive sex or gender, we should imagine this proverb implying that males who need to cook must find the right ingredients. As proverbially true as it is in Yorùbá that "without a cause, women are never named Death-Took-the-Heir-Apparent" (Bí kò bá nídìí, obìnrin kìí jẹ́ Kúmólú), the face-value meaning does not preclude the fact that men, too, get to be named Kúmólú (Death-Took-the-Heir-Apparent) only when a strong cause indicates it. In other words, the foundation of a proverb's significance concerns more than the explicit phrases of the inventoried saying.

Subordinating medium to content, as face-value studies do, ranks prevailing interests and explicit contexts very high within meaning construction factors.

The structure that holds contents together ranks not so high because it merely serves to contain the spirit of immediate and remote production circumstances. Hence those who translate "ọ̀rọ̀" as "speech" or "communication" in the "Word's Horse" proverb emphasize context in their understanding of the nature of the proverb. For them, speakers ride the word's horse to fit performance contexts to their broader cultural (or semantic) antecedents. We quote proverbs, they imply, to bring the authority of the past to bear on current interactions and to press communal influence on the processing of delivered messages. The proverb's face value calls, maybe not whips, conversations into linear cultural order. Proverb users mount the steed of proverbial words to instate age-old semantic coherence handed down from one epoch to another. Proverbs are considered capable of transporting the past into the present because their anonymous, communal, and ancient authorship underwrites a system of quotation and of manifesting reasonableness within a speech community. By quoting a proverb, the speaker reassures listeners that the expressed thoughts are not arbitrary: "A child knows that the proverb used by the scolding parent was not made up by that parent. It is a proverb from the cultural past whose voice speaks truth in traditional terms. It is the 'One,' the 'Elders,' or the 'They' in 'They say,' who direct. The parent is but the instrument through which the proverb speaks to the audience" (Arewa and Dundes, "Proverbs and the Ethnography of Speaking Folklore," 70). In this conception of folk historicist reasoning, the most effective and easily communicated ideas in quoted proverbs recreate the past, even if the audience—the child, for example—cannot recognize its details. The gloss—ideational meaning, according to Norrick—attached to proverb inventories are apparitions of cultural presence. In face-value readings of proverbs, the horse rider in the "Word's Horse" proverb either revives or discovers something or catches up with it in every quotation. While quoting proverbs is not unlike citing "the Bible, Shakespeare or any other source felt to be part of the cultural heritage of the community as a whole," the proverb user is deemed to "disappear as an individual directive agent" (Norrick, *How Proverbs Mean*, 26).[11]

Accounting for difference is the main problem here: How is the past not the present? What separates the literal from the figurative, the event from its textuation, culture from the individual, text from contexts, and so forth? To my mind, proverb use does not remove difference in these binaries, in spite of the eminent logical sense proposed by the communicationist and face-value models discussed above. The folk recognition of the difference between the present and the past, for example, is evident in their quoting the past. The act of quoting, assuming that it is the past that is being quoted, makes temporal difference perceptible. The surface meaning of the quoted text plies the similarity of the occasion at hand with antecedents. By the same gesture, however, the difference between the two temporal spheres is marked. I have not come across a proverb about proverbs that claims to portray meaning, intentions, logical relations, cultural ethos, age-old wisdom, and the like, in their naked forms. To the contrary, proverbs speak of the capacity to generate similarities, differences, and comparisons: "Ohun tó bá jọ'hun la fi ń wé'ra wọn" (Semblance is the basis of comparison), says one Yorùbá proverb. The common English translation of a similar proverb in Igbo reads "Where one thing stands another will stand by it." Proverbs, it seems, do not make things stand on their own. In the "Word's Horse" proverb, the proverb becomes the horse only in the course of a continuing, contingent set of exchange activities. Without the loss of words, the horse is a horse, and the word is the word. Proverb users ride the horse made available to them when the word is lost. The proverb does not promise recovery or, in other words, a return to the sameness of equilibrium.

Proverb anthologists concede that meaning glossaries attached to proverbs cannot fix proverbs for good and place them outside of the relentless comparisons within which meanings are hatched in conversations. Most anthologists plead that inventoried meanings are only samples and that the theoretically indeterminable number of contexts in which a proverb can appear makes any interpretation provisional. This admission does not go far enough, because it does not reflect the centrality of polyvocality—not just polysemy—to proverb pragmatics.[12]

The importance of the play of difference to the being of proverbs is remarked most poignantly in what Raji-Oyelade names as "postproverbials," that is, new sayings that command attention and instantly get into the inventory by flaunting their awareness of tradition in the way they distort the logic and syntax of older texts. In one such popular "de-formation," the pathos-filled adage "Màálù tí ò nírù, Olúwa ní í lẹ́sinṣin fún un" (As for the cow that has no tail, God swats flies for it) becomes "Màálù tí ò nírù, ó wà ní Sábó" (As for the cow that has no tail, it is at the livestock market) ("Postproverbials in Yorùbá Culture," 77; translation modified).[13] In postproverbials, the supplementary structure of the new, flippant creation betrays the not-quite-not-original status of the older proverb while facetiously brandishing the new ones' dubious claim to originality. When "Ẹṣin iwájú ni àwọn tẹ̀yìn ńwò sáré" (The leading horse is an example to other racers) becomes "Ẹṣin iwájú ló gba ipò kìnní" (The leading horse takes first position), the supplement fills the syntactic slots in the original differently and marks for emphasis the significant role of substitution in proverb use. The supplement's hyper-competence betrays the arbitrary character of the canonical form. The logic and syntax of disaffirmation in postproverbials defame allegedly ponderous wisdom, and privilege profane literalism over high poetry. From within the culture, they loosen the hold of tradition on proverb use. Raji-Oyelade praises these schizoid constructions, which simultaneously recognize and misrecognize antecedence as the product of fecund thinking and imagination. Only those who are competent in the workings of tradition but who do not hold them sacrosanct can invent such texts, his research shows.

The playful marking of difference is not native to only postmodern sensibilities, I would like to think. The postproverbial's refusal to cede authority to the original's temporal priority and the straight-faced commitment to the possibility of reconfiguration both manifest foundational features in proverb structure. Only a proverbial sentiment would, for example, hail the spoken word as "ọ̀rọ̀, ajepomápọ̀nọ́n" (the word, one that subsists on red palm oil without soiling itself). In this epithet, the meaning of proverbial words does not arise organically from what they ordinarily signify; palm oil's substantive redness loses its determinant power in the discursive realm, where cold indifference rules. The word, as it were, bleaches the redness out of palm oil and absorbs its residue. The aphorism's force field nullifies substantiveness.[14] I am not arguing that proverbs erase difference without trace. They do not; after all, we still know that the word "ate" the palm oil. My argument is that proverbs manage the differences between the past and the present, between literality and figuration, and between commentary and inscription by transforming the alleged substantive elements of each term so that comparisons that generate meaning can continue to be made.

How, then, should we think about the relationship of the contents of largely preformed texts like proverbs to their quotation context? Do preformed texts come with antecedent contexts that affect usage? What is the role of antecedent situations in how proverbs create intertexts? These theoretical considerations are well illustrated in students' responses to the proverb used as an essay prompt in the January 1963 University of London's GCE O/Level Yorùbá examination: "Ẹní bá sọ̀kò sọ́jà, ará ilé ẹni ní í bá" (If one throws a stone into the crowded market, it hits a relative) (Rowlands, "The Illustration of a Yorùbá Proverb," 250; translation modified). Rowlands observes in his analysis of 214 scripts that an overwhelming number wrote supplementary narratives with a full complement of characters, events, and plots. The story elements were drawn from published collections of folktales, a school reader, and personal experiences. A very small group invented original stories, and a still smaller proportion (precisely, six percent) approached the question "in a manner which one might be expected to adopt in an English essay," in other words, without reference to a narrative supplement.[15] Rowlands views the students' manner of essaying as the continuation in modernity of Yorùbá tradition's "association of proverbs and moral tales" (251). Failing to acknowledge the value of supplementarity in the symbiotic relation of proverbs and narratives, Rowlands implies that Yorùbá students, contrary to what they are taught in schools about essay writing, rely on tradition's ready-made content and form to construct evaluative arguments, even in a situation that calls for a unique, synthetic exposition.[16]

The "Stone-throwing" proverb is also discussed in Alàgbà Ṣùpọ̀ Kòṣémánìí's *Òwe àti Àṣàyàn Ọ̀rọ̀ Yorùbá*, a book that reverses the convention of using story-telling occasions to exercise a stray proverb or two; here, proverbs are the primary subjects, and stories create contexts. Before I get to Kòṣémánìí's handling of this proverb, I want to say a little more about the book's unique approach to proverb analysis. The book consists of six extended dialogues between an elderly male, Alàgbà Kòṣémánìí (literally, "Indispensable Elder"), and two younger men. Unlike the founding exchanges in Fágúnwà's fiction that we will see in chapter 3, the conversations open with an obviously literate young man, Ọmọ Baba (Child of the Older Male), seeking instruction from Alàgbà (Elder) on proverbs and idiomatic expressions. Unlike the insistence in many ethnographic works that proverbs cannot be genuinely elicited outside of a "natural" context, the old man gladly agrees to teach his young ward. He even encourages the young man to take written notes and bring along an audio recording device. These two characters are not social equals, although their interaction is dominated by banter. The second young man, Adéṣínà, joins the conversation during the third dialogue. The dramatic dialogues began as a talk show on the radio network of the Ọ̀yọ́ state government's broadcasting service. The book is neither an anthology of proverbs nor a conventional scholarly analysis, yet the serious venture of gathering and analyzing proverbs occasions its being.

The young interviewers approached the right person to remedy their cultural lack probably because they knew that "It is only in the mouth of the elder that the kola nut is ripe" (Ẹnu àgbà lobì ńgbó).[17] But because one does not take to monotheism without monotheism taking something away from the convert (A kìí gba ìgbàgbọ́ kí ìgbàgbọ́ má gba nǹkan lọ́wọ́ ẹni), the age-appropriate consultant asks his acolytes to create a permanent record of his expertise for their future reference. In the give-and-take exchange, the orality/literacy scholarly axioms about things moving from voice to letter, from the old to the young, and from the past to the present appear to have percolated down to the folk. The exchange dynamics also indicate that proverbs can be a topic of formal inquiry to the "folk" outside of "natural," conversational contexts. I have commented this much on Kòṣémánìí's book's milieu to highlight the flexibility of contexts and also to reiterate the point proved in the response of Yorùbá students to the University of London examination that the bald citation of a proverb can cause the elicitation (and possibly the creative invention) of a context. For the University of London candidates, as well as for Kòṣémánìí's students, contexts are contingent and contrived; they may serve as backdrops for proverb usage just as easily as a quotation can instigate the creation of contexts.

I want to return to the "Stone-throwing" proverb and the topic of contexts. At the beginning of the third section in Kòṣémánìí's book, Ọmọ Baba asks whether all proverbs are associated with long narrative accounts of real-life contexts, whether proverbs are condensed records of events. The old man answers that "Gbogbo òwe tí àwa ń pa pèlú gbólóhùn méjì-méta wònyí ló ní ìsèlè kan tàbí méjì tó ṣu wón" (All these short sayings are caused by some events) and adds a few moments later that "Àwọn ìtàn tí ó ṣu àwọn òwe wònyí ni ibi tí okùn wọn ti fà wá" (The stories are the origins of the proverbs) (*Òwe àti Àṣàyàn Òrò Yorùbá*, 40–41). Kòṣémánìí's word choice implies more than a straightforward affirmation, however, because he does not admit that the events (ìsèlè) narrated in stories associated with proverbs are historical. He also does not say that they cause the proverbs, historically speaking, although his selected predicator, "ṣu," means "to excrete" as well as "to birth." Although he suggests causality (okùnfà) in his expansion of the first answer, the responses indicate that the proverb's primary relationship to past events is to the discursive transformation in stories that are probably best understood as allegories (ìtàn olówe).[18]

Adéṣína asks the question about the "Stone-throwing" proverb: "Baba, mo tún gbó tí àwọn ènìyàn máa ń sọ pé, bí a bá sòkò sójà, ará ilé ẹni níí bá. Ṣé ẹnì kan ti sòkò sójá rí, tí ó lọ ba ará ilé wọn ni àbi èwo ni àbùrò máa sòkò sí ọjà tí òpò ènìyán wà?" (Sir, I also hear people say that if one throws a stone into the crowded market, it hits a relative. Was there a time a person threw a stone into the market and injured that person's relatives; why the saying about throwing stones into a crowded marketplace?) (*Òwe àti Àṣàyàn Òrò Yorùbá*, 65–66). Kòṣémánìí responds with a tale of origin (ìtan tí ó bí òwe yìí) (66) that contains nothing about stone throwing or the market; it includes, however, doing harm to blood relatives inadvertently when the malicious intent to injure an innocent party misfires.

Kòṣémánìí's narrative speaks of a wealthy man who, because he detests beggars, decides to get rid of a particularly pesky alms seeker, to whom he gives a pouch of venomous snakes disguised as a bag of gifts. The rich man's children, who see their usually stingy father give away a bag they think is filled with money, waylay the poor beggar, steal the pouch of snakes, and get bitten. These are not completely innocent children, the story indicates with a little detail; they harvested the snakes for their father. Stone throwing comes in at the end of the story, when the village chief who adjudicates the case of snake poisoning brought by the rich man against the beggar rules in favor of the latter. According to Kòṣémánìí,

> Baálè ní òrò bàbá olówo dàbí òrò ẹni tí ó sòkò sí ọjà, tó rò pé òtò ni ẹni tí yóò bá sùgbón tí òkò tí ó sọ sàdédé orí ará ile rè. . . . Láti ọjó tí Baálè yìí ti sòrò yìí ni òrò náà ti di òwe. (*Òwe àti Àṣàyàn Òrò Yorùbá*, 68) (The village chief says that the rich man's case resembles that of a person that throws a stone into the market thinking that it will fall on a targeted person but watches it hit a relative. . . . The chief's words have been a proverb since then.)

In this account, the terms of the chief's judicial warning (ìkìlọ̀) that later became a proverb are, on their own, elements of an allegory. The stone-throwing coda is a micro-narrative that further allegorizes the longer story about two character types, the wicked Rich Man (Bàbá Olówo) and the Poor Beggar (Alágbe). The only historical (referential) relationship between them is Kòṣémánìí's retelling of the story of the chief who first used one illustration to conclude another. In the sequence of events, the alleged origin of the proverb is a narrative commentary within another narrative about the inadvertent consequences of a deliberate intent to harm another person. It cannot be clearly established that the proverb, the chief's quoted words, did not predate the story of the wicked rich man. If the chief's words—"the rich man's case resembles" (ọ̀rọ̀ bàbá olówo dàbí)—are taken literally, his reference must be to something that happened before the case at hand. As such, the proverb issues not from the story of the allegedly causal event but from the chief's admonition, a supplement that relies on an antecedent case. The purported ante-textual events of the "Stone-throwing" proverb and the case of "The Rich Man and the Poor Beggar" proverb supplement but do not cause the chief's words. The chief's words, now the "Stone-throwing" proverb, refer to another set of events and story.[19]

Following the imperative that most studies of proverb meanings observe, Kòṣémánìí's proverbs are used in context. But contexts here are no less synthetic than the proverbs they explain. After describing his mission at the beginning of the book, and after Kòṣémánìí has welcomed him, Ọmọ Baba ventures a proverbial opening, saying: "Wọ́n ní bí ń bá ń yá kì í tún pẹ́ mọ́" (If it unfolds briskly, the completion never takes long). The old informant completes the saying with "Òwe Láàńtètè" (Láàńtètè's proverb), an attribution that the young man does not know exists. Ọmọ Baba therefore follows up with "Kín ni Láàńtètè ṣe baba, tí òwe náàa fi jẹ́ tirẹ̀?" (What did Láàńtètè do that makes the proverb his?). Kòṣémánìí supplies the context by telling the story of an enthusiastic father who, in anticipation of his child's birth, starts preparing pediatric care potions soon after his wife becomes pregnant. Although the story does not clarify whether the words were invented by Láàńtètè or by observers of his anxious behaviors who attach the saying to his acts, the alleged originator's name, "Earnestness" in English, is an allegorical device for summarizing the contents of the proverb attributed to him. Láàńtètè, the agent of contextualization, refers not to a historical person but to a figurative invention.

Kòṣémánìí broadens the meaning of context to an extent not normally realized in proverb studies. He, for instance, collapses what we generally call meaning and context into one unit. When asked to explain "Èèyàn bí ìgbín ní í he ìgbín, ẹni bí ahun ní í rí ahun í he" (People like snail choose snails, people like tortoise find other tortoises) (*Òwe àti Àṣàyàn Ọ̀rọ̀ Yorùbá*, 13), Kòṣémánìí says, "*ìtúmọ̀* òwe yìí ni pé, *nígbà tí* dìndìnrìn àti wèrè bá fẹ́ jà tàbí tí àwọn aláìmọkan méjì tàbí aláàbọ̀ làákàyè méjì bá fẹ́ fi ìṣe wọn dí ọlọgbọ́n lọ́wọ́ ni àwọn àgbà tó bá wà nítòsí yóò pa òwe yìí fún wọn" (This proverb *means* that *when* an imbecile and a mad person are about to fight, or when the habitual ignorance of two ill-informed persons threatens to disrupt a wise person's focus, elders around use this proverb) (13). Meaning equates context in this example. A short while later synonymy gets into the mix when Kòṣémánìí adds substitute proverbs (13). Because Kòṣémánìí uses one proverb as the meaning (ìtúmọ̀) of another on several occasions, it looks like meaning for him implicates substitution and deferment. He says " 'Bí a bá ń kí wọn n'írè, wọn kìí jẹ́ láéláé, ṣóńṣórí ọmọ owú ni wọ́n fi í jẹ́ ni' *túmọ̀ sí pé* 'a kì í yínmú, kí a tún máa súfèé' " ("If you greet iron workers in the forge, they never answer, they only tip their nose in response" *means that* "the person who curls his or her lip to show disbelief cannot whistle at the same time") (7). The expressions on either side of "means that" are two different, complete proverbs. Kòṣémánìí also offers two contextual explanations: (1) the cultural situation of the blacksmith's forge (7–8) and (2) an imagined conversational situation that justifies a speaker's deliberately rebuffing a distraction that threatens to take him or her off course. Meaning, contexts, and synonymy— an array of substitution and supplementation—circumscribe proverb usage.

Going by Kòṣémánìí's words, context (àsìkò, or, ìgbà tí a ńlò ó), meaning (ìtúmọ̀), and function (ohun ti a ń lò ó fún) are all related. Contexts for him involve more than "natural" dialogue situations. That the exchange on the proverb about greeting blacksmiths at work occurs in a pedagogic context (ẹ̀kọ́ṣẹ́ òwe [*Òwe àti Àṣàyàn Ọ̀rọ̀ Yorùbá*, 11]), and not within a "natural" forge, implies that contexts are not completely separate entities that proverbs visit only when invited. The prohibition in Akan societies of the "direct elicitation of proverbs" outside of natural conversations seems not to apply to Kòṣémánìí's Yorùbá community. As Yankah reports, in Ghana "one cannot sleep except in a dream," that is, "without discourse, one does not tell proverbs" ("Do Proverbs Contradict?," 5). To Kòṣémánìí, the indispensable (Yorùbá) elder, dreams are ultimate discursive inventions, not the unvarnished natural facts that the surface meaning of the Akan proverb represents them to mean.

Perhaps the most important achievement of Kòṣémánìí's book is its handling of proverb meaning as performative speech acts, iṣẹ́ tí à ńfi ṣe (the task we use them to accomplish). Kòṣémánìí recodes the transporter model that thinks of proverb communication in terms of actions fully formed in the cultural past in more versatile ways. The blacksmith's forge conversation referred to above further unfolds thus:

ỌMỌ BABA: Òwe wo ni a tún le lò dípò òwe yìí? (What proverb can we use in place of this?)

ALÀGBÀ ṢÙPỌ̀ KÒṢÉMÁNÌÍ: Etí kìí gbéjì. (The ear does not take in two at a time.)

ỌMỌ BABA: Ṣé *ìkìlọ̀* ni òwe yìí tàbí *ìbàwí*? (Is this proverb a *warning* or a *reproval*?)

ALÀGBÀ ṢÙPỌ̀ KÒṢÉMÁNÌí: À ń fi òwe yìí *pàrọwà* fún ènìyàn ni. (The saying is employed to *mollify.*) (*Òwe àti Àṣàyàn Ọ̀rọ̀ Yorùbá*, 8; emphasis added)

The substitute proverb "Etí kìí gbéjì" (The ear does not take in two at a time) says that physiological limitations recommend that a person in the middle of an utterance must resist distractions. The linear structure of timing in speaking and hearing, this proverb notes, physically debars the stacking of spoken (or heard) sounds. Processing spoken words one at a time, as the fully engaged blacksmith in the forge does, is "natural." Important as this observation about physical limits seems, its discursive transformation in a proverbial speech act is perhaps more important: "The ear cannot take in two at the same time" simply mollifies, it does not warn, says Kòṣémánìí. The supplement does not clarify a natural fact; it effects a desire.

Proverb Meaning and Performative Speech Acts

When proverb scholars discuss meaning, do they speak of synonyms, of syntax-dependent logical relations, or of syntax-defying performative effects? Kòṣémánìí's terms, words in accord with the spirit with which J. L. Austin exposed the inadequacies of construing ordinary language meaning as approximations of thoughts and acts fully realized prior to representation for meaning, make this question pertinent.[20] In Austin's formulation, performative utterances fit contexts for words and words for context, but do not describe or report something already done. In his famous example, the party that says "I do" at a marriage ceremony is not reporting the doing of a marriage but "indulging in it" (*How to Do Things with Words*, 6); the saying is the doing. The speaker who says "Pèlépèlé làá pa àmúkùrù abẹ́ ẹpọ̀n" (The gnat nested in the folds of the testicular sac ought to be picked very gently) could not be reporting a unique experience, if the quotation is a proverb. Tense and syntax notwithstanding, if the metaproverb that says proverbs do not lie is to be believed, the saying does not report something done in the past. The statement is also not "historical," in the ordinary sense of transferring verifiable facts about a specific event, because its reference is present with the utterance. Were an earnest interlocutor to seek clarification by asking, "Is that true?," the person would have misconstrued the utterance and would have opened the path to an inadvertent postproverbial. It is remarkable in this regard that the thousands of lines of dialogue between Kòṣémánìí and his young students contain no line of "Ṣé òótọ́ ni?" (Is it true?) regarding the *meaning* of a proverb. It seems as if a proverb may be incorrectly applied but not falsely so.

Austin's accounts of how words do things by their being spoken is very useful for addressing the trouble with proverbs. Humans do something by saying something because factors other than correctly spoken words guarantee the coming to pass of the desires articulated. Felicitousness rules and conventions stipulate the correct words to be said by what persons, the right ways to put them, and under what conditions. Austin blurs the distinction between utterances that report already accomplished acts and those that bring reportable acts to life and demonstrates that every saying of words constitutes a doing of things: "the utterance of certain noises, the utterance of certain words in a certain construction, and the utterance of them with a certain 'meaning' in the favorite philosophical sense of that word, i.e., with a certain reference" constitutes "the performance of a locutionary act" (*How to Do Things with Words*, 94). Every meaningful utterance turns ordinary noises into linguistically significant sounds according to prevailing grammatical rules and effects a worldly act as the semiotic community permits. Of course, Austin excludes poetry and jokes from ordinary thing-doing words, an issue I address below.

Locutions, or semiotically intelligible speech, consist of sound (noises), grammar (the instrument of subjecting of noises to the rules of a particular language system), and reference (distributing the rule-governed grammar into directives that are to be followed within a specific language and sociopolitical environment). Thus Austin says,

> When we perform a locutionary act, we *use* speech: but in what way precisely are we *using* it on this occasion? For there are very numerous functions of or ways in which we *use* speech, and it makes a great difference to our act in some sense . . . in which way and which *sense* we were on this occasion "*using*" it. It makes a great difference whether we were advising, or merely suggesting, or actually ordering, whether we were strictly promising or only announcing a vague intention and so forth. (*How to Do Things with Words*, 99)

The locution "Can I have that piece of meat?" could be a question, a request, an order (an illocution), or a complaint (a perlocution). A university dean who responds to his colleague's report on students' plagiarism with "Fail them all" could be issuing an order to be obeyed, or mocking an officious colleague. Austin's point is that the link between well-formed statements and the acts they effect is not completely subject to the strict dictates of either grammar or cultural antecedents.

I have no evidence of either Kòṣémánìí's formal academic credentials or his camp among semantic theorists. Undeniable in the dialogues he anchors is the tendency to think of the effect of proverb use in terms analogous to Austin's. Almost every proverb Kòṣémánìí explains is attached to a performative act, a sample list of which is offered here.

ìkìlọ̀ or kìlọ̀ ìwà (warn[ing])   8, 17, 24, 27, 29, 65
ìbáwí (reproval, blame, scold)   8, 16
pàrọwà (mollify, soothe)   8, 38
pa lẹ́nu mọ́ (resist)   17
rán ni létí or ṣí ara ẹni létí (remind) 18, 19
ṣe òòṣà ìfura (self-awareness)   21
láálí (curse out)   22
bú (insult)   29, 69
ṣèfẹ̀ or ṣe yẹ̀yẹ̀ (mock)   37
pègàn aláṣejù (condemn excess)   65
làyé (explain)   82

It is not uncommon for one proverb to perform more than one speech act, or for different sayings to effect a common act. In one case, six different sayings are reported capable of being used to scold an unduly boisterous person:

1. Ohun tí ó bá jọ'hun ni a fi í wé 'hun; èèpo ẹpà jọ pósí ẹ̀lírí; àtàǹpàkò jọ orí ahun. (Semblance is the basis of comparison; the peanut shell resembles a tiny mouse's casket; the thumb resembles a turtle's head.)
2. Ipaṣẹ̀ làá mọ àrìnjọ. (Footprints reveal the nature of the company.)
3. Ẹni tí yóò yá ẹgbẹ̀rún ọkẹ́ tí kò ní bíyá (ṣan), kó ti ibi ọkẹ́ kan bẹ̀rẹ̀. (The debtor who cannot afford to repay two million should try borrowing twenty thousand first.)
4. Ìyàwó tí yóò gbọ́ràn, kì í fi ojojúmọ́ bú ọpa. (The obedient bride does not swear every time.)
5. A kìí tẹ̀ túfọ̀ ajá. (Delivering the sad news of a dog's death does not require a conference of elders.)
6. A kìí yọ́ "bá mi kí ìyá mi lóko" sọ. ("Greet my mother when you get to the farm" need not be whispered.) (*Òwe àti Àṣàyàn Ọ̀rọ̀ Yorùbá*, 22)

In an even more intriguing case, one proverb carries two contradictory speech acts of commendation and denigration:

ỌMỌ BABA: Ó ní itọ́ pẹ́ lẹ́nu, ó di wárápá. (He said if the saliva stays too long in the mouth, it becomes epileptic foam.)

ALÀGBÀ ṢÙPọ̀ KÒṢÉMÁNÌf: Bẹ́ẹ̀ ni, wọ́n parí rẹ̀ báyìí pé, . . . egbò pẹ́ lẹ́sẹ̀ ó di jàkùtẹ̀, bí obìnrin bá pẹ́ nílé ọkọ àjẹ́ ní í dà. (Yes, the saying is completed thus . . . an untreated sore becomes elephantiasis, a long married woman becomes a witch.)

ỌMỌ BABA: Baba kín ni ọ̀rọ̀ jàkutẹ̀ àti àjẹ́ ti jẹ́ nínú ọrọ wárápá? (Sir, what has elephantiasis got to do with epilepsy and marriage with witchcraft?) (*Òwe àti Àṣàyàn Yorùbá*, 36)

The old man explains that epileptic foam is to sputum as witchcraft is to a woman's longtime marriage because a cultivated habit becomes second nature over time. (Of course, the biology of the premise is not scientific and the syllogism about marriage is inaccurate.) In discussing the proverb's meaning and usage, Kòsémánìí says:

> Nígbà tí wọn bá fẹ́ fi oníwà buburú tàbi oníjàngbọ̀n kan ṣe yẹ̀yẹ́ ní àwùjọ ni wọn í fi irúfẹ́ òwe yìí ṣèfẹ̀ pé ó tún gbé iṣẹ́ rẹ̀ dé. . . . A tún le lo òwe yìí fún ẹni méjì tí wọn sì ńṣe dáadáa. (*Òwe àti Àṣàyàn Ọ̀rọ̀ Yorùbá*, 37) (This type of proverb is used to publicly ridicule a habitual trouble maker who is about to start another one. . . . We can also use this proverb to commend upright citizens.)

As Kwesi Yankah has argued in "Do Proverbs Contradict?," the proverb in question does not contradict itself. Unlike Yankah's informants, however, Kòsémánìí would accept the contradiction of the two perlocutionary acts as normal.

Invoking J. L. Austin's performative to unify the three sides of Kòsémánìí's explanation of proverb meaning (context, function, and meaning) would be easily dismissed if I were to leave unaddressed Austin's excluding poetry, stage acting, and joking from ordinary language. In his original thinking about performatives, Austin argued that "normal conditions of reference" are suspended in artistic usage because their ordinary signification is hollow or void: "A kìí ran ọmọ tí kò gbọ́n" (One should not speak in ironies to an unwise child), Austin would have said, had he been working with Yorùbá expressions (*How to Do Things with Words*, 22). The Kòsémánìí dialogues afford us two counterarguments without resorting to Derrida.[21] First, as noted above, "natural" (for Austin, "ordinary") contexts are contrivances of speechmaking and not just the other way around. Kòsémánìí and his acolytes happily make up contexts as they go, without sounding extraordinary or unduly literary—Austin, by the way, does the same. Second, Austin's axiomatic submission about the literary uses of language does not consider proverbial texts wherein figuration and literality routinely accommodate each other. For Kòsémánìí, the danger that ironic speech poses to unwise youngsters is a discursive (which is to say historical and cultural) formulation, not a "natural" fact. Ọmọ Baba and Adéṣína, not so wise at the beginning of the book, undertake the cultural education they need. Most important, if the link between locutionary noises (sounds), their illocutionary effect (the production of an impetus to do something following the grammatically correct articulation of meaningful noises), and their perlocutionary consequences (on the "feelings, thoughts, or actions" of the hearers) is not organic but conventional, as both Kòsémánìí and Austin show, there is no ordinary, nonhistorical, linguistic ground to exclude poetry, proverbs, and other allegedly "nonserious" genres from the class of impact-producing utterances. Austin seems right only because historical, extralinguistic institutions that set out the broad outline of how words should mean have excluded literary languages from ordinariness. I should say in conclusion that proverbs mean according to the standards of effecting perlocutionary consequences within particular speech communities. They always say what they mean but never in the "face value" manner often attributed to them in cultural studies. They appear never to fail to mean what they say because they enforce propriety, not truthfulness. In the language of Alàgbà Kòṣémánìí, Indispensable Elder, the individual for whom a "proverbial" use of language is meant cannot but recognize it (Bí òwe bá jọ tẹni à á mọ̀ ọ́).[22] To conclude where the discussion began, citing a proverb iterates not the unanimity of thought concluded in the past as traditions; proverbs facilitate, that is render intelligible, commentary making among disputants seeking diverse, interest-serving ends in the present.

Notes

1. Like the proverb (òwe), comparison (àfiwé), riddle (àló), narrative (ìtàn), and interpretation and translation (ìtúmọ̀) all imply folding, entwinement, comparing, and, in the case of meaning, unwrapping or unfolding.

2. Here is the plot summary: conversation turns wayward; speakers use the proverb to chase it down; speakers return the conversation to its proper track.

3. The "Word's Horse" proverb is a rather strange statement, given that the horse is a prestige item of conspicuous consumption in traditional Yorùbá societies, including those closest to the savannah. Proverbs, of course, are not an elitist speech form. Furthermore, horses are not native to historical Yorùbá kingdoms. They were introduced from the North and used mainly by the cavalry in war and for ceremonial purposes at other times. Ajibola records two other relevant proverbs about horses: "A kìí kí 'yàgò' fún ẹlẹ́ṣin àná" (The "make way" honor accorded a horse rider does not extend beyond that moment; that is, deference ceases when the eminent horse rider loses his or her status) and "Ẹní gun ẹṣin, ilẹ̀ ló ṁbọ̀ (The horse rider is bound to dismount) (qtd. in Law, "A West African Cavalry State," 1).

4. Another rendering says "Ẹyin lohùn, bí ó bá balẹ̀, fífọ́ ló ńfọ́" (The voice is an egg; once it falls, it cracks).

5. The difference between metaphor and simile is important only in the English translation because in Yorùbá both terms are àfiwé (comparisons).

6. The new elaboration of the proverb's meaning seems to assume that the material word is not subject to these manipulations. While a directive might be retracted, the fact of its having been uttered (its ọ̀rọ̀) cannot.

7. Ojoade opens his essay on proverbs about proverbs with a similar phrasing ("African Proverbs on Proverbs," 20).

8. The prominent use of inscriptions in Ifá divination, as we saw in chapter 2, does not quite agree with this view.

9. This is the only topic about which Owomoyela agrees with those he normally portrays as misguided readers of African sensibilities. See *African Difference*, 143–163, especially the section subtitled "Gender and Proverb Usage." See also *Yoruba Proverbs* (12–14). Olajubu, too,

adopts face-value signification in her use of proverbial evidence ("Seeing through a Woman's Eye").

10. Schipper admits in the opening page of her more comprehensive, transcultural, and suprahistorical analysis of proverbs and women that "those who look for differences will only find differences, but those who look for similarities will find out what people experience or have experienced jointly" (*Never Marry a Woman with Big Feet*, 1). The book teases out the similarity of women's general denigration. For a critique of insufficiently historical gender studies in Yorùbá societies, see Oyěwùmí, *The Invention of Women*.

11. Proverb users are so constructed because their texts lack verifiable authors; after all, a person who loves quotations and who uses Shakespeare's words is never thought to have ceded control to the Bard.

12. Proverbs stand apart in discourse flow, and because their contents are usually at odds with the subject matter at hand, they threaten topic coherence (see Norrick, *How Proverbs Mean*, 16, 18, and 69). However, because we assume that our own epoch-bound unity ideal for conversations defines good speech across time, we tend to explain away the significant difficulties that proverbs constitute for linear thought flow by focusing on how the hidden cultural meaning serves discursive and semantic unity.

13. In *Rẹ́rẹ́ Rún*, Òkédìjí makes his protagonist's tragedy highly memorable with the "broken" proverbs Láwúwo mouths when he loses control of his labor union and, as a result, his mental faculties. The difference between those utterances, which the playwright calls "Òwe Láwúwo" (Láwúwo's peculiar proverbs), and postproverbials is that the latter are clever manipulations of sound minds and playful hearts. Adéẹ̀kọ́ (*Proverbs, Textuality, and Nativism*, 64–81) discusses Láwúwo. Yusuf proposes a positive use of English and Yorùbá postproverbials—he calls them "counter-proverbs"—for battling misogyny (see "Countering Mysogyny" and "A Semantics Classroom Connection").

14. The phrasing is originally from Derrida's *Of Grammatology*, 18.

15. Of the 201 scripts, 30 "are based on a written source," the story of Aṣeeremáṣékà in a Yorùbá third-grade reader; 45, the largest number, turn on the jealous co-wife motif; 23 are stories of "treachery inspired by envy, the hope of gaining an advantage" or revenge; 20 deal with the experience of a wickedly vindictive fellow; excessive cruelty stories are also another large class among stories that do not revolve around failure of recognition. Among 30 stories that depend on "failure of recognition," 23 are traditional and 7 deal with contemporary experience.

16. As it stands, this conclusion looks weak without a contrastive analysis of how similar students responded to "essay" prompts in other languages.

17. Translation is Owomoyela's (*Yoruba Proverbs*, 409–410).

18. My usage of allegory as "ìtàn olówe" refers to (1) the storytelling genre that Deirdre LaPin identifies as specific to Ìbàdàn—ìtàn tá ń fi pòwe or the narrative "used to tell a proverb" ("Story, Medium and Masque," 33) and (2) the translation of the literary term in the first volume of *Yorùbá Metalanguage*, edited by Ayọ̀ Bámgbóṣé (3).

19. The origin story of the "amúnikọluni, aláǹgbá orí èṣù" (a-creature-that-pushes-one-against-others, the lizard on the Èṣù shrine) saying reiterates the incidental—and not causal—relationship of stories to proverbs (Kòṣémánìí, *Òwe àti Àṣàyàn Ọ̀rọ̀ Yorùbá*, 45–48). See also 54–56, 61–62, and 66–68, where Kòṣémánìí shows that etiological narratives refer to perceived first time of usage.

20. I have not been able to consult Yusuf's 1996 University of Lagos (Nigeria) dissertation on speech act theory and proverbs. Going by his published articles that I have read, however, he seems to favor the "face-value" approach to proverb meaning.

21. These issues have been thrashed out in abrasive exchanges between deconstructionists and speech act theorists. See Derrida's "Signature Event Context" and "Limited Inc abc . . ." and Searle's "Reiterating the Differences" for the initial record of the debate. Searle expands on Austin in his chapter on figurative language in *Expression and Meaning*. J. Hillis Miller (*Speech Acts in Literature*) describes the sources of the differences between deconstruction and speech act theory.

22. I first articulated the viewpoints argued in this chapter in a paper written for a collection of essays to honor the memory of Oyekan Owomoyela (1938–2007), Ryan Professor of African Literature at the University of Nebraska, Lincoln. His deep and sustained analysis of Yorùbá proverbs for over four decades in three significant collections and annotations, and in numerous articles, easily make him dean of proverb studies in African literatures and oratures.

3 Reading, Writing, and Epistemic Instability in Fágúnwà's Novels

THE ONLY EPISODE about divination of any type in all D. O. Fágúnwà's novels happens in the first one, *Ògbójú Ọdẹ Nínú Igbó Irúnmalẹ̀*, when on his second lone venture into the place Wole Soyinka rendered in English as "the forest of a thousand daemons," the protagonist, Àkàrà-ògùn, tries to decipher what the day has in store for him by casting kola nut seeds. To get the perfect day Àkàrà-ògùn wants, two of the four kola nuts ought to fall face down and two face up, but that does not happen, even after many attempts, so he decides to make his own good augury, using the proverb "Ọwọ́ ara ẹni ni a fi í tún ọ̀ràn ara ẹni ṣe" (With his own hands does a man mend his fortune) as if it carries a cultural endorsement of his violation of the divination process:

> Mo tìkara mi ṣi ojú méjì sí òkè mo da ojú méjì dé mo wí pé, "Ọwọ́ ara ẹni ni a fi í tún ọ̀ràn ara ẹni ṣe bí ìwọ obì yìí kò bá fọ rere n ó fọ rere fún ọ." (22) (With my own hands I turned two up and faced two down saying, "With his own hands does a man mend his fortune; if you kola pieces will not predict good, I will predict that good for you.") (37)[1]

As I argued in chapter 1, object casting and the inscription dictated by how the cast objects present are not subject to the diviner's personal motivation. Àkàrà-ògùn's manipulation clearly violates that writing rule. He ought to have left alone the nut casting system and focused on the commentary stage, where, still relying on the proverb about will and fortune, he would have figured out the sacrifices necessary for making the untoward augury less inauspicious. Before midday, the brave hunter chases a deer into a cave, where he is promptly bound and enslaved. Every element of his armor—spells, charms, incantations—fails, and he does not regain his wit until he realizes that he "had failed to reckon with God" (41). Critics such as Afolabi Olabimtan debate whether the God invoked here is Christian or Yorùbá, as if the two are incompatible. In my argument about cultural being, the specific identity of that God is not very relevant to a deeper understanding of living as Yorùbá. The character of the divinity on which a Yorùbá person calls comes from the commentary part of divination, the part in which a client applies gumption and self-reflexivity to the narrative accompaniment of inscription, which is frequently suffused with proverbs. After Àkàrà-ògùn's captivity forces him to reflect soberly, he realizes his error of enthusiasm. Àkàrà-ògùn's gesture definitely constitutes an attempt at a radical rewriting of the divination process; it does not, however, undermine the fundamental position of inscription, even if the God he calls on for intercession is Christian. A perfect day, in the end, still requires that two divination kola nuts fall face up and the remaining kola nuts fall face down. The referent of the proverb he mistakes to be an inscription of willful bravado expresses nothing other than a pragmatic commentary on the necessity of creativity in the right way to respond to revealed inscriptions. The inscription system, this episode reveals, resists the individual's autocratic will. Àkàrà-ògùn's dabbling, I argue in this chapter, reflects the profound epistemic questions that confronted practices of being Yorùbá in the years between the twentieth-century world wars. The attempt to reorder the basis of organization of life we witness here operates on two levels. First, the brash hunter wants to forcefully determine the character of the "letter" that the divination object casting should reveal. Second, he then justifies the disruption with a cultural communication theory of the proverb which, in essence, is a self-serving "referent" (or interpretation) he has devised all by himself. In this chapter, I place Akara-ogun's experiment in divination writing, reference, and proverb use in a line of other actions that illustrate Fágúnwà's evaluation of of epistemic changes in his Yorùbá storyworld; in chapter 4, I illustrate how the novels normativize and render as most acceptable one of the changes, a male-dominated worldview.

I open this chapter by discussing some discovery fundamentals in orality scholarship and how those fundamentals manifest in the works of Fágúnwà critics, who see in him a self-conscious attempt to outline features of a modern African history of consciousness. I describe Fágúnwà's representation of shifts in intellectual consciousness by analyzing first the terms of the exchanges between the self-conscious and self-appointed representatives of the passing generation and their younger amanuenses. I then propose that the older, male "oral" storytellers in Fágúnwà's novels enjoy no special intellectual status that could be called "traditionally" Yorùbá, and that neither are the young, also male, scribes they convince to record their experiences inherently "modern." While the two sets of Yorùbá-speaking men gather in Fágúnwà's novels under the auspices of the durability advantages of writing in the ordinary sense, neither concedes that the pre-alphabetic era is incompatible with the contemporary period; they both stress continuity over breaks. As I show later in the chapter, the continuity story works because it conceals the unfolding disruption in strategies of commentary making about lived experiences by foregrounding the commonalities of orality and literacy as subjects of narrative. I conclude the chapter with an analysis of the influence of Fágúnwà's interpretation of the Yorùbá concept of historical timeliness (òlàjú) on the dominant internal movements of characters and plotting in his novels.

Literacy in Orality: Conceptualizing Fágúnwà in Literary History

The history of speech technologies produced in orality scholarship, particularly those patterned after what Brian Street calls the "autonomous model,"[2] presumes that oral language is not an invention but an instinctively given fact of being human. Since it is found naturally, everywhere, oral language is believed not to have been engineered, and its referents, because they do not depend on antecedent material corpus, are deemed prior to emanations of meaning generated in subsequent technologies.[3] When writing was invented, for example, it could only subsist on "the exquisitely intricate structures and references evolved in sound," language's "natural habitat" (Ong, *Orality and Literacy*, 85).

Orality and literacy scholarship premises large theoretical propositions about the evolution of human consciousness on the presumed permanent dependence of other mechanics of speech dissemination on the primordial referents of oral language. For example, eras that predated writing used language in its "untechnologized" forms and are said to have been eras of attentive listening, overwhelming immediacy, warm interpersonal interactions, and dominating phenomenal presence. Those societies that did not invent alphabetic techniques appear to have been incapable of conceptualizing language as a phenomenon. Since those societies failed to think of records of events as following a structure that consists of anything other than recollections, the need to develop instruments of physical repositories in which things could be "looked up" never arose. Walter Ong articulates these allegations succinctly:

> Oral cultures . . . have no dictionaries and few semantic discrepancies. The meaning of each word is controlled by . . . "direct semantic ratification," that is, by the real-life situations in which the word is used here and now. The oral mind is uninterested in definitions. . . . Words acquire their meanings only from their always insistent actual habitat, which is not, as in a dictionary, simply other words, but includes also gestures, vocal inflections, facial expressions, and the entire human, existential setting in which the real, spoken word always occurs. (*Orality and Literacy*, 47)

The axioms remain largely unrevised by Jack Goody and Ian Watt:

> The transmission of the verbal elements of culture by oral means can be visualised as a long chain of interlocking conversations between members of the group. Thus all beliefs and values, all forms of knowledge, are communicated between individuals in face-to-face contact; and, as distinct from the material content of the cultural tradition, whether it be cave-paintings or hand-axes, they are stored only in human memory. ("The Consequences of Literacy," 306)

In an oral society, to speak is to mean, and to hear is to understand. Archival definitions could serve no practical purpose; words did not "accumulate the successive layers of historically validated meanings" (Goody and Watt, "The Consequences of Literacy," 306).[4] As the general history is written, meanings that are independent of speaking and understanding—that is, those that are free of hearing—came with engineered language.

In the flat world so constructed for oral peoples, verbalized thought is generally perceived as agglutinative, prolix, and meant for temporizing. Tradition is deified, speculation is shunned, and consequential memory is tethered to spectacular conflicts. Leading thinkers and performers in oral and traditional societies sporadically succeed in breaching the limitations that oral speech imposes on knowing by adapting the acoustic properties of oral language in formulas that depend on sound and time. Thus, among the personalities that could be passed off as intellectuals in traditional societies,

> thought must come into being in heavily rhythmic, balanced patterns, in repetitions or antitheses, in alliterations and assonances, in epithetic and other formulary expressions, in standard thematic setting (the assembly, the meal, the duel, the hero's "helper," and so on), in proverbs which are constantly heard by everyone so that they come to mind readily and which themselves are patterned for retention and ready recall, or in other mnemonic form. (Ong, *Orality and Literacy*, 34)

Because oral peoples do not engage in falsifiable abstractions, and because their polities are ruled with heavy-handed traditions, their advanced thinkers reduce the ever threatening chances for social conflict by memorializing their laws in rhythmic formulas. Proverbs, for example, are not ordinary "jurisprudential decorations, but themselves constitute the law" (35).

Probably because they more readily permit a serious study of African forms than any other model of writing the history of consciousness, orality scholarship's assumptions have served theorists of African culture who seek to construct the organic unity of pre- and postcolonial expressions very well. Principal terms in orality studies afford African discovery frameworks that can be used to explain the characteristics that differentiate Africa's writing and thought from other traditions. Orality paradigms, for instance, permit a credible premise for arguing the case for an influential African past for modern writing, including those written in languages introduced after European conquest. Hence African literary and cultural criticism treats folkloric and unwritten verbal artifacts as embodiments of tradition; written forms, considered to be so only if they are alphabetic, are considered modern. Influences traceable to Homer, the Bible, Shakespeare, Tolstoy, and Conrad are all deemed equally modern, and those attributable to Chaka, a nineteenth-century Zulu hero, and Ọ̀rúnmìlà, the ageless Yorùbá patron deity of lyrical divination and prognostication, and, as argued in the previous chapter, commentary generating systems of inscriptions, are judged traditional.

Textual Africanity in literary history is generally measured by structural affinity to oral and precolonial forms. This yardstick is considered proper because oral traditions bear the originary marks of African cultural resilience.[5]

Trends in the criticism of the writing of two Yorùbá men, Amos Tutuola and D. O. Fágúnwà, best manifest the operations of orality axioms in African literary histories. After Tutuola was initially rejected by highbrow African readers, later critics rehabilitated him and rescued his work for significant contemporary development by attributing the peculiar tendencies of his narratives to the influence of the oral storytelling traditions from which he could not wean himself. Emmanuel Obiechina's defense of Tutuola's founding position in Anglophone West African literature invokes the closeness of his style to the oral traditions thus: "The uniqueness of Tutuola's work rests on his ability to assimilate elements peculiar to the oral tradition with elements peculiar to the literary tradition: in other words, to impose a literary organization upon essentially oral narrative material" (*Language and Theme*, 50). The paradoxical assertion that Tutuola is unique because his work is very traditional becomes the source of analytical curiosity, and his "un-novelistic" narrative exemplifies "a transitional stage in the formal artistic evolution from a purely oral narrative tradition to a purely literary narrative one" (50).

Abiola Irele's work on the manifestation of tradition and individual talent in the narrative arts of D. O. Fágúnwà, Amos Tutuola, and Wole Soyinka—all Yorùbá men—provides a more extensive illustration of the historiographic tendency. Irele places the three writers on the orality/literacy and tradition/modernity binaries differently, with Fágúnwà, the only one who wrote in Yorùbá, very close to the left side of the oppositions because he is more oral and more communal than are Tutuola and Soyinka, who both write in the English language. Fágúnwà is traditional because his imageries and symbols tend to be less individualized, and such is his case because his consciousness, his material language, and his sensibility are still very oral. Fágúnwà projects a vision of humanity whose place in the order of things appears fixed. His text "stands for the universe, inhabited by the obscure forces to which man stands in a dynamic moral and spiritual relationship" ("Tradition and the Yoruba Writer," 81). Since Fágúnwà's medium, the Yorùbá language, is not yet literate enough, he cannot idiosyncratize symbols for his own particular visions of existence. Still ensconced "within the framework of a particular complex of cultural reference" (84), Fágúnwà's allegories and symbols tend to be too communal and unindividuated; he is so deeply immersed in tradition that Tutuola, "a poor imitator" of Fágúnwà and an "inferior artist who has taken advantage of the historical prestige of English to overshadow the creator and master of the new Yorùbá novel" (86), expresses "a contemplative quality" (89) that could not be found in Fágúnwà. The more technically accomplished Fágúnwà emerges as the more traditional of the two because his style is more oral:

In all of Fagunwa's stories, a distance seems to separate the characters and events that he presents from the deepest feeling of the author himself. This impression of a dissociation between the narrative content and the writer's response is reinforced by Fagunwa's habit of didactic reflections and constant asides to his audience. The result is that the world Fagunwa presents, despite its vivid realization, acquires a certain objectivity and the drama that he depicts a certain explicitness whose meaning seems to stand apart from any activity of his own artistic consciousness upon his material. ("Tradition and the Yoruba Writer," 89)

Irele's ranking of Wole Soyinka as the most contemplative of the three Yorùbá men further demonstrates that Fágúnwà's overwhelmingly traditional world derives mainly from the oral status of his chosen language. Soyinka carries the literate's sensibility adroitly, while Tutuola handles the same in less than steady poise. Fágúnwà, of course, lacks it. In Irele's estimation, Soyinka emerges the most competent and introspective user of a literate and cosmopolitan language because he is the most eccentric and idiosyncratic user of tradition in his plotting, significant characterization, and individuated visions of the world. Irele theorizes implicitly that African writers are bound to tradition because they depend on a more oral and traditional African language, and that in the historical continuum represented by Fágúnwà, Tutuola, and Soyinka, intellectual consciousness progresses from Yorùbá to English, from oral to literate, and from tradition to modernity. Irele's conclusion that "the work of Fagunwa and Tutuola grow out of a living tradition, and in the writing of Wole Soyinka, we find a personal appropriation and re-interpretation in new terms of a Yorùbá cosmology, so that it exists in his work as an authentic mode of vision" ("Tradition and the Yoruba Writer," 100) reflects a grounding paradigm of orality studies that nonliterate media tend to be communitarian.[6]

Fágúnwà critics within Yorùbá studies argue differently. They do not begin by assuming that the non-European language or culture are necessarily oral, and do not try to plot the evolution of a written consciousness out of the preceding oral tradition. It is common in Yorùbá literary criticism for Fágúnwà to be adjudged the least Yorùbá—in other words, the least traditional—of modern writers despite his universally acclaimed status as an inventor of novel forms. In the same issue of the journal in which the Irele essay discussed above first appeared, Afolabi Olabimtan, a Yorùbá-language poet, novelist, and literary scholar argues a different view of Fágúnwà's use of tradition. He says that Fágúnwà's myths are more Hebraic than Yorùbá, and that his privileged theology is more biblical than animist:

Fagunwa ... has used with tremendous success traditional material to suppress some traditional beliefs for the purpose of preaching Christian ideals. He takes God as the central, all-governing source and measure of morality. The

Yorùbá believes that it is each person's character, Ìwà, that is important to him as a means of receiving salvation, not a deity. But Fagunwa avoids attributing any of these and similar beliefs to the Ifá literary corpus which is the great "store-house" of Yorùbá culture inside which one can find all the traditional wealth and glory of the Yorùbá people. (Olabimtan, "Religion as Theme," 111)

In Olabimtan's view, Fágúnwà fell victim to European missionaries, who knew that storytelling acculturated their congregations' communities and, therefore, "encouraged the late Fagunwa to write a story book with traditional background in order to teach Christian ideals, and to suppress such elements of traditional religion as could be detrimental to the growth of the Christian religion" ("Religion as Theme," 111).[7] In a similar reading, Ayọ̀ Bámgbóṣé attributes a great part of the writer's historicalness to his creative domestication of his eclectic literate readings, drawing on Arabian Nights tales, Aesop's fables, and allegorical Christian writing, particularly John Bunyan's *The Pilgrim's Progress* (*The Novels of D. O. Fagunwa*, 23). Unlike Olabimtan, Ayọ̀ Bámgbóṣé praises Fágúnwà for subordinating these various literate sources to the Yorùbá folktale's narrative structure.

Confluence of Vanguards: The Teller and the Editor

Fágúnwà's novels start in agitation, typically when looming mortality causes the narrator to write an account of his life for posterity. Thus moved by the possibility of his dying without the world knowing of his remarkable deeds, the accomplished older male protagonist intrudes upon an easily convinced younger writer-editor, who passes down—in the form of the text in front of the reader—a version of his recording of the older man's recounted exploits. This internally propelled drive to tell a story always happens very close to the time of writing and, beyond the highlighted need to preserve things in writing, it usually has no apparent effect on the content or structure of the episodes recounted. Nonetheless, a narratively sustained form of agitation moved by pressures other than the narrator's will and desire inheres structurally in the plotting. In three of the five novels,[8] the longest recollections concern a journey undertaken at the behest of a king who presses on the most brilliant male professionals in his domain the urgent need for an expedition to procure from foreign lands some ideas or objects that are important to peaceful and orderly governance. Perhaps because the narrator-protagonists' fervent expressions of the desire for self-preservation sound patently admirable to their first literate audience (that is, the writer-editor who scripts each story), the psychological and political disquiet that motivates self-accounting in Fágúnwà's popular, forest-based novels is not perceived as a record of doubt about the narrator's self-understanding of his place in society. Readers, following the writer-editor's lead, accept on face value the older man's stated wish. The unmistakable anxiety that surrounds the mouth-to-letter exchange supervised by the old man is overlooked, and each king's motive for sending away the most accomplished technical and military professionals in every novel is never held suspect.

Thus, there are two crucial seeds of generating stories in Fágúnwà's novels: (1) an older man who is afraid of being lost to history narrates biographical adventures to a younger male editor who is co-opted into creating a project that preserves memories; (2) the central event in the older man's recounted stories is about a time when rulers of city-states, seeking development and peace, convinced their most accomplished citizens, usually under the leadership of the storyteller, to risk their lives in order to procure key instruments of communal advancement. These grounds of biographical self-accounting, I am arguing in this chapter, are symptoms of significant disruptions in the construction of normative means and manners of relating to the world during Fágúnwà's formative social milieu during the twentieth-century interwar years. As suggested in the brief discussion in the opening paragraph of this chapter, of Àkàrà-ògùn's botched attempt at divination writing, the venturesome hero should take charge of how his day is to go. However, Àkàrà-ògùn's retreating into the norm of commentary making, as hinted at the beginning of this chapter, reiterates the irrefutability of the material inscription's role in lived sociocultural changes. It is obvious in many of the exchanges that Fágúnwà's old men understand that durable narratives must outlast the physical presence of either the teller or the scribe, the oral storyteller or the writer. What we learn from Fágúnwà is not the transition from orality to literacy as such. The exchanges between representatives of the society's gradually expiring present—occupied by both the old and the young, the teller and the writer—and its unfolding future that frame Fágúnwà's novels denote some epistemic instability in a changing world that is not yet quite fully understood, but to whose inevitability the community has reconciled itself.

I want to shift attention to the staged dialogues between the old and the young, the teller and the writer, and the hunter and the village schoolteacher that frame the novels. The first novel, *Ògbójú Ọdẹ Nínú Igbó Irúnmalẹ̀*, opens with a long editorial remark:

> "Èyin ọrẹ́ mi, bí òwe ni a ńlu ìlù ògìdìgbó, ọlọ́gbọ́n níí jó o, ọmọràn ní sì í mọ̀ ọ́. Ìtan tí n ó sọ yìí, ìlù ògìdìgbó ni; èmi ni ẹni tí yóò lu ìlù náà, èyin ni ọlọ́gbọ́n tí yóò jó o, èyin sì ni ọmọràn tí yóò mọọ́ pẹ̀lú. Àwọn àgbà a má a pa òwe kan—ẹ kò bi mí bí wọ́n ti ńpa á dan? Wọ́n ní, 'Bí eégun ẹni bá jóo're orí á yá ni.' Tótó ó ṣe bí òwe o." (7) ("My friends all, like the sonorous proverb do we drum the agidigbo; it is the wise who dance to it, and the learned who understand its language. The story which follows is a veritable agidigbo; it is I who will drum it, and you the wise heads who will interpret it. Our elders have a favourite proverb—are you not dying to ask me how it goes?—they tell it thus,

'When our masquerade dances well, our heads swell and do a spin.' Forgive my forwardness, it is the proverb which speaks.")

We learn on the next page that the presentational voice in this passage belongs to a privileged writer-editor to whom was recounted over several days the tale that the reader is being invited to enjoy. This direct address to the reader is not a part of the received story, but an interposition created by the scribal recorder who, between the time of listening and translating into book form the words he heard, has evolved from a mere recorder of stories told to a presenter and interpreter of the narratives he hears. Very soon the register of appropriate reception shifts from dance's graceful movements and festive drumming to quiet, lonesome reading:

> "Ṣùgbọ́n bí ẹ bá sì ńfẹ́ kí ijó yin dára, ohun méjì ni ẹ ó ní láti ṣe: èkiní ni pé, nígbà tí ẹnì kan bá ńsọ̀rọ̀ nínú itàn yìí, ẹ ó fi ara yín sí ìpò olúwa rẹ̀ ẹ ó máa sọ̀rọ̀ bí ẹni pé èyin gan an ni. Bí ẹnìkan bá sì ńda ẹnikejì lóhùn ẹ ó ka itàn náà bí ẹni pé èyin ni ẹ jókò tí ẹnìkan ńba yín sọ̀rọ̀ ti ẹ sì ńfún olúwa rẹ̀ ní èsì tí ó yẹ." (1) ("But for a start, if you want this dance to be a success, here are two things I must request of you. Firstly, whenever a character in my story speaks in his own person, you must put yourselves in his place and speak as if you are that very man. And when the other replies, you must relate the story to yourselves as if you, sitting down, had been addressed and now must respond to the first speaker.") (7)

Without a marked transition, dance becomes monologic drama; pleasures of one aesthetic do join another.

The exuberant impresario is caught at a crossroads of modes: telling, listening, writing, reading, drumming, and dancing. One could attribute the admixture to the scribe's less than dexterous handling of metaphors and accept the old storyteller's belief that tradition could somehow be handed down to posterity without any interference from the medium of printed letters. It is, however, more accurate to perceive the editor's conflation of play-filled metaphors as an effort to manage the symptoms of the agonistic reality that confronts the self-conscious writer given the task of faithfully preserving the received traditions of an era whose spirit he is unqualified to share. In the narrative proper, which readers will soon encounter directly on their own, the listener-writer, now characterizing himself as a presenter to a contrived live audience, does not dance or drum, but listens and writes all the time when the events are narrated. He does not participate in the events handed down to him in the stories, and no part of the novel indicates that he has independent means of verifying the old man's claims.

Other incongruities appear in the preliminary materials of the story, particularly in the expression of the older teller's preference for the written preservation of experience and the writer's reversion to spoken proverbial wisdom. The teller invited himself to the mouth-to-mouth transmission of experience with words that show a preference for writing's superior durability: "Bí mo bá sọ fún ọ lónìí, tí ìwọ kọ ọ́ sílẹ̀ dáradára, bí ọjọ́ mi bá tilẹ̀ pé tí mo kú, àwọn ọmọ aráye kò ní gbàgbé mi" (2) (If I pass it on to you now and you take it all down diligently, even when the day comes that I must meet my Maker, the world will not forget me [8]). The old man's sense of "diligent" or befitting written records encompasses conventions of representation, not just lexical accuracy, and also signals his willingness to move away from inherited modes of preserving and disseminating knowledge. While the fear of being forgotten points back to the old man rather than to the historical significance of his accomplishments, the novel gives the power to convene the audience proper for the old man's spoken tale to the authorial location governed by the writer-editor. The writer's report of the second day of narration begins thus:

Nígbàtí ọkùnrin yìí lọ tán tí mo padà dé ilé, mo pe àwọn aládugbò mi jọ, mo pe ọ̀rẹ́ àti ojúlùmọ̀ mi mo sì pe àwọn ìbátan mi pẹ̀lú mo ro gbogbo nkan wọnyí fún wọn. Ẹnú yà wọ́n gidigidi gbogbo wọn sì fi ohùn sí i pé kí àwọn jí wá sí ilé mi lówùrọ̀ ọjọ́ kejí kí ọkùnrin nì to dé, kí àwọn ba le gbọ́ ìtàn tí ọkùnrin náà yóò tún sọ, nítorí ìròhìn tèmi kò ní le tó àfojúbà ti wọn. Lóòótọ́ bí ilẹ̀ ti nmọ́ hàì ní ọjọ́ kejì ni wọ́n dé, nígbàtí ọkùnrin náà papa sì fi ma wọ ilé, ilé mi ti kún kò gba ẹsẹ̀ mọ́. Kí ilẹ̀ tó mọ́ ni mo ti pàṣẹ kí àwọn ọmọ ọ̀dọ̀ mi ṣe ìtọ́jú oǹjẹ, kí ó sì tó di pé ọkùnrin náà bẹ̀rẹ̀ ìtàn rẹ̀, mo gbé agbọ̀n ẹko mẹ́rin sílẹ̀ fún àwọn àlejò wọ̀nyí mo sì wa ẹran sí àwo fún wọn. Olúkúlùkù jẹ ó yó ó sì mu omi. (21) (When the man had departed and I had returned home I called my neighbours together; I summoned friends and acquaintances, sent for my relations also and recounted this affair to them. They were greatly amazed and all resolved to wake early the following morning before my stranger arrives, so that they might themselves listen to the man's adventures, for my re-telling could not . aspired to their own participation. True enough, sharp on the moment the new day began to break, they began to arrive, and by the time that the man himself entered my house it was filled to overflowing and could hardly take another pair of feet. Before dawn I had ordered my servants to prepare food, and so before the stranger began his tale I placed before my guests four baskets of ẹko and ladled meat into dishes for them. Each and every man of us ate to satisfaction and drank.) (35)

By virtue of his residence and social ties, the writer in this passage controls the old storyteller's access to his audiences, including a live group of listeners.

The divergent criteria used by the teller and the writer to demarcate and manage story time is further evidence of the unsteady collaboration between the two agents of story (and knowledge) delivery; the teller prefers accurate recollection, while the writer privileges narratological consistency. The first storytelling day coincides with the return home of the protagonist, Àkàrà-ògùn, after his first expedition to Irúnmalẹ̀ Forest. He declares "Bẹ́ni ìtàn ìgbà èkíní mi ní igbó

burúkú nì pári" (20) (Thus ends the story of my first sojourn in this most terrify-
ing forest) (34) and equates a stage in his life with the movement of the day. In
accordance with this plan, events in the second journey are compressed into the
second storytelling day. Time gets complicated when the story expands to involve
other exceptional characters on the Mount Lángbòdó trip, and the narrator begins to justify his severe abbreviations of lived experiences with lack of storytime
and, surprisingly, insufficient print space. The compressed account of Kàkó's fight
with Wèrè Ọrun in the City of Birds is explained with: "Ìjà ọjọ́ náà kò ṣe sọ tán
sínú ìwé yìí, nítorí àkokò ńlọ" (65) (Alas, that day's fight cannot be recounted fully
in one book, for time is flying) (91). The old man extols the virtue of silence as he
elides the details of what his fellow travelers saw in the city of animals:

> Ṣùgbọ́n mélo ni kí nsọ, mélo ni kí nrò, melo ni kí nwí nípa àwọn ohun tí ojú
> wa rí ni ibi tí mo kà sílẹ̀ wọnnì! Wọ́n pọ̀ ju ohun kíkà lọ—dídákẹ́ ló ya. (66)
> (But how many should I recount, how many tell, how much can I tell you
> about the many encounters in these places I have mentioned! They were more
> numerous than lips can tell—the rest is silence.) (93)

He exhorts in the same breath that "Ọ̀pọ̀lọpọ̀ ìdinà ni a tún bá pàdé ṣùgbọ́n nkò
rí àyè sọ wọ́n tán nísìsiyi" (66) (Many hindrances did we encounter but there is
not time to tell you everything (93–94). At the end of the group's second day at
Iragbeje's house, Àkàrà-ògùn admits:

> Bẹ́ni a gbádùn títí ilẹ̀ fi ṣú ó wa ku ọjọ́ márun tí a ó lò ní ọdọ̀ Ìrágbèje ṣùgbọ́n
> nkò ní lè sọ àwọn ohun abàmì wọnnì tí oju wa rí àti etí wá gbọ́ ní ọjọ́ máràruń
> náà nítorí àkokò ńlọ. (94) (And so we made merry until nightfall: there re-
> mained five days of our stay with Iragbeje, but I cannot tell you all the marvels
> which our eyes witnessed and our ears heard during these five days, for time is
> flying.) (130)

The narration then skips to the seventh and last day of the visit. The storyteller
explains his near total silence on what the few that made it back home experienced on the return journey with "Nkò ní lè sọ ohun tí oju wa rí ní ìrìnàjò wa ti
àbọ̀ yìí fún yin nítorí yóò ti pọ̀ jù" (100) (I will not be able to tell you of the various adventures of our return journey for they are too numerous) (138). After his
summary account of the less than rousing reception they got after having been
away for so long—even the king who sent them has only faint memories of them—
the narrator says: "Báyìí ni ìtàn ìgbàtí mo lọ sí Òkè Lángbòdó parí. Ẹ̀yin ọ̀rẹ́ mi
gbogbo, ìba tí ng ó sọ fún ayé mọ lákokò yìí ni èyí" (101) (And thus ends the story
of our journey to Mount Langbodo. My friends, here ends all that I mean to tell
the world at this time) (139).

It is significant that on the first two storytelling days narrative duration is
determined by the movement of the sun, an arrangement that violates perfor-

mance conventions in the old narrator's allegedly oral society of origin, where the enjoyment of twice-told tales ensues either at twilight or under the glow of the moon. Àkàrà-ògùn, ostensibly the embodiment of traditional wisdom in *Ògbójú Ọdẹ*, cannot tell stories at night, perhaps because his writer needs daylight to see the scribbling in his notebook. It is understandable therefore that daytime, for Fágúnwà's writer-editor, is story time and that worthwhile storytelling deserves the suspension of daytime labor. The novelty of the emergent leisure (storytelling) and work regime shows not in the explicitly narrated event but in the brief references to narrative time-management decisions. It is easy to conclude that the old man's immediate audience and, by extension, the novelist's, does not consist of traditional subsistence farmers who cannot afford to miss daytime work. These listeners—and readers who encounter them in the pages of the novel—can skip daytime work for a few days to enjoy an extended good story.

A closer scrutiny of the justifications quoted above shows that decisions about time and event elaboration in *Ògbójú Ọdẹ* could not have been made by the older man. First, given the storyteller's status as a wealthy, highly respected retired hunter and leader of a professional cohort, time available to tell a story ought not be a scarce commodity. In addition, the "space" referred to in these statements cannot be some physical dissemination location, because spoken stories, except when stored electronically, do not occupy space as such. Every Yorùbá knows that plenty words cannot fill up a basket ("Ọ̀pọ̀ ọ̀rọ̀ kò kún agbọ̀n"). It should be more productive to read the quoted internal time-management statements as originating from the writer-editor rather than from the history-bearing figure. I will refer again to an event in the City of Birds at which the storyteller is reported to have abbreviated his account of a crucial fight with "'Ìjà ọjọ́ náà kò ṣe sọ tán sínú *ìwé yìí*, nítorí *àkokò ńlọ*'" (That day's fight cannot be recounted fully in *this book*, because *time is flying*) (65; my translation and emphasis). The first underlined phrase relates to the physical limitation of the book form; the second, to the time available for the narration that precedes the writing of the book. Although the two references to time and space are about the protagonist's lived experiences, in practical terms, the speaking, live storyteller does not know what "ìwé yìí" (this book)[9]—a creation of none other than the writer-editor—looks like.

The fraught narrator-recorder cohabitation in the prequel narrative, *Igbó Olódùmarè*, is even more pronounced. The novel opens with the teller ambushing the writer who, because of a recent bereavement, does not welcome his midnight guest. The man of experience forces a second glance by screaming at the writer, who now recognizes his visitor as Àkàrà-ògùn, the old storyteller. Because another speaking and writing session starts immediately, the reader can assume that a pleasant and probably profitable working relationship was established after the publication of the earlier story and novel. For the new story, the teller speaks with certainty about the accumulated wisdom in his head, and positions all

Black people as his inspiration, suggesting that the listening forest should suffice for an audience:

> "Ki ọwọ́ bọ àpò rẹ, bóya ohun ìkọ̀wé le wà níbẹ̀, gọngọ á sọ lónìí, mo ní iṣẹ́ láti rán ọ sí àwọn ọmọ aráyé, nítorí ọ̀rọ̀ pàtàkì ńbẹ ní agbárí, beni ìmọ̀ràn tí ó nílárí ńbẹ ní àtàrí, nítorí náà mo fi orúkọ́ àwọn ènìyàn dúdú bẹ̀ ọ́, jọwọ́ dọbálẹ̀ lórí àpáta, kí a fi àpáta ṣe tábìlì wa, kí èmi dúró gẹ́gẹ́ bí alága, kí ìwọ dúró gẹ́gẹ́bí akọ̀wé, kí ewéko igbó sì dúró gẹ́gẹ́ bí ọmọ ẹgbẹ́ fún wa." (5) ("Dig into your pocket; perhaps the tools of your trade are conveniently lodged in there. Today, the crook of the drum will reverberate, for I have a message to the children of the earth through you; great issues are lodged in my skull and great lessons in my forehead. Therefore I implore you in the name of the black race, stretch yourself out on this rock, let us use it as a desk. I shall stand in as chairman and you as the scribe, while the leaves of the forest remain like members of the union.") (9)

While the encounter is presented as a meeting of two creative minds, the older man speaks like the convening authority as he recounts the wonderful exploits of his father, Olowo-aiye.

Things switch inexplicably in the middle of the novel (on the second full day of storytelling), when Àkàrà-ògùn pulls out a sheaf of his father's written autobiographical papers and instructs that the writer should cease taking down a told story and begin to record a tale to be read to him:

> "Nígbàtí ó wọlé mi ní ọjọ́ kejì ó mú ìwé tí baba rẹ̀ fi ọwọ́ ara rẹ̀ kọ hàn mí, nínú ìwe yìí baba rẹ̀ sọ ìtàn ara rẹ̀ láti ìgbàtí ó ti wà ní ọ̀dọ̀ Ọba Igbó Olódùmarè ó sì sọ ọ́ dé ibìtí ó ti padà wá sílé. Ìgbàtí Àkàrà-ògùn ti fi eléyìí hàn mí tán ni ó ti jòkó rẹgẹ̀jì lórí àga, ó ní kí nka òn sí bí ẹni pé Olówó-aiyé ni òn, ó sì fi ara rẹ́ sí ipò bàbá rẹ̀ òn ńka ìwé náà fún mi èmi náà mú ohun ìkọ̀wé mi, mo jòkó bí ó tí yẹ kí ẹnití ńkọ̀wé jòkó, mo ńba iṣẹ lọ." (53) ("When he came into my home the following day, he brought with him the manuscript that his father had written with his own hands and showed it to me. On those pages, his father had narrated his own story from the time of his stay with the King of the Forest of Olodumare till that moment when he finally returned home. Having displayed the script and spread himself comfortably in a chair, my visitor stressed that I should regard him as if he was himself Olowo-aiye, now assuming his father's voice. Thereafter he began to read to me. I sat attentively as one who takes a dictation and plunged into work.") (71)[10]

This disruption makes manifest all the previous insinuations about Àkàrà-ògùn's literacy awareness in *Ògbójú Ọdẹ*, the sequel. We see clearly now that the storyteller's historical time is not completely ignorant of alphabetic writing and reading. By reading his father's written words and asking the recorder to convert these into a book, Àkàrà-ògùn forces his editor to rewrite.

The story given to Fágúnwà's readers of *Igbó Olódùmarè* contains a transcriber's rendition of his audition of Olowo-aiye's self-authored words read aloud by his son, Àkàrà-ògùn. In this exchange, the literate, oral raconteur experiments with trying to read his father as he wrote himself down and having a captive writer record that experience. But because we readers do not have the father's book, we cannot estimate the current scribe's accuracy or follow Àkàrà-ògùn who, unlike us, does not read *Igbó Olódùmarè*, the story he partly dictates. He, too, cannot evaluate the accuracy of the writing he has commissioned. Hitherto, Àkàrà-ògùn has been recounting from memory things he has heard. Now, he reads so that another person can rewrite things heard from an already written account. The editor's writing, in theory, duplicates Olowo-aiye's papers as read out by his son, and the novel presents a story of writing (the editor transcoding what he heard read) that ostensibly reproduces a story that has already been written (Olowo-aiye's papers) and that has been folded inside another written story (the editor's transcription of Àkàrà-ògùn's telling and reading aloud of his father's life). The many levels of writing, reading, and rewriting in the middle of *Igbó Olódùmarè* cast doubt on the axiom about writing's permanence and durability spouted by Àkàrà-ògùn at the beginning of the earlier novel. The mere fact of literacy does not satisfy Àkàrà-ògùn, who now insists on print reproduction.

Although there is little to go by on the chronological ages of either the editor or his informants, textual evidence allows us to speculate that literacy is already four generations deep in Àkàrà-ògùn's society, if we assign one generation each to Akowediran, the father of Olowo-aiye (the main character in *Igbó Olódùmarè*), who is the father of Àkàrà-ògùn (the protagonist of *Ògbójú Ọdẹ*), and the editor. Given that Yorùbá-language literacy got to the hinterland in the 1840s and that the editor could be Fágúnwà's alter ego, the underlying chronology of the stories is historically probable.[11] Fágúnwà's novels could thus be interpreted as offering critical insights into the slow spread of the literate sensibility in interior southwestern Nigeria until the early decades of the twentieth century. We can note in that regard that the common strategy for those who created the earliest literate archives of Yorùbá verbal traditions involved visiting the interior and recording the words of male elders.[12]

In Fágúnwà's stories, literate elders, who perhaps have seen the published words of even older males in print, emerge from nowhere to seek out a young writer to whom are told captivating stories of past heroic exploits that deserve preservation. As noted above in the discussion of the textual maneuvers for the control of the narrative high ground and dominant representational perspectives, the exchanges between the older and younger men involve some tension that ordinary historical archives cannot note. The older tellers, although literate, epitomize a fading ethos—multiple wives, a belief in magical prowess, obedience to kingly authorities, allegiance to multiple deities, anthropomorphizing elemental forces—of a community in which editors are among those who now determine what is worth preserving in culture. Some of the passing practices—for example, satisfying the competing needs of several deities at the same time—no longer bring comfort to the leading characters, although these men are not yet completely invested in the newer patterns of being in the world—for example, following one universal deity, schooling, and unbridled individualism. The teller and the writer both desire tangible signs of progression, both horizontal (ìlọsíwájú) and vertical (ìdàgbàsókè), for their societies. That is why the older men agree to go on dangerous expeditions on behalf of the community even after retirement. They embrace the newness promised by future dawns, yet will not entertain the thought of abandoning origins or antecedents (orísun). Hence the leading cadres of the knowledge and discovery expeditions always return home. The younger writer-editors, in contrast, usually have no hometowns ascribed to them, and their sense of rootedness is often opaque beyond the received tales that are handed down to them. The usually nameless writers show no interest in genealogy and, with the exception of Akíntúndé Béyìòkú in *Adiitu Olodumare*, we do not see them headed anywhere. Within the symptomatic analysis being offered here, it is clear that parameters of knowing and being are in flux across the dominant generations whose experiences are narrated in—and who also narrate—the novels. The essence of Fágúnwà's commentary about movements in lived cultural life is translated to exchanges about the function of the durability of biographical experiences recounted in, and as, alphabetic story writing.

Being Yorùbá, Being Modern

The foreword of *Ìrìnkèrindò*—the chronological endpoint of Fágúnwà's trilogy about three great hunters loosely bound by their attachment to one beloved, but unnamed, hometown—would serve as a good beginning for a content analysis of the uncertain epistemic shifts in the storyworld of his adventure tales. The novel is dedicated to teachers and other chieftains of the formal schooling system in colonial southwestern Nigeria, including representatives of the indigenous high clergy of the Anglican Church, and Yorùbá traditional royalty.[13] Among these, Bishop Phillips's citation stands out:

> "Ìgbésí ayé Bishop S. C. Phillips ní ǹkan pàtàkì láti kọ́ ọmọ Yorùbá. Ó jẹ́ ẹni tí a nílàti má a ránti láti ìran dé ìran wa. Ẹ̀yin náà mọ̀ pé àbùkù àwa Yorùbá ni èké ṣíṣe, àti sọ òdodo a máa ṣòro fún ni. Bí o bá wí fún ẹnì kan pé 'Máṣe bá mi lo Yorùbá,' ìtumọ̀ ọ̀rọ̀ rẹ ni 'Máṣe puró fun mi.'" (Fágúnwà, *Ìrìnkèrindò*, v–vi)
> ("Bishop S. C. Phillips's life has a lot to teach Yorùbá people. He is a person we have to remember through and down the ages. You know as much as I do that falsehood is our stock in trade as a people; telling the truth is rather difficult

for us. If one person were to tell another, 'Do not play Yorùbá with me,' it means 'Do not lie to me.'")

We have here extradiegetic evidence of how epistemological uncertainty bothers the novelist. To the Christian Yorùbá writer, it is scandalous that colloquial speech equates Yorùbá being with blatant lying and advertises duplicity as a cultural trait about which one need not be ashamed. The novelist believes that the axiom contradicts the community's long view of itself:

> Ìgbà tí a bá sì wo bí ojú Yorùbá ti là tó kí Gẹ̀ẹ́sì tilẹ̀ tó gòké, tí ó sì jẹ́ pé kò sí ẹyà kan ní Nigeria tí ó lè wípé òun lajú ju Yorùbá lọ títí di òní olónìí, ẹ ó rí i pé bí a bá le mú irú àbàwọ́n báyìí kúrò lára wa ìlọsíwájú wa yóò má a ya gbogbo ará ayé lẹ́nu ni. (Fágúnwà, *Ìrìnkèrindò*, vi) (When we consider how widely open Yorùbá eyes have been from before the advent of whites till the present moment, you will not but conclude that our progress will keep surprising the whole world, were we to rid ourselves of this singular stain.)

On the one hand, Yorùbá culture has been exceptionally enlightened, before the whites came and before the advent of alphabetic systems of reading and writing. In colloquial terms, Yorùbá eyes were wide open long before colonization and Christianity reached Yorùbá-land. On the other hand, modern descendants of these long-civilized people seem not to care that their manner of speaking represents their interactions with the world and with one another as driven by falsehood, as if advancement and falsehood can cohabit peacefully among a people. To demonstrate that duplicity does not define Yorùbá being, Fágúnwà holds up the example of Bishop Phillips, a Yorùbá man who rises to the pinnacle of his calling because he is straightforward and honest. Fágúnwà uses Bishop Phillips's name to remodel the terms of proper Yorùbá being:

> Bishop Phillips fi han ni pé kì í ṣe gbogbo ọmọ Yorùbá ni o ńpurọ́. Tani ẹni náà ní òde ayé yìí, yálà dúdú, yálà funfun tí ó le wípé Bishop Phillips bá òun lo Yorùbá? Kò sí, àfi ẹni tí ó bá ma pe àgùntàn ní màlúù, tí ó pe mọ́tò ní kẹkẹ́, tí ó pe Ọmọ́túndé ní Akíntúndé, tí o pe ará ayé ní ará ọrun. Òótọ́ nìkan ni Bishop yìí máa ńsọ, gbogbo ènìyàn sì ti mọ bẹ́ẹ̀ fún un. Àpẹẹrẹ ni èyí fún gbogbo wa. Bí ẹrù bá ńbá ọ láti sọ òótọ́ má ṣe gbàgbé Bishop Phillips Olódodo nítorí Bishop yìí tí ó jẹ́ aṣájú pàtàkì fún ni kò fi èké kọ́ iwọ àti èmi. (Fágúnwà, *Ìrìnkèrindò*, vi) (Bishop Phillips shows us that lying does not define Yorùbá being. Who in the world, black or white, will accuse Bishop Phillips of "being Yorùbá" with him or her? No one, except for that individual who habitually mistakes a sheep for a cow, calls an automobile a bicycle, refers to Omotunde as Akintunde, confuses a living person for the dead.)

In short, Bishop Phillips is a Yorùbá whose worldly comportment is un-Yorùbá. One would be mistaken in thinking that these prefatory declamations are not central to Fágúnwà's narrative considerations. On the contrary, his books are filled with characters that are neither here nor there culturally: Kurembete was punished with two mouths that speak two incompatible languages (*Ògbójú Ọdẹ*, 43); Kako is neither human nor beast; and Aroni has lived for so long that he remembers Solomonic times in the Bible (42).

Anxiety about uncertain grounds of knowing and governance is even more prominent in the plots of Fágúnwà's stories. The central quest of the first novel starts when the king of the protagonist's unnamed city tasks the bravest and wisest men of his domain to procure from the king of Mount Lángbòdó the secret ingredients of social harmony and civil peace (*Ògbójú Ọdẹ*, 49–50). Unrest, until this point, has not been a concern in the city. Upheavals are in the bush, and they are all reported as experiences of the hunter-protagonist, whose calling diverts him periodically from the comfort of home. But narrative silence about civil unrest in the city ought not preclude us from reading other elements of the story symptomatically, particularly the social and physical locations of those the king sends on the expedition. The leader, the retired Àkàrà-ògùn, is a confidant of the king. Next to him in order of presentation is Kako, born of two different species of wild spirits, lives out of town in the terror-filled Igbó Ńlá, a forest reserve of terrible creatures. Several other notables command unusual skills, such as magical body temperature control and exceptional comprehension of the language of birds. One is a metrosexual singer and dancer, another a three-eyed (two eyes in front and one in the back) hunter raised by monkeys. Completing the leadership list are a man of patently superior discerning, Ìmọ̀dòye, and a lethally accurate archer, Ẹfòìyẹ̀. In cliometric terms, the journey happens after the long nineteenth-century Yorùbá wars, when Ṣódẹkẹ, Ògèdèngbé, and Ògúnmọ́lá, all mentioned in a motivational speech (57), entered legendary lore. Historically, the postwar timing of the events in the novel witnessed the spread of Western Christian missions and the gradual entrenchment of British colonization in southern Nigeria, two developments that demanded intellectual expansion and imposed governance mechanisms that require resources obtainable only in foreign lands. The competences needed for the age that gave birth to Fágúnwà's writing seem to be so lacking that the king sends away the most accomplished of the kingdom's professional cadre to acquire them. (It may also be the case that the king wants to get rid of the powerful men.)

In *Ìrìnkèrindò*, Fágúnwà returns to the same historical time and city. Ìrìnkèrindò did not go on the Lángbòdó trip led by Àkàrà-ògùn (in *Ògbójú Ọdẹ*) because his father had sent him to recover a younger brother lost in another city. Sometime before the return of the Lángbòdó group, the same peace-desiring king commissions an expedition of another set of experts, this time to Òkè Ìrònú (Mount of Thought), where they will find and bring back the seeds of the tree of Reason. The pool of men available to Ìrìnkèrindò is not as storied as those led by Àkàrà-ògùn, probably because the pool is already badly depleted; one is such a glutton that any kingdom will like to keep him away. The king's charge deserves to be quoted fully because it focuses on the modernization theme that binds the narrative together:

Mo fẹ́ kí o wá ṣe aṣájú àwọn ọdẹ míràn, kí ẹ wá lọ sí Òkè Ìrònú, tí m̀bẹ nínú Igbó Elégbèje, kí ẹ wá lọ ká èsò igi ìrònú fún mi wá. Igi Ìrònú ni ó fún ìlú náà lórúkọ, abàmì igi ni igi ìrònú, baba mi sì ti ńsọ̀rọ̀ rẹ̀ fún mi kí ó tó di pé títán dé bá a, tí èmi wá gun orí oyè. Bí ènìyàn bá sì gbin igi náà sí orísun omi ní ìlúkílùú ẹnikẹ́ni tí ó ba mu nínú omi ibẹ̀ yóò di ọlọ́gbọ́n pátápátá. Bẹ́ẹ̀ kíni gbòǹgbò ìgbéga òde aiyé pátápátá? Mo ṣe bí ìrònú ni. Àìronú ní ḿmú kí ènìyàn jalè, tí ḿmú kí ènìyàn ṣèké, tí ḿmú kí ènìyàn ṣátá ọmọnìkejì, tí ḿmú kí ènìyàn rẹ́ ọmọnìkejì jẹ. (11) (I have this desire to assign you to lead another special delegation of hunters on a voyage to a certain place named the Mount of Thoughtfulness, which has its location in the Forest of a Thousand and Four Hundred Deities. There is a certain tree in that country whose name is thoughtfulness. It is the fruit of this same tree of thoughtfulness which interests me and which I desire you to pluck for me. This Tree of Thoughtfulness is it that gives the country its fame, for a mysterious tree indeed is the tree of thoughtfulness. My father has told me a lot about this tree in his time, that if this tree is planted close to the source of any municipal water supply, whosoever drinks of it would be instantly transformed to a wise person. And yet what is it that forms the root of the universe in the absence of this thoughtfulness of which we speak? It is the lack of thoughtfulness that leads a man into stealing and lures him to speak vile of his neighbour.) (17–18; Adeniyi's translation modified)

The king lists other unmistakable fruits of thoughtfulness:

Ìrònú ni ó wà ní ìdí ẹ̀rọ mọ́tò, òn ni gbòǹgbò rélùweè, òn ni ọmọ ènìyàn fi ńfò lójú ọrun, ìrònú ni pàtàkì ohun ìjà oníṣẹ̀gùn, òn ni ó wà ní ìdí egbòigi, paríparí gbogbo rẹ̀, bí ènìyàn bá wà tí ó wípé kò sí ǹkan tí Olódùmarè le ṣe, aláìronú ni. Agbára ìrònú pọ̀, òn ni ìyàtọ̀ tí ó wà laàrin àwọn ọmọ ènìyàn àti àwọn ọmọ ẹranko. Nítorí náà, Ìrìnkèrindò, ìwọ ọmọ Oyíndaiyépọ̀, bá mi wá èso igi ìrônú lọ. (11) (It is the thought which ignites a motor-car's engine, forms the base of the railways and provides the wings by which men frolic about in the skies. Thoughtfulness it is that makes victor of a warrior and forms the foundation of healing. To crown it all, if you catch a man in the process of saying that God is of a little potency, such a man is clearly suffering from the lack of thought. Myriad powers give company to Thoughtfulness and it marks the difference between men and beast. Therefore Irinkerindo, son of Oyindaiyepo, go now and fetch me this fruit which carries the name of Thoughtfulness.) (18)

Till now, everyday Yorùbá speech represents automobiles, railways, aviation, and pharmaceutics as gains (or signs) of civilization's progress (nǹkàn ọ̀làjú). The magical seed Ìrìnkèrindò is to secure will enhance reason and the manufacture of appliances that make life easier.

Modernization soon becomes an explicit subject in the story, when Ìrìnkèrindò and his men reach the city of Èdìdàrẹ́, where the people live contrary to the norms known to the traveling men. Òmùgọ́diméjì (Foolishness II), the king of Èdìdàrẹ́, unlike the king who has sent Ìrìnkèrindò and his men on their errand, has shut off his eyes to discernment. As the baffled narrator puts it: "Kò sí ọba kan pàtàkì tí ó le fi ojú ara rẹ̀ sílẹ̀ títí ìlú fi ma burú tó bí a ti bá a nì" (40) (No king of worth would, while his eyes remained wide open, permit his territory to deteriorate to such lamentable condition of collapse" (58). It seems that Òmùgọ́diméjì (Foolishness II) lives in darkness and cannot follow the progression of time and civilization trends, and that obvious incongruities do not strike him as such. Probably because Èdìdàrẹ́'s backward march into darkness contradicts the story's progression toward reason's light of self-awareness, the narrative lingers in the city more than in any other place.

Ọ̀làjú, or Enlightenment

Before proceeding with the analysis of Fágúnwà's narrative concerns with modernization's reason and light in *Ìrìnkèrindò*, I want to consider in some detail the ramification of the term "ọ̀làjú," the word used to characterize the essential ingredient lacking in Èdìdàrẹ́. The study of emic African notions of modernity, progress, and modernization that is most often cited is J. D. Y. Peel's "Olaju," an article that grew out of an incidental discovery in his 1974 field trip for his research on the historical sociology of the Ilésà kingdom in postindependence Nigeria.[14] Asked in a random sample to name the "causes of social change" in their city, Peel's respondents used the word "ọ̀làjú" "far more spontaneously" than any other. Although Peel was struck by the semblance of the word—whose literal English translation would be "lightening (or opening) up of the eyes"—to what studies of modern thought refer to as "Enlightenment" in plain English, he doubted the historical depth of the usage in Yorùbá lexicon: "It is impossible to say how ancient such usage is, if it was coined to refer to the modern enlightenment which is associated with experience of Europe or if it was ever explicitly used before Yorùbá had dealings with Europeans" (Peel, "Olaju," 144).

Dictionaries help little in tracing a sure history of "ọ̀làjú," partly because the extraverted history of dictionary making in Yorùbá has produced only one monolingual volume, Delano's *Atúmọ̀ Èdè Yorùbá* (1958). R. C. Abraham's *Dictionary of Modern Yorùbá*, the only dictionary Peel consulted, contains Yorùbá entries but only English definitions.[15] The bilingual *Dictionary of the Yorùbá Language*, sponsored by the Church Missionary Society, one of Delano's acknowledged sources, makes no reference to "ọ̀làjú" and does not associate literacy with illumination of any sort. To make up for the recognized deficiency in dictionaries, Peel supplemented Abraham with historical conjectures from the evidence in missionary reports compiled by nineteenth-century Yorùbá clergy-men in the Anglican Church.

Bilingual dictionary evidence, survey results, and available missionary ar-chives led Peel to conclude that the general tendencies of missionary and mer-cantile groups to speak of " 'opening up' Africa" and of " 'replacing darkness' " with light might have influenced the adoption of a similar sociohistorical register of "ọlàjú" (having to do with the opening of the eyes) as the Yorùbá frame-word for modernity and modernization. In other words, Iléṣà male household leaders that Peel polled in the 1970s viewed modernization and historical process as enlighten-ment probably because missionary and mercantile metaphors of intellectual pro-gression had trickled down to the population. Whatever other uncanny links the Yorùbá term might have to the English-language Enlightenment, Peel believes that in 1974 Iléṣà, ọlàjú "is metaphorical . . . a social state or process of increased knowl-edge and awareness, which is a condition of greater effectiveness and prosperity." He adds that "as the individual, unmetaphorically, becomes 'enlightened' by open-ing his eyes, a society does so through opening itself to experience of the outer world" ("*Olaju*," 144). As glossed by Peel, "là" (to split open) is the root morpheme in "ọlàjú," a term whose rich and intriguing polysemic entanglements encompass explanation (àlàyé), demarcation (ààlà), and drawn line (ilà, or, ilà). Peel warns be-fore going further in his analysis that "the student of culture must carefully set such elements as 'values,' 'ideal factors,' 'indigenous concepts,' etc., in their con-texts of use, if he is to avoid the facile arbitrary assumption that a culture is en-dowed with some power of self-propagation" (159). He then demonstrates that the concept his informants name as "ọlàjú" distills a set of specific historical practices about the acquisition of knowledge—particularly new techniques—with implicit and explicit acknowledgment of ties to power, material well-being, and access to upward social mobility. Peel reasons that "*olaju* was first definitely used . . . to refer to the cultural package brought from outside by, above all, the missionaries" (147) and understands his respondents to have used the term figuratively to mean a spe-cific kind of "enlightenment" that amounts to "a social state or process of increased knowledge and awareness, which is a condition of greater effectiveness and pros-perity" (144). Peel makes eminent sense within his adopted model of Yorùbá his-tory, one which proceeds on the firm belief that Yorùbá ethnogenesis is recent and is largely a creation of print literacy midwifed by the introduction of Christian missionaries—particularly early literate indigenous Christians—and by the in-strumentality of returned captives and Afro-Brazilian repatriates.[16] In this view of Yorùbá history, a pan-Yorùbá metacritical term such as "ọlàjú" could only have been of recent provenance.

Peel offers several descriptions of the term: (1) "the cultural package brought from outside by, above all, missionaries" ("*Olaju*," 147); (2) "the acquisition of the knowledge and techniques of Europe through the 'opening up' of the country" (148); (3) "part of an official programme of development" (148); (4) "a precondition for *individual* advance and for communal advance principally as an aggregated effect of that of successful individuals" (150); (5) "opening the eyes to the wider system, and acquiring the literary skills necessary for a really close acquaintance with its working" (154); (6) "the symbol of a particular party [the educated, technocratic, professional cadre] in the community but one linked to the universally-held value of communal aggrandisement" (154). Peel reads his informants to be have exposed in "ọ̀làjú" a historiographic metaphor that conceals its own historical origins in the dual legacies of nineteenth-century Christian missionary work and the British colonization of the Yorùbá hinterland at about the same time.

Notwithstanding Peel's commendable representation of nonacademic accounts of how "ọ̀làjú" captures historical significance, some of the responses offered by the Iléṣà men he surveyed demand a more expansive outlook than his analysis admits. To the question, "What changes have been for the better?" ("*Olaju,*" 142)—the exact Yorùbá phrasing is not printed—some answered "Ilera ti po si, olaju ti po si," a statement he translated as "We've become healthier, and *more* enlightened" (142; emphasis added). The sense of quantitative accretion reported in the phase "more enlightened" does not quite capture the durative entailment of "pọ̀ sí i." The response "Olaju de si *i*" (143) is translated and interpreted to mean "Olaju has come right up." A more loyal translation, one that is not beholden to the view that the concept is a recent metaphor for constructing and managing emergent power relations, might have glossed this statement as "Olaju arrives more," or as "A more bounteous olaju arrives," or even as "Olaju arrives more bountifully." The answer, "Olaju ti a ri be dara ju ti tele lo, sugbon o ku die ko to" (143) is rendered as "The olaju we know is already better than what was there before but there's still a little way to go before it's complete." To my mind, this respondent is periodizing "ọ̀làjú" in a way that is not truly reflected in the translation. The Yorùbá phrasing implies that there was some "ọ̀làjú" before now— whichever way "now" is dated—and that the previously existing "ọ̀làjú" is less satisfying than the current one. Duration and change are implied, too, in the statement "Enia o ku mo bi i ti atijo nitori hospital t'o wa bayi. Olaju isin Imale ati Igbagbo de," which Peel translates as "People don't die like they used to, because of the hospitals we have now. Olaju of Islam and Christianity has come" (143). The second sentence suggests antecedence or something prior in time. Here, "ọ̀làjú" is an adjective that describes the gains of two world religions, neither of which is represented as the creator of "ọ̀làjú." Instead, they brought their own, admittedly different and efficient, conditions of "ọ̀làjú." The syntax of the statements made by Peel's informants indicates that there might be a longer history to "ọ̀làjú" than Peel's article acknowledges.

It ought be considered significant that "ọ̀làjú" belongs to a family of Yorùbá words whose meanings are not, perhaps, exhausted by post-1850 Iléṣà contexts. Other "là" references are "àmà" (demarcation), "ìmà" (drawn line, facial marks included), and "àmàyé" (explanation). It is equally important, I will add, that several terms relating to splitting are conjoined to other body parts besides the eye: "lawọ́" (generous, or open palms), "lahùn" (speak freely, or open voice), "lara" (be envious, or open body), and "làyà" (frightened, or open chest). While "ọ̀làjú" does not appear as a free entry in Delano's dictionary, it shows under "akọ̀wé": "Ẹni tí o le kọ̀wé tàbí kàwé, ẹni tí ó ńṣe iṣẹ̀ ìwé kíkọ́ tàbi kíkà, ọmọwé ọ̀làjú" (A literate person, one who works in a reading and writing profession, an enlightened educated person). Delano includes under the meaning of "là": "(1) hàn, tan ìmọ́lẹ̀; Ọ̀run là sóri ilẹ̀ (appear, shine light. The sun shines on the earth.) (2) Fọ́ wẹ́wẹ́; Igba iya mi la si meji. (Break into pieces. My mother's crockery broke in pieces) (3) Gbàlà; Omo na nikan lo la. (Extricate safely. Only the child got saved or survived)." He also reports intransitive forms of the verb: "(1) ṣe eto larin enia meji, la ija (n. Olola [arbitrator]) Settle a matter or dispute between two individuals."

"Ọ̀làjú" clearly implicates activities and events that have to do with physiological indices of wakefulness. Its range of reference includes bodily movement, spatial awareness, and diurnal changes. "Ọ̀làjú," in short, concerns the placement of discursive bodies in their time and space. The properly placed—and therefore responsive—body takes optimal advantage of the particular social environment, and the one that is not so well placed falls behind in time and space (e.g., eyes are shut when not sleeping, stumbling into open ditches, running into visible walls, unable to distinguish dawn from dusk). Peel's argument that his informants might have used the term metaphorically does not preclude the possibility that "ọ̀làjú" 's semantic cluster relates to words that denote far more than a recent intellectual coinage. Other terms of "sight" and spatio-temporal "being" include "ojúmọ́" (dawn, literally "the brightening of the eyes or face or clarity"), "ìtìjú" (bashfulness or proper self-restraint, literally "shutting [also pushing] of the eyes"), "ìrójú" (endurance or the displacement [also distortion] of the eyes or face). These words also connote ethical and moral relations. Lacking ọ̀làjú or àìnítìjú (self-restraint), and suffering from àìnírójú (weak will), regardless of the specific steps attached to them at any historical time, are always character flaws that individuals so afflicted must strive to remedy.

Hence I argue that ọ̀làjú denotes the irreplaceable, irrevocable, repetitive, constant movement of the socially responsible individual and community. People whose eyes are open (ẹni ọ̀làjú) wake up at the right time, recognize newness when it appears, and pay their due to it by assimilating themselves into the unfolding routines. Definitely, "ọ̀làjú" involves newness. But it also involves promptness and propriety (in the sense of appropriate responsiveness or responsibility to social stimuli). Yorùbá semioptics, as it were, ties temporality in some fundamental way to a notion of visuality, or the ability to read and interpret the movement of time in relation to the space occupied.[17] It may not be accurate to say that "ojú dúdú" (benighted eyes) is the opposite of "ọ̀làjú," as Peel suggests, unless "ojú dúdú" refers to the effect (experience, feeling) of eyes shut close. Modernization (ọ̀làjú) that lacks morality (ìtìjú) will yield not benighted eyes (ojú dúdú), but mistaken temporality (ọ̀làjú òdì).[18]

Peel reports a questionnaire respondent thus on the worthy gains of development: "Olaju ni fi aiye dara ju ti atijo; awon enia nse irinajo, gbogbo ohun ti awon si ri l'ohun ni won mu wa sibi" (It's olaju that makes the world better than it was before. People travel, and everything they see abroad, they bring here) ("*Olaju*," 142). This statement, which could have come straight from Fágúnwà, indicates that "ọ̀làjú" is not static and that it has always been there. As Fágúnwà asserts in the preface to *Ìrìnkèrindò*:

> Ìgbà tí a bá sì wo bí ojú Yorùbá ti là tó kí Gẹ̀ẹ́sì tilẹ̀ tó gòké . . . kò sí ẹ̀yà kan ní Nigeria tí ó lè wípé òun lajú ju Yorùbá lọ títí di òní olónìí. (vi) (When we consider how widely open Yorùbá eyes have been from before the advent of whites, . . . [we realize that] there are no other people in Nigeria whose eyes are open wider.)

According to this statement, "ọ̀làjú" is not exclusively Yorùbá; other people have it too. But not all people have it in equal measure: the Europeans have it more than the Yorùbá, and the Yorùbá have always had it more than other Nigerians.

Reading, Writing, and Modernization in Fágúnwà

Concerned about "ọ̀làjú," Fágúnwà's heroes worry about time and how it unfolds. The time of ancestors, beyond traceable genealogy, is not important to them. However, the future, especially the welfare of the unborn and of those who have much to live for, drives storytelling. The expedition leaders accede to their king's requests because they care about how the dawn (ojúmọ́) of other days will open. They travel to Lángbòdó and Òkè Ìrònú to improve the community's experience of tomorrow, the next ojúmọ́. Each expedition leader agrees to his king's requests because he is reminded of the need to care for how ojúmọ́ will unfold (là). For Fágúnwà, "ọ̀làjú" is the foundation of free living. Any people who lack its fortune and refuse the chance to embrace it when the opportunity to do so appears deserve to be subdued and taught the approach to being. This is the case with the Èdìdàrẹ́ people in *Ìrìnkèrindò*. They lack ọ̀làjú and they seek neither social progress (ìlọsíwájú) nor upward growth (ìdàgbàsókè), three deficiencies that the Yorùbá-speaking expeditionists on the way to the Mount of Thoughtfulness find unconscionable and use as pretexts to subdue and colonize the Èdìdàrẹ́. It was considered appalling that the king accepts the rampant oppositeness and incongruities that define his people (40, 58). The administrator imposed on this hapless community is instructed to install a governance system that ensures timely proportionality in all things social. The novel also indicates that ọ̀làjú has something to do with self-conscious restraints (ìtìjú) (50) without which up-to-date motions might devolve into soulless gestures. Citizens of Aláṣejù (Excess) country enjoy modernization when they ride their automobiles, bicycles, and motorcycles (Wọ́n ní mọ́tò, wọ́n ní kẹ̀kẹ́, wọ́n ní alùpùpù, ọ̀pọ̀lọpọ̀ nǹkan ọ̀làjú ni wọ́n ní), but their mindless punctuality (Àṣejù wọn nípa ètò ṣíṣe) is unbearable. The entire city goes to dinner at the same time; at table, the movement of hands from plate to mouth is synchronized countrywide, and whoever moves out of time is jailed. In Fágúnwà's scale, this city is modern but uncivilized; it focuses on punctual timing but gives no regard to proportion and individuality. Its inscription systems leave no room for commentary.

The King's Death, Narrative Closure, and Transition in Consciousness

Something is always off about the kings at the end of each novel. They are either too old to remember things or too sick to continue. In either instance, passing on to a new order is always necessitated. The significance of regime change at the end of *Ìrèké Oníbùdó* is so obvious as to require no glossing, a feature that the narrative observes by reporting the closure in just two sentences. The narrator, who is now wise in the art of advance governance, succeeds the king who sent him on the errand of discovery, although he was born in a faraway community where he is not of royal descent. He is elected king by popular acclamation: "Gbogbo àwọn ọmọ ìlú ti pa ohùn pọ̀ pé èmi ni kí wọ́n fi jọba, kò sì pé tí mo dé tí mo fi gun orí oyè, mo jọba ní ìlú tí kì ìṣe ìbẹ̀ ni a ti bí mi" (140). (The citizens unanimously decided that I should be made the king, and not long after I returned, I ascended to the throne in a city in which I was not a native.)

The last part of the quoted comment indicates an epochal change in Àlùpàyídà (Transformation) country, the nodal point of a cosmopolitan, modern, democratic, peaceful transition to a regime led by a techno-philosopher. At the time Ìrèké comes to power, he controls advanced knowledge of ethical and moral governance and guidance, the secrets of curing a royal intractable ailment, and has lived with sheer brawn, Kumọ́fẹ̀hìntì, in close quarters for a long time. The positive ending of the story suggests that the new developments in Àlùpàyídà signal progress and uplift, two variants of ọ̀làjú.

In *Ìrìnkèrindò*, the story in which ọ̀làjú is most explicitly illustrated, the travelers to the Mount of Thoughtfulness successfully procure the seeds only after walking along a pathway filled with poisonous reptiles and climbing atop a tree whose trunk consists of only thorns. As in *Ìrèké Oníbùdó*, the end of the story marks a new beginning for the protagonist, who leaves his hometown permanently, perhaps filled with thoughtfulness, to live in affluence with his wife in a faraway town.

Igbó Olódùmarè, the most complex of the narratives, is a misadventure of sorts in which Olowo-aiye, the protagonist, and later a group of other hunters, are lost in the bush until Olowo-aiye is rescued by a storytelling sage who instructs him in ethics. Indeed, all of Fágúnwà's protagonists operate in worlds they do not understand and are able to navigate only uncertainly. They live in times when a little path connects the homestead to the densest forest, when the most accomplished hunter can get lost in the bush, when royal succession lines are amenable to changes, when existing measures of ọ̀làjú negotiate their relevance in emergent ones, and when polytheism, while not repudiated, is held suspect. This is also a time when polygamy ruins families, and monogamy nurtures affluence and comfort, even for men. Literacy is not strange, but neither is it widespread. Amidst the flux, institutions of recognition survive. The experienced storyteller who has lived through the changes, the younger writer-editor recording the older man's words, the internal audience convened by the writer-editor exchange commentaries, many times literally so as extradiegetic sermons. Reflections on transformation (àyípadà), upward growth (ìdàgbàsókè), forward movement (ìlọsíwájú), and modernized civilization (ọ̀làjú) are repeated in different forms.

The metacommentaries on ethics and epistemic changes take a decisive turn in *Àdììtú Olódùmarè*, Fágúnwà's last novel. At the age of fifteen, Àdììtú, with just primary school education in hand, leaves home hungry, heads into the bush, and becomes a foraging hunter-gatherer. After having lived in the wild for seven years, he stumbles into the city of Ajédùbúlẹ̀, carrying an elephant tusk he has earlier picked up from a heap to which his pet lion had led him. Àdììtú hits sudden wealth in ivory trade and inherits money and property—a goldfield, a rubber plantation, twelve houses, twelve cars, and six trucks—from his deceased friend. By the time he returns to Ìlákọ̀ṣẹ, the only named hometown of any of Fágúnwà's heroes, his parents have died of hunger. In their memory, Àdììtú endows a scholarship fund for a course of studies in "ẹ̀kọ́ nípa ìwà" (44), a course in ethics of being. Àdììtú seems to have realized that modernization (ọ̀lájú) alone is inadequate for a fulfilling existence in a town that is indifferent to the sufferings of the poor and the old. Because its people have turned their backs on each other and do not respond to one another any more, the eyes of Ìlákọ̀ṣẹ people are not quite properly opened, despite their tarred roads, good schools, and churches. The city will regress closer to the Èdìdàrẹ́ state, if its citizens do not give considerable self-conscious attention (ìrònú) to the grounds of being in their community. Àdììtú's endowment reminds his people, as Ìrágbèje theorizes during a storytelling session in *Ògbójú Ọdẹ*, that the essence of ethical being is diffused and is to be found in everyday interactions among all citizens: "Ìwà lẹwà; ẹwà kò sí níbìkan" (95). Àdììtú's scholarship funds could therefore be interpreted to mean an investment in cultural self-examination, the singular end to which are directed

Fágúnwà's novelistic reflections on institutions of storytelling, listening, writing, and reading.

Notes

1. Unless otherwise stated, the translations are from editions listed in the bibliography. I have tone marked all the Yorùbá words, although that is not the case in the original stories, because this makes comprehension easier for the contemporary reader. For the same reason, I have also followed prevailing orthography. In each quote, the first page number refers to the Yorùbá original and the second to the English translation.

2. "The model assumes a single direction in which literacy development can be traced, and associates it with 'progress,' 'civilization,' individual liberty, and social mobility. It attempts to distinguish literacy from schooling. It isolates literacy as an independent variable and then claims to be able to study its consequences" (Street, *Literacy in Theory and Practice*, 2). For Street's very strong criticism of this model, see 19–65.

3. Jacques Derrida provides a sustained critique of that view of oral language in the first two chapters of *Of Grammatology*.

4. Although Goody seems to have modified these axioms in *The Domestication of the Savage Mind*, his insistent anchoring of the transition from mythological thinking to scientific reasoning on the divide between orality and literacy confirms the old metaphysics.

5. See Irele, "African Imagination," and Scheub, "Review of African Oral Traditions," for influential conceptions of these tendencies. Jane Wilkinson ("Between Orality and Writing") agrees with both Irele and Scheub. Eileen Julien (*African Novels*; see the Introduction) is more skeptical.

6. We should consider it important that Emmanuel Obiechina puts Amos Tutuola at the exact point Irele places Fágúnwà. In Irele's study, based on the writing of Yorùbá men, Tutuola is twice removed from tradition and broaches the modern sensibility. Fágúnwà, however, is only once removed from tradition since he writes in a largely oral language. See also Wilkinson, "Between Orality and Writing," 42–43; Smith, "D. O. Fagunwa," 10–12; Schipper, *Beyond the Boundaries*, 99–106; Okpewho, *Myth in Africa*, 203–221.

7. See also Ogunsina, *Development of the Yoruba Novel*, 76–80; Ogundipe-Leslie, "Poetics of Fiction," 93.

8. *Ògbójú Ọdẹ Nínú Igbó Irúnmalẹ̀, Igbó Olódùmarè*, and *Ìrìnkèrindò Nínú Igbó Elégbèje*. The other two will be cited for support as the discussion demands.

9. This is probably the reason Soyinka substitutes the indefinite article "a book" (ìwé kan) for the definite article "the book" (ìwé yìí) used in the original text.

10. Soyinka moves moves this episode from its place at the beginning of chapter 4 in the Yorùbá novel to the end of chapter 3 in his English translation.

11. Bámgbóṣé (*Novels of D. O. Fagunwa*, p. 4) draws a direct line from the novelist to the editor character. See Barber's extensive analysis of the role of editors in the development of early Yorùbá language popular print literacy in the early 1900s in her introduction to *Print Culture and the First Yorùbá Novel*.

12. Historical examples include E. M. Lijadu's collections of divination stories, Samuel Johnson's *History of the Yorùbás*, and I. B. Akinyele's *Iwe Itan Ibadan* and Odumosu's compilations of medicinal herbs and processes. The struggle between the textual locations occupied by the literate teller and the writer-editor in Fágúnwà's novels signals an unfolding epistemic fight that a Lijadu or a Samuel Johnson might not disclose.

13. The honored individuals include Professor Margaret Read of the University of London, Mr. R. A. McL. Davidson (head of the Education Department in Nigeria's colonial administration), Bishop S. C. Phillips, Rev. Sijuwade, Oba Olagbegi II of Ọ̀wọ̀, Mrs. J. A. Mars, Miss J. V. Herklots, Mr. L. Murby, Principal of Igbobi College, Lagos, and Mr. D. R. G. Gwynne-Jones, Principal of Government College, Ìbàdàn. Adeniyi's English translation (Fágúnwà, *An Expedition to the Mountain of Thought*) excised the preface. Soyinka's translations of the other two installments in the trilogy (Fágúnwà, *Forest of a Thousand Daemons* and *Forest of Olodumare*) also exclude the author's preliminary remarks.

14. A Google Scholar search on August 10, 2012, reported seventy-two citations in digitized publications.

15. The dictionary drew from just twenty-two books that include Fágúnwà's novels, five books of poems and songs (mainly by Obasa and Sowande, two early poets), one collection of proverbs, the Church Missionary Society's bilingual dictionary, two years of the newspaper *Akede Eko* (1940–1942), and two primers. Chief I. O. Delano does not indicate that he referenced nonliterary usage of any word.

16. The opposing tendency accepts a longer view of origin and stresses the continuity of ritual practices (see Olupona, *City of 201 Gods*; Apter, "Yoruba Ethnogenesis from Within").

17. I first encountered that word in Moyo Okediji's dissertation, "Semioptics of Anamnesia."

18. Two other development terms used by Peel's respondents, "ìlọsíwájú" (forward movement) and "ìdàgbàsókè" (vertical growth) address only spatial relations and do not incorporate the movement of time as ọ̀làjú does.

4 Sex, Gender, and Plot in Fágúnwà's Adventures

Two main thought streams dominate considerations of sex and gender ethics in Fágúnwà's works. One asserts that the stories "negate [the] marginalization of females and reject the peripheral roles assigned to female folk in the post-colonial Yoruba society" (Adeyemi, "Representation of Gender in Fiction," 97). This judgment relies almost exclusively on a facile reading of the behaviors of the hero's lover in the final novel, Àdììtú Olódùmarè. It is stressed in the older, more perceptive stream that the novels portray "no profound observation on women," even though the life of females, going by their frequent appearances in the men's adventures, seems "to be a fascinating topic for Fagunwa" (Bamgbose, Novels, 60). In other words, while females are critical to the stories, the narratives make them serve only ends that promote men's interests. Both sides determine the preoccupation with females in the novels to be responses to preexisting consensus in the author's environment. Adeyemi believes that Fágúnwà opposes the larger, Yorùbá, culture's historical maltreatment of women, while Bamgbose demonstrates that the author "merely follows views commonly held by the Yorùbá" (60). One can refute these polar views with historical references to standard-issue ethnographic studies and argue instead that the ideal nuclear, conjugal, monogamous love favored by the leading men of the stories was not a widespread "Yorùbá" manner when Fágúnwà began writing in the 1930s and that the "traditional Yorùbá" woman's subservience that Àdììtú Olódùmarè is praised for repudiating existed nowhere in the form Adeyemi presupposes.

As the following discussion will show, disagreeing with the two positions summarized above does not mean that Fágúnwà's females are best left alone. The approach to follow should begin by viewing writing and storytelling structures as reality production practices and not as devices fit only for reporting already fully constituted sociocultural consensus. In one of the earliest sophisticated readings of the sociological ramifications of Fágúnwà's art, Molara Ogundipe-Leslie urges critical readers to focus on the novelist's aesthetic constitution of the presumed Yorùbá contents of the stories. Ogundie-Leslie enjoins enthusiastic scholars whose justification of the realism-defying elements of Fágúnwà's stories relies exclusively on the ostensibly Yorùbá worldviews of the stories to not draw any conclusions about the text without first examining the provenance of the aesthetic object in their hands. According to Ogundipe-Leslie, "It may be a more fruitful and more manageable task for us to attempt to see how these concepts of reality and existence are mediated by art—in this particular exercise, in the medium of fiction" ("The Poetics of Fiction," 86). Ogundipe-Leslie insists that worldviews do not inhabit narrative aesthetics as worldviews but in, and through, the brokerage of formal conventions. *Ògbójú Ọdẹ*, for example, does not report the state of historical Yorùbá culture. The Yorùbá society of that novel does not question its "slave-holding and gerontocratic oligarchy," subjecting the individual "to the will of a master, or a hierarchically superior person and an over-all will whose *metaphor* is the Oba" (87; emphasis added). Olabiyi Yai disagrees with the relevance of this example by asking "To what extent can we say that the Yoruba society was a gerontocratic one? What was the significance of gerontocracy if it existed? Was it based on socio-economic privileges?" ("On Omoralara Ogundipe-Leslie," 120). But he does not discredit Ogundipe-Leslie's main argument that the Fágúnwà critic "should try to reach the reality expressed by the writer through the formal character of each work and, from the yield, make deductions about our social and historical condition" (89). Aiming to evaluate construals of the ethics of gender and sex advanced in the stories, in the rest of this chapter, following the parameters Ogundipe-Leslie outlines, I propose a study of how narrative progression and character focalization in Fágúnwà's novels are deployed to create in Yorùbá the acceptability of a male-dominated worldview.

From Àkàrà-ògùn to Àdìítú, love drives all the leading men in Fágúnwà's five novels. These leading men put themselves in harm's way for the love of their homelands. They travel from one end of the earth to another to share their love of storytelling with young writers. Their love for fellow adventurers knows no bounds. Among the cardinal lessons they learn during their public service journeys, lessons they impart at the many subsequent storytelling sessions they convene for their biographers, none surpasses their repeatedly professed discovery of the supreme advantages of monogamous, heterosexual love. In this chapter, I go beyond the men's manifest proclamations on love to examine the reasons those beloved (and the not-so-beloved) female partners of the storytelling male adventurers do not accompany them on the journeys of self-discovery and community improvement that structure each novel. I analyze how critical changes in the many heroic, self-directed plots that define Fágúnwà's fiction typically occur at the expense of women. The two main claims that drive the discussion are: (1) that the central adventures driving narrative progression in the forest tales pursue a male worldview that is not fully supported by other story elements, and (2) that character focalization during significant turns of events tightly restricts reading to an overwhelmingly male-determined ethics of gender relationships. These two narratological, writing, considerations pitch to readers gender norms that are not fully supported in the storyworld but are, through commentaries, recommended as what should be most desirable. The gender relationship preferments of the narrator impose themselves textually between observed behaviors and recollections. I argue in this chapter that Fágúnwà's famed emphasis on narrative formalities—such as symbolic naming and fantastic settings, and memorable characterization, actions, and language use—betrays, even in its conspicuousness, a mistrust of the reader.

Travelers Wanted? Only Men Need Apply

As I observed in chapter 3, the need to reach a predetermined destination—Mount Lángbòdó, Olódùmarè Forest, or the Mount of Thoughtfulness, for example—handed by the king to the heroic adventurers and their cohorts anchor movements in the forest novels. The quest to reach that destination, usually formulated by the king to address a social need, and rarely meant to satisfy personal ambitions, sets the heroes on inexorable man-making paths that will at some point make them realize that men must not but act in manly ways, or "ọkùnrin kò ní ṣàì ṣe ọkùnrin" (*Adiitu*, 78). The men know where they are headed but often do not know how to get there, and the efforts they make to carve an itinerary typically constitute a good part of the experience narrated. Àkàrà-ògùn, a universally famous, brave hunter (ògbòjú ọdẹ tí òkìkí rẹ̀ sì ti kàn káàkiri gbogbo aiyé [*Ògbójú*,50]), is persuaded out of retirement by the king to gather seeds of harmonious living from Mount Lángbòdó, at the frontier of this and the other world and to which he will navigate his way without a roadmap. Olowo-aiye heads into Olódùmarè Forest—an enchanting wilderness in which snails are larger than turtles—in search of nǹkan ńlá, lofty objectives (*Igbó Olódùmarè*, 10). The men of Ìrìnkèrindò's group, dispatched by their king to collect the fruit of introspection (èso igi ìrònú) from the Mount of Thoughtfulness, tumble from one happenstance to another, including encounters with the king of the country of the witless contrarians (Èdìdàrẹ́). Ìrèké Oníbùdó is bogged down for seven years in the forest until he is captured by the one-eyed, slave-owning Olú-igbó, who he overcomes by driving a nail through the occiput. Ìrèké Oníbùdó soon finds himself underwater, wherein rules Àrògìdìgbà the mermaid. For killing a dragon lizard, he earns himself a wife (who soon dies) and high political office. He survives a trap set by his deceased wife's half sister and has to travel with two other men to procure a medication for his ex-father-in-law's ailment. Relentless poverty leads Àdììtú into the bush at the age of sixteen, and he finds contentment there. He, too, has no roadmap when, seven years later, he exits the forest into a thriving town in which, as its name, Ajédùbúlẹ̀, announces, commerce sprawls splendiferously. After selling for a small fortune the elephant tusk he is carrying, he begins a rewarding life in high trade. One exception to the male hero's sojourn in the enchanted forest plot is the story of Ìfépàdé, a female adventurer in *Ìrèké*

Oníbùdó, who suddenly leaves town of her own volition in search of Ìrèké, her rescuer and lover: "O di ẹrù rẹ̀ kò sì sọ fún ẹnikẹ́ni, òun náà fi ìlú sílẹ̀" (She packed her luggage, said nothing to anyone, and she too left town) (91). But the woman's will to take a risk away from the domestic sphere is soon appropriated by the lover in whose tale we encounter her. Ìfépàdé's unique, short-lived, radical departure from home is quickly reined in as male-motivated, and she is denied the opportunity for self-definition. Indeed, she dies six days after the marriage that halts her travels (97).

Maleness is not incidental to the plot developments. Even a casual reader will notice that the self and social improvement discoveries gained at the end of the stories are presented as things only men can acquire. In each of the unnamed cities at the starting point of the heroic experiences, it so happens, without any explanation offered, that only men dare to go into the bush to earn the social status high enough to catch the king's attention. Ìrìnkèrindò posed his appointment as a test of his readiness to take over his deceased father's responsibilities. In the king's words, "Eléyìí náà ni yóò sì fi han gbogbo ènìyàn irú ọmọ tí ìwọ ó jẹ́ẹ̀, yálà bí o bá ní le tó ẹru baba rẹ gbé" (This task will demonstrate to all the type of heir you will be, whether you are adequate to inheriting your father's duties) (*Ìrìnkèrindò*, 11). Probably because that part of the story is recounted by his son, details of Olowo-aiye's motivation in *Igbó Olódùmarè* are simply attributed to his exercising "hunterly" will and curiosity: "Bàbá mi . . . múra ní òwúrọ̀ ọjọ́ kan báyìí tí ó bá igbó abàmì kan lọ lẹ́bàá ìlú wa láti lọ ṣe ọdẹ" (8) (My father prepared one morning to venture into a singular forest near our town to hunt (14). Ìrèké Oníbùdó leaves town to follow his mother's death bed advice (47). With no more than an elementary education to his name, Àdììtú leaves his hometown to save himself from the poverty that eventually led to his parents starving to death (31). Unlike the equally poor Ìrèké Oníbùdó, Àdììtú explicitly ties manliness to his decision to pursue far away from his place of birth his chances for upward social mobility. During the internal dialogue the sixteen-year-old has with himself about who to inform of this decision, he resolves not to disclose the plans to his mother out of regard for her womanly sensibilities (31) because the strong, discreet man ought to minimize the chance of exposing a woman to emotional distress.

Similar statements of self-conscious maleness are made by leading characters in other novels. Àkàrà-ògùn notes the gender pattern in the community's response to the valedictory honors accorded his group as it leaves for Lángbòdó—men scowl in sadness, while women weep without restraint (*Ògbójú*, 57). When Olowo-aiye leaves home, he counsels his people not to mourn if he fails to return because they should know that daring the uncertain is universally masculine. As manhood demands, he should leave ("ọkùnrin ńlọ" [*Igbó Olódùmarè*, 10]), he tells his family. Ìrìnkèrindò, announcing that his aspiring to manliness requires him to step confidently and proudly into his father's shoes, proclaims, "Bàtà ti bàbá mi fi sílẹ̀, mo ti pinnu àti fi ẹsẹ̀ mi sí i, ọnà tí ó ti ńtọ̀ rí, mo ti pinnu àti máa tọ̀ ọ́" (12) (The sandals which my father left behind I have strapped to my feet; the road on which he trod I am fully primed to tread [19]). Perhaps the narrative feature that most reveals the male burden borne by the forest trilogy is that named leaders in each installment are all called "akọni," or male-humans in literal English rendition.[1] This brief discussion of narrative beginnings in Fágúnwà's stories indicates that declarations of self-certainty about manliness is integral to readying each hero for his perilous travel. They are all aware that only those willing to pay the price of manhood can confront the wilderness of existence. Even in the two novels where the ends to be achieved by the main journeys are not that certain at the beginning, only self-driven and self-directed males are predisposed to risk their lives and, after triumph, attain heightened self-awareness and gain access to high social standing.

Need Help Traveling? Call Your Mother

The information presented thus far about females in Fágúnwà's stories not leaving home paints only a partial picture. At every major turn in each narrative, the male adventurers encounter women, although usually after the women have transformed into witches, dead mothers' spirits, helpful angels, and other quasi-human figures. The females lurk in different guises along the routes waiting to help the often lost males rediscover their paths. Each heroic male leader successfully negotiates almost every difficult frontier he traverses because a female figure shows up, usually after a powerful plea of helplessness to the Almighty. In one instance, the manly hero literally cries for his mother. I will illustrate this with Ìrèké Oníbùdó's travails. The hero's polygamous father, Ìrèké-Aiyé, ruins his family's fortunes on the thirty-one women he marries after his stable and mildly prosperous relationship with one wife. He dies a broken person, and the hero's mother, his first and constant wife, soon follows, but not before she urges Ìrèké Oníbùdó to seek a better chance for himself somewhere else. At his first stop, Ìrèké Oníbùdó begins to make a life for himself working as a laborer for a kind, monogamous gentleman he meets in the bush. Trouble begins when this employer takes a second wife, and the story takes another turn because Ìrèké refuses to reciprocate the new woman's illicit love overtures. The spurned woman turns her husband against Ìrèké, who is driven away. The young boy, who has left home to make a man of himself because he has inherited no patrimony, is further displaced and unwittingly sent along on his life journey by a different set of machinations caused by a female acquaintance. Although women do not accompany Ìrèké on this leg of his journey, we see one victimize him significantly.

His troubles with women continue when he swims out of the coastal city of Èrò Ẹ̀hìn (62), only to find himself aboard a merchant ship that soon capsizes and sinks to the bottom of the ocean, where he is imprisoned by Àrọ̀gìdìgbà, the mermaid. The narrated description emphasizes her womanly dimensions: "Kò tilẹ̀ jọ ẹja rárá, ó dàbí ọmọbìnrin ó sì di irun orí rẹ̀ wìnnìkìn" (She does not resemble a fish at all, looking like a maiden with a gorgeously plaited coiffure) (64–65). The major obstruction that this feminized character becomes in the events that follow threatens to end Ìrèké's life.

Although Ìrèké is much younger than the other brave males of the hunter trilogy, his abject helplessness while held in the mermaid's custody, and his manner of overcoming his terrors, are identical to what happens in the terrestrial encounters in Olódùmarè and Irúnmalẹ̀ Forests. Help comes to Ìrèké unexpectedly while he is asleep one night in the mermaid's dungeon: his dead mother shows up magically to comfort him and to assure him that she will summon otherworldly legions to help him execute the mermaid's humanly impossible tasks. Ìrèké breaks down when he learns of his second task: to cultivate and harvest a plantation of yams in twenty-four hours. In tears, he cries out for his mother: "Mo wọ inú ilé mi lọ mo sì bẹ̀rẹsí sọkún mo ńké pe ìyá mi" (I disappeared into my cell, began to weep, and started calling out for my mother) (67). Being a true and good mother, the still unnamed woman answers, bringing help from the land of the dead. For the third and pivotal task, Ìrèké is asked to fight "Ewúrẹ́ ìbẹ̀rù" (Fearsome Goat), a beast raised by Lucifer to torment creatures around the mermaid's palace. Days before the scheduled conflict, the mermaid lodges Ìrèké in her mother's den of witchcraft, where he is to be killed before the appointed date. Meanwhile, Ìrèké's dead and all-seeing mother knows that he will not survive the mermaid even if he defeats the goat. To prepare him for the double danger, Ìrèké's spirit-mother teaches him the necessity of developing the will to withstand a determined threat if he wants to be a man: "Múra bí ọkùnrin lóníì o, ṣe bí akọni ọkùnrin, jẹ́ kí ọkàn rẹ le bí òkúta tí ẹnikẹ́ni kò lé borí" (Arm yourself like a man, act like a manly man, harden your resolve to become like a rocky obstacle that no one can scale) (69). She also brings over again otherworldly forces to help her son destroy the mermaid (71). Ìrèké loots Àrọ̀gìdìgbà's palace, and when he arrives at his next stop—above water, in Àlùpàyídà—it is with enormous wealth.[2] In subsequent encounters, the spirit mother's gift of a magical dagger proves critical in other fights. Ìrèké's election later as king of Àlùpàyídà is due principally to the help rendered by the ghost of a dead mother who was utterly powerless while she was alive. The critical roles played by the employer's seductive wife, by the life-threatening mermaid, and by the spirit mother constitute significant conflicts and resolutions that define Ìrèké's life journey. The observation made earlier that women do not travel in Fágúnwà still stands. However, the observation needs to be added that men continue largely because females help them. It is also true that the women are dismissed as soon as they are done help-ing the men. Some unarticulated factors of the social environment seem to make it impossible for the women to do wonderful things, heroic motherhood included, as ordinary mortals.

The narrative formula discussed above creates a contradiction. On the one hand, the outer story flaunts the manliness purposes of traditional adven-ture plots; on the other hand, female activities, unlike in the inherited tale type, are necessary for the successes of the male adventurers. The women do not leave home and thus do not enjoy the adulations of heroic departure and return-ing. However, they rule with extraordinary powers, stepping in and out of the stories unbound by time and space constraints, the thoroughfares and byways of the men's itineraries. Overall, it looks like Fágúnwà wants women to travel, but not in the way men do. Perhaps because the principal males are confounded by their dependence on females, they constantly repeat to themselves (and to their primary listeners as they speak to the writer-editor) axioms about the nature of males and females in asides and homiletics. As they find themselves at the mercy of females, they reassure their egos, if only rhetorically, of the strictures that limit the range of women's activities in the social order they are working to preserve and improve.

Male Town, Female Town; Being Men, Being Women

The last leg of Ìrèké Oníbùdó's man-making journey offers an excellent illustration of the sex role quandary in the plots of Fágúnwà's novels. For a few days, Ìrèké and his two fellow travelers (Èrò-ọkàn and Kùmọ́fẹ̀hìntì) stop at a city populated exclu-sively by men, which the narrator interprets to be the creator's warning about what social life would be like without women: "Àpẹrẹ tí Ẹlẹ́dàá ṣe láti fi hàn bí ayé ọmọ ènìyàn ìbá ti rí bí kò bá sí obìnrin" (The Creator's example to show the world what *humanity* would have looked like were there to be no females) (108; emphasis added). Word choice in the narrator's gloss about the city betrays the novel's vacillation on how to correlate sex and social order. A generous reading of the description will take "ọmọ ènìyàn" (human offspring) to be a substitute for hu-manity in general. However, since the only population in reference here consists of only males, it will not be entirely uncharitable to take "ọmọ ènìyàn" (humanity) to mean strictly men. Readers soon discover, as Ìrèké recounts its features, that this community is not a homosocial Eden, notable among which is the inhabitants' general disregard for the care of the body. Ìrèké observes further that because the men do everything for themselves without the assistance of female companions, and because it is impossible to differentiate socioeconomic production activities by sex, not much wealth is created:

Owó kò pọ̀ ní ìlú náà tó nítorí wọn kò rí àyè ṣiṣẹ́, wọn ní láti wá oúnjẹ ara wọn kí wọn tójú ilé, kí wọn pọn omi kí wọn sì ṣe oníruúrú iṣẹ́ tí obìnrin ńṣe. (108) (There is not much wealth in the city because they have no time to work, they have to cook, take care of the home, including fetching water and performing other sundry tasks that women do.)

We have here another sign of consternation. First, the report acknowledges the economic consequence of domestic work. But the quantification is less than full, in that domesticity is reported as impoverishing for the men who are compelled by circumstances to engage in it. Furthermore, since this town harbors no females, the sexist notion of "iṣẹ́ tí obìnrin ńṣe" (sundry tasks that women do) should not ordinarily apply except in comparison to what Ìrèké and his internal audience know to be the norm. It is also within this frame of reference that the description of the allegedly natural toughness and roughness of the male city's inhabitants can be understood:

Kò sí nǹkan tí ó rọ̀ ní nǹkan wọn, ijó wọn le, orin wọn le, ìlù wọn le, bí wọn bá ńṣiré, iré líle ni wọn máa ńṣe, ṣe ni wọn á máa lé ara wọn tí wọn á máa lu ara wọn. (109) (Nothing is soft about them, their dance is hard, their singing is hard, their drumming is hard, they play hard games, chasing themselves up and down, beating up each other without care.)

Without the comparative knowledge of other places, the ostensibly manly attributes imputed to these males do not quite make sense. Ìrèké notes as well that the men's city is clean, although the homes are in disarray; their cuisine passes muster, although it is not remarkable. Unfortunately, the narrator does not report the peoples' self-understanding of their own ways. The observations narrated are those of the male heterosexual on his way to becoming the king of Àlùpàyídà. Ìrèké binds maleness to manliness, although evidence in the city of men gives no support to that conclusion (109).

Five days after leaving the city of men, the traveling party arrives at the city of women. As in the city of men, biological reproduction here is asexual. Citizens of the female city, too, do not care about appearance, and many go about naked, neglecting to conceal their bodies. Ìrèké is also confounded by the females' ability to do all things that males do elsewhere: they cultivate large farms, raise abundant yams, produce more than adequate various produce, run and jump, and ride horses. Compared to the city of males, however, the females gossip a lot (111), and their homes are not well kept. These negative judgments, we should note again, are valid only in relation to the gender order in Ìrèké's world and are completely unremarkable, except for comparison to occurrences in the city of men. The reason for the untidy homes, according to Ìrèké, is that the females' preoccupation with other aspects of life leaves them no room for domestic care. Although domestic care impoverishes males, as noted above, ignoring the same tasks does not make the women richer. Ìrèké also notes that the females are excessively fearful, cry easily, are exceedingly compassionate, have weak laws, don't follow rules, and are devoted religionists (112). In short, they are soft. The grounds to question these observations are too numerous and obvious to recount. It should be sufficient simply to note that the weeds in the streets of the female city could not have been caused by the women's lack of strength—they are, after all, accomplished farmers—and also that Ìrèké's general negative characterizations barely disguise an unwarranted fear of women working outside of the home.

At the level of basic biological and socioeconomic production and reproduction, living in the male city and in the female city is identical. But because the narrator/protagonist comes from a city where males live like men and females have become women, and men's ways are the norm for no evident cause, the narrator extrapolates divine wisdom as the reason the features of life in that world are normative and the contradictions he witnesses in the female city and male city are aberrant. According to Ìrèké,

> Ọgbọ́n Ẹlẹ́dàá pọ̀ púpọ̀ tí ó dá ọkùnrin àti obìnrin sí òde ayé, àwọn ọkúnrin dúró bí egungun àwọn obìnrin sì dúró bí ẹran ara ènìyàn. Láì sí egungun ara kò lè ṣe nǹkan, láì sí ẹran, egungun kò lè ṣe nǹkan. (112) (Inestimable is the Creator's wisdom for creating men and women, men standing for the skeleton and women for the flesh. Without the skeleton, flesh is of no value, and without the flesh, skeleton is useless.)

To reiterate, the observed experiences in the male city and the female city do not agree with the "egungun" (hard, brittle bones of the skeleton) and "ẹran" (soft, malleable flesh) binary generalizations about gender that Ìrèké claims to derive from them. The narrator takes advantage of the authority of his storytelling position to raise to cosmic superiority the dual sex/gender system of his own lived world and to discount the value of the different experience he experiences in other places.

To recap, Fágúnwà's men travel to seek fortune and intellectual instruments of social good; they sometimes marry along the way, but always return to the homestead to carry on an improved life. During the journey, found or conjured females play determinative roles in how the itineraries shape up, usually easing, but not infrequently aggravating, how difficulties are overcome and goals achieved. Female figures, without being privy to the heroes' overall plans, often serve as linkers and binders of the random eventualities that constantly threaten the men's tales of desire and becoming. These feminized life and narrative agents are self-sacrificing and rarely seek personal credit or accommodation within the journeys. Also, they are rarely human and, therefore, have no personal interests to protect or seek in their contributions to the ends achieved by the male wards they rush to help.

Wives, Witches, Fiancées, and Other Lovers

The adventurers' settled, intimate lives, either before or after their main journeys, involve memorable women—Àjẹ́dìran, Ìpọ́njúdìran, Ìfẹ́pàdé, Ìfẹ́pínyà, Iyúnadé, Kàkó's fiancée, the writer-editors' wives, and so forth—with whom they spend considerable time. These women, unlike those who smooth the rough segments of the life road traveled by the heroes, are idealized as wives, mothers, and mates. Narrative affairs, as they concern this set of characters, are different from the measures applied to those discussed above. I want to shift the discussion to how Fágúnwà constructs the domestic norm for these women. I will restrict the discussion to how the pattern of focalization[3] in the retelling of the women's experiences differentiates between men and women and secures from the reader greater attention and identification for the men.

The forest novels cede the dominant voice to the homodiegetic narrator, the main male adventurer who is also the main character in the story he recounts of the exploits he either foments or leads others to attain. The consequence of this privileged narrative position is that the heroes serve as influential cultural spokespersons, as controllers of readers' access to events and characters, and also as the main selectors of disclosure protocols or how the story is going to be told. Characters can speak through the narrators to the reader (in the case of the forest novels, the listening audience gathered at the writer-editor's home) in the form of direct quotes. They might report only what characters see, or what they think of what they see. In other words, the nature of the narrator in these stories makes it serve more than just being disinterested agents of a purportedly Yorùbá culture bound by space and time. The narrator is also the main focalizer, the agent "that sees and, seeing, causes [others] to be seen" (Bal, "Narrating and Focalizing," 244). The narrating agent, who also presents itself as the main doer in the chain of actions given to the reader (and listeners), "selects actions and chooses the angle from which to present them" and "with those actions creates the narrative" (244–245). Because the seen passes through the narrator, Bal recommends that narrative analysis should separate "the vision through which the elements are presented" from the concerns of "the voice verbalizing that vision" (*Narratology*, 143). Characters, being approximations of bodies that exist in space and time, cannot but see. Narrators, being factors of storytelling, do not always see, but always present what characters have seen, and fit perception into discursively intelligible and semiotically proper conventions. No social body, it is commonly known, tells as it sees, proverbial assertions to the contrary notwithstanding.

In hierarchically organized societies such as the ones in Fágúnwà's novels, the telling agent—say, the mouth—is prohibited from reporting everything that the seeing agent—say, the eye—passes to it. This implies that the telling agent's burden of presentation is different from that of the seeing organ. The eye, for instance, cannot not see what lies within its visual field. (It could frown, or wink, of course.) The mouth, however, can choose not to speak even if it is open, and when it speaks, the utterance need not correspond to what the sight organ sends across. One can even argue that the speaking agent that reports every construct passed on to it will one day be destroyed by its indiscretion. Bal represents the story of the eye's incapacities as a storage (or memory) problem (*Narratology*, 147).

To the reader, the focalizer, "the point from which the [story] elements are viewed" (Bal, *Narratology*, 146), is bipolar. From one perspective, it keeps the extent and proportion of things apprehended and works like the eye; in another, it functions like the mouth because it limits what is disclosable. In actual narration, readers see through the focalizer's "eyes and will, in principle, be inclined to accept the vision presented by that character" (146). Focalization can be internal (with an agent who is a character, who need not be the narrator, from inside the story) or external (with an agent who need not be a character in the fable but usually the narrator). It seems impossible to have an external focalizer who is not a narrator. In contrast, internal focalization is always character-bound but not necessarily narrator-bound. The focalized object can be "perceptible" or "imperceptible" (e.g., dreams, internal dialogues).

One of the main contributions that feminist narratology has made to the phenomenology of reading is to demonstrate the many ways that stories map sex onto gender. For example, tear-jerking, sentimental novels report suffering from the victim's perspective and typically focalize events such that readers can "participate emotionally from the subject-position of the oppressed" (Warhol, "How Narration Produces Gender," 183). It is also well known that depth of field and angle of vision do prompt the reader to favor particular responses over others, especially in relation to the presentation of conflicts that determine plot turns (events that have causal or other consequential impact on progress, stasis, reversal, victory, defeat, fulfillment, disappointment, or some other outcomes).

Fágúnwà's man-making forest novels rarely afford the reader a sympathetic gaze on the domestic, female companion of the heroic males, even when they endure undeserved distress. The suffering of Ìrèké Oníbùdó's mother, which could have been the exception, is subordinated to her husband's conjugal incontinence and the beginning of her son's journeys into wealthy manhood.[4] A fuller illustration of the narrative denial of sympathy to female companions is to be found in the treatment of Kàkó's fiancée in *Ògbójú Ọdẹ*. When Àkàrà-ògùn travels to Igbó Ńlá to recruit Kàkó for the Lángbòdó trip, he meets his friend on the last day of an obligatory seven-year courtship and conclusion of elaborate marriage rites that Kàkó, filled with the patriotic love stoked by Àkàrà-ògùn's words alone, breaks off unilaterally and wantonly. Àkàrà-ògùn, in retrospect, describes the breakup as utterly wrong: "Ìwà àìdára pátápátá gbáà" (52) (It was most unbecoming behavior) (75). While this statement reflects Àkàrà-ògùn's moral position, his management of focalization, him being the narrator, renders the summary judgment a rather tepid exoneration. In the next paragraph, the telling of the encounters shifts to a report of Kàkó's nameless fiancée asking what she might have done to provoke that level of disregard from her beloved almost-husband, close companion of seven years. She puts her plea in the form of vindicating questions that list the many unwomanly infractions that she believes might turn away a man—conjugal infidelity, poor housekeeping, inhospitality, selfishness, incompetent cooking (53). The woman's choosing the ordinarily second person plural, but also seniority marking and deferential, pronoun used for addressing superiors reflects her abject self-subordination, a position from which she recovers two paragraphs later. Kàkó's answer does not reciprocate his fiancée's use of respectful pronoun. He concedes, however, that she has been a perfectly monogamous consort (53), as he justifies his boorishness thus:

> Ìgbà tí nǹkan bá dé, ó dé náà ni: bí ojú bá mọ́ igba ewé á máa wọ̀ ní orí igi; bí ilẹ̀ bá sí ṣú igba ẹranko á máa rìn nínú igbó—ohun gbogbo ni ó ní àkokò wọn: àkokò eré, ọ̀tọ̀ ni; àkokò ìjà, ọ̀tọ̀ ni; àkokò ẹ̀rùn, ọ̀tọ̀ ni; àkokò ayọ̀, ọ̀tọ̀ ni pẹ̀lú; àkokò lílọ mi nìyí, ọ̀ràn dandan sì ni kí nlọ. (53) (When a crisis comes, it comes, and that is that. At twilight, hundreds of leaves slumber on the bough; come darkness and beasts roam the forests in their hundreds—there is a time for everything; a time to play, a time to fight; a time for tears, a time even for joy; this is my time for a departure, and my going will yield to nothing.) (76)

Because the heavily biblical language of the prose is not the focus here, that feature of the diction will be bypassed.[5] This is also not the place to analyze time and timeliness in Fágúnwà. The focus is on sex and focalization in relation to the management of narration.

At this critical moment, Àkàrà-ògùn—the narrative agent on whose version of events both the internal audience and the reader must rely—shows his friend earnestly invoking impersonal laws that govern the movement of the heavens and other natural elements to justify the correctness of his actions. According to the terms of the report, Kàkó's fiancée is doomed because she wants to tether the movement of the seasons—"mú ọjọ́ so lókùn" is the expressive formula in everyday Yorùbá speech—the natural force into which Kàkó has turned the journey that Àkàrà-ògùn (the narrator) has committed himself to lead. The woman's calling on the bonds of passion and undying affection does not register significantly for Àkàrà-ògùn and his friend. Kàkó moves on undeterred, obeying the call of timeliness like western educated professionals, the class that writes novels: "O mú kùmọ̀ rẹ lọ́wọ́, o fí àdá rẹ̀ sí àkọ̀, ó ńlọ kíákíá bí ìgbà tí àwọn alákọ̀wé bá ńkánjú lọ sí ibi iṣẹ́ wọn" (53) (He simply grabbed his club, stuck his matchet in its sheath and walked on briskly as when the office clerk hurries to his place of business) (76). When the woman speaks back, she addresses an empty space, and her switch to the regular second person singular pronoun sounds somehow out of time. She grabs Kàkó, demanding that he should look for a means of getting rid of her literally: "Ó dì mọ́ Kàkó ó ní, 'O kò ní ílọ lónìí, o ní láti wá bí o bá ti máa ṣe mí sí' " (54) ("She wrapped herself tightly round Kàkó saying, 'You are going nowhere, not until you find some way to dispose of me' ") (76).

This is how Àkàrà-ògùn reports the next series of actions:

> Inú bí Kàkó nígbà tí ó pẹ́ ti obìnrin yìí ti dì í mú, ó yí ojú padà ó sì fa àdá rẹ̀ yọ ó ní, "Ìwọ oníkúpani obìnrin, ìwọ àjẹ́ obìnrin, ìwọ tí ó ńfẹ́ dí mi lọ́nà ibi iṣẹ́ mi, o kò mọ̀ pé kí ilẹ̀ tó pa òṣìkà, ohun rere yóò ti bàjẹ́! Kí Ọlọ́run tó dá èmi lẹ́bi n ó dá ọ lẹ́bi tìrẹ̀." Bí ó ti wí báyìí tán ó ṣá a lágbede-méjì díẹ̀ ló sì kù kí ó bẹ́ ẹ já, obìnrin náà sí ṣubúulẹ̀ ó ńjẹ aporó ikú ó sì ńkígbe Kàkó, ó ké e lọ sí Ọ̀run: Ẹ̀rú bà mí gidigidi. (54) (Kàkó grew truly angry. His face was transformed and he pulled out his matchet, saying, "Woman of death, mother of witchery seeking to obstruct my path of duty, know you not that before earth destroys the evil-doer, much good has already suffered ruin! Before God adjudges me guilty I shall pass sentence on your guilt." And, having spoken, he slashed her amid-riffs, and lacked only a little for the woman to be cloven clean in two; she fell on earth, twitching in the final throes of death crying the name of Kàkó, crying his name into the other world. Great indeed was my terror.) (77)

Changes in voice and focus in this paragraph are revealing. The woman's desperate clinging to her lover (and murderer) is reported in the distancing third person; that is, in relation to the homodiegetic figure who interjects his feeling of fear ("Ẹ̀rú bà mí gidigidi" [Great indeed was my terror]), not moral abhorrence, to close the report. Àkàrà-ògùn's expressed eyewitness fear cannot effectively induce the reader's sympathy for the murder victim, because the narration places her suffering at a distance. Moreover, the previous paragraph, which privileges Kàkó's words over hers, has already positioned her as an impediment to the anticipated national epic journey in which the narrator is fully invested.

Keeping his position outside of the events, the autodiegetic narrator, Àkàrà-ògùn, surreptitiously justifies Kàkó's actions by telling the reader (and the internal audience) that it is the woman's persistence that vexed Kàkó, who the narrator, we already know, has judged indispensable to the success of the Lángbòdó trip. In other words, the narrator accepts Kàkó's indignation, positioning the murdered woman as an obstacle, probably because he too has an interest in Kàkó's abandoning the domestic bliss he has enjoyed with his woman. The moral and ethical claims she addresses to Kàkó more or less inculpate Àkàrà-ògùn as well. The insinuated third-person justification of Kàkó's anger slips into a verbatim, direct-voice report of what Kàkó said as he drew his machete to cut down his not-quite-not-wife, and Àkàrà-ògùn, in effect, allows the reader into his friend's mind. That closeness is denied in the presentation of the victim's pain and woes in the quick step back to the third person voice of the homodiegetic eyewitness who plants himself between the reader and the victim. The woman's exact words about the agony of death ("igbe oró ikú") are edited out. The telling of the woman's last moments prioritizes Kàkó's acting on his anger over the unnamed woman's pain. The narrator's sympathy and aesthetic focus lie with Kàkó. Indeed, later at home during the nine-day break before the start of the Lángbòdó journey, other brave hunters joke about the episode during drinking bouts:

> Ọpọ̀lọpọ̀ ìgbà ni a sì ńlọ máa kí [àwọn ọ̀rẹ́ wa] tí gbogbo wa máa ńyí òde ẹmu kiri, ìgbàkigbà ti a bá sì sọ̀rọ̀ kan ti Kàkó àti ìyàwó rẹ̀ gbogbo wa á máa ṣe yẹ̀yẹ́ pé: "Pa mí kí nkú ṣe orí bẹnbẹ sí ọkọ, ìyàwó Kàkó." (54) (Many times we did go and visit [our friends], and we all together would set out on palm wine rounds; whenever the conversation turned on the matter of Kàkó and his wife, they all would tease him saying, "Deal-me-death thrusts her neck at the husband— such was the wife of Kàkó.") (78)

Whatever sympathy a reader, especially a sensitive and ambitious young male, might have developed for Kàkó's quasi-wife is sure to evaporate here because the two male eyewitnesses (Àkàrà-ògùn and Kàkó) probably retold the event to fellow male, heroic avatars (akọni) in ways that stress her expressions of love as foolhardiness.

The specific terms attributed to the victim must not be overlooked. Kàkó's referring to a tenacious female as "àjẹ́" (witch) repeats a formulaic method of placing at critical turns (usually at the beginning) females whose man(hood)-stunting acts steel, and sometimes cause, the will-for-progress in principal male characters. Àjẹ́dìran (literally, "witchcraft runs in the family")—Àkàrà-ògùn's mother, we should remember—is an ageless witch ("ògbólógbòó àjẹ́") who is shot and killed by her husband after having transformed herself into an antelope that he mistakes for a true beast. Because their male companions get better at their resolve to triumph after killing them, it is not difficult to view Kàkó's consort and Àkàrà-ògùn's mother as storytelling props intended to serve as enabling impediments, their being implacable witches notwithstanding.[6]

The account of Ìrèké Oníbùdó's beginning provides a different view. Ìrèké's father ruins his family by marrying many women, as observed above, and also by allowing himself to be deceived into putting all his money in a failed joint-stock venture (47) in which one of his younger wives—simply described as "ọmọ olówó kan" (a certain rich man's daughter) to imply spoiled upbringing—convinces him to invest. All the wives, including the rich man's daughter who gets him into the misbegotten venture, desert the man after the unfortunate turn. Only the first wife, the hero's mother, remains loyal.[7] While there is no causal link between the decline in wealth and status and the terminal illnesses of the hero's parents, the juxtaposition of the two events in narrative sequence insinuates some relatedness. It is also perhaps not incidental that Ìrèké is the first child of these two otherwise solid citizens. The autodiegetic narration founds the fable on the ill-considered machinations of the father's frivolous wife. As with Kàkó's wife, this enabling impediment does not enjoy the dignity of a name. The unnamed mother who sends her son (and the novel's narrator) forth has to be cleared off the narrative deck as a condition for the departure and self-discovery of the narrator, who serves simultaneously as the story's hero.

The significance of focalization and sympathetic positioning of the reader appears in bolder relief in the report of the death of Ìrèké's mother:

Ìgbà tí ó ṣe, àìsàn kọlu ìyá mi. Mo ṣe ìtọ́jú rẹ̀ dé ibi tí ipá mi tó, nígbà tí ò ṣe, àìsàn náà túbọ̀ ńburú sí i, ní òwúrọ̀ ọjọ́ kan báyìí, ìyá mi pè mí ó bá mi sọ̀rọ̀ ìkẹhìn rẹ̀ ó ní:

"Ìwọ ọmọ mi, Ìrèkè-ońibùdó, bí mo ti ńwo ọ̀rọ̀ mi yìí, nkò rò pé mo lè yọ nínú àìsàn yìí, bẹ́ẹ ni nkò ní nǹkankan sílẹ̀ fún ọ. Mo fi ọ́ lé Olódùmarè lọ́wọ́, bí mo bá ti kú tán, ṣe ni kí o jáde ní ìlú kí o máa lọ sí ibikíbi tí o bá rí. Baba rẹ ti ta gbogbo nǹkan tí mo ní kí ó tó kú ó sì fi mí sílẹ̀ ní ìhòhò ní òde ayé, báyìí ni ayé mi bàjẹ́ lójú mi, nkò ṣe ẹnikẹ́ni ní ibi rí, nkò sì hu ìwà ìkà sí ọmọnìkejì, jọ̀wọ́ Ọlọ́run Ọba, má ṣàì tún ẹ̀hìn mi ṣe. Bá mi tọ́jú Ìrèkè-ońibùdó nínú ayé, má ṣe jẹ́ kí ó kú sí wàhálà bí èmi. Bí ọmọ yìí bá pàdé ìyọnu lóde ayé, Olódùmarè yọ ọ́, bí ó bá pàdé wàhálà, Olódùmarè yọ ọ́, bí ìpọ́njú owó bá sì dé bá a, Olódùmarè má ṣàì yọ ọ́ nínú rẹ̀ dandan."

Báyìí ni ìyá mi sọ, nígbà tí ó sì dákẹ́ ó ní ki nwá gbé òun lọ́wọ́ mo sì gbé e, àfi gbígbe tí mo gbé e tán tí ó mí kanlẹ̀ lẹ́ẹ̀kanṣoṣo, ó dákẹ́ lé mi lọ́wọ́. (47–48)

(It came to pass that my mother fell gravely ill. I took care of her to the limit of my powers, but she she got worse as time went by. One morning, my mother called me and spoke to me thus:

"Ìrèkè-ońibùdó, my child, as I see things at this moment, I do not believe that I will make it out of this sick bed. Unfortunately, I have nothing for you to inherit. I put you in God's good care. When I am dead, you should leave leave this town and travel to wherever you may find fit. Your father pawned off all my belongings before he died, and he left me on earth without any clothes on my back. He brought me undue misfortune, I who never thought evil of any one and did no wickedness to no one. Almighty lord, do not forget to take care of my affairs when I am gone. Take care of Ìrèkè-ońibùdó, let him not die of strife like me. When he meets trouble, save him, when he confronts a strife, save him, should he face financial distress, save him with all your might."

Thus my mother spoke. She extended her hand to me. As soon as I held it, she took one very deep breath and expired in my hands.)

The movement of narrative voices in this passage is dexterous. It opens with Ìrèké talking about himself and his mother from the perspective of a caring son's deserving of the final blessings about to be received. That speaker recedes soon, to allow the mother to address the narrator (and the reader) directly and, in consequence, to authenticate the details that Ìrèké has already rendered about his dead father's profligacy. Although it is still Ìrèké's view of things, the change in voice assures the reader that this is not just an aggrieved son complaining about his father. In the middle of the mother's words, her addressee changes to God without any formal rhetorical marking, and Ìrèké directly witnesses his mother's prayer for his well-being. Readers are more likely to "cry" for Ìrèké's mother than for Kàkó's fiancée, not because one woman is more virtuous than the other, but, mainly, because Ìrèké's mother is closer to the narrative agent, who happens to be the male hero in both instances, than Kàkó's fiancée is. The guiltless mother victimized by her husband speaks in her own words to a doting narrator who makes her speak directly to the textual audience. The intimate distance and sympathetic listening obvious in this episode contrasts to what obtained with Kàkó's fiancée. In both cases, the narrative agent benefits from the women's suffering: Ìrèké's mother encourages him to leave home and start a life that culminates in the novel itself; Àkàrà-ògùn distances himself from the victimized woman and tries to absolve himself of Kàkó's criminal indifference. Focus manipulation in the two examples assuages conscience and clears narrative grounds for the leading traveling men.

But these are not misogynistic texts. That is why I conclude this chapter by commenting on the dissonance between the impression of unassailable male dominance created in the main narratives and the protofeminist concerns propounded outside of the fables, usually in the prefaces, dedication pages, and narrative prologues. My first example is from the revealing mixture of textual voices on the last four pages of *Igbó Olódùmarè*. First, the writer-editor marks the conclusion of his ostensibly verbatim scripting of Àkàrà-ògùn's reading aloud of his father's already written autobiography. These are the recorder's words:

> Báyìí ni bàbá òrẹ́ mi kọ apá kan ìtàn ìgbésí ayé rẹ̀ sílẹ̀. Ọjọ́ méjì ni mo sì gbà kí ntó kọ apá kan yìí náà tán, mo kọ̀wé títí gbogbo èjìkà ńro mí gooro, Àkàrà-ògùn tí ó jẹ́ ọmọ Olówó-aiyé ni ẹni tí ńka ìtàn náà fún mi. (162) (Thus did my friend's father conclude one part of his life story. It took two days for me to transcribe this part, I wrote until my shoulder ached to crack, Àkàrà-ògùn the son of Olowo-aiye being the one who read out the transcript for me.) (219)

These words alert the novel's readers, who could not have been in the live audience that listened to Àkàrà-ògùn's reading of his father's autobiography, that the writing/scripting agent (who is not the narrator) is twice removed from the text he helped create. The novel, which has incorporated the read autobiography, returns to Àkàrà-ògùn (the internal reader of the protagonist's written words) after the brief interjection quoted above. Àkàrà-ògùn now addresses the live audience assembled to listen to him read his father's autobiography and watch the writer-editor record his words. Àkàrà-ògùn urges the crowd to identify their life work and pursue it diligently. He also thanks the sitting writer and prays for his long life and well-being:

Mo dúpẹ́ púpọ̀ fún iṣẹ́ tí o ti ńṣe fún mi láti ọjọ́ tí mo ti ńtọ̀ ọ́ wá wọnyí mo ṣe àkíyèsí pé iṣe náà kò jọ ọ́ lójú ṣùgbọ́n kàkà bẹ́ẹ̀ ó ńfún ọ ní ìrẹ̀lẹ̀ ni . . . Kí Olódùmarè fún ọ ní ẹmí gígùn; kí Ọlọ́run fún ọ ní ìbàlẹ̀ ọkàn; kí Ẹlẹ́dàá má ṣàì fi aláfíà jíńkí rẹ. (162) (I thank you greatly for the work you have done for me from the day I sought you out, and I observed that you have not considered it a big deal, on the contrary, it has merely enabled you to acquire greater humility . . . May God grant you a long life, may God grant you peace of mind. May God not fail to make you a gift of good health.) (219–220)

He proceeds to draw a curtain on the performance with these words: "Ó tó àkokò ná wàyí tí mo ní láti padà lọ sí ibi tí mo ti ńwa, bí Ọlọ́run bá sì dá ẹmí sí, ọjọ́ ḿbọ̀ tí a ó tun fi ojú rí ara wa" (162) (It is time I returned home, if God preserves our lives, the day is not far when we shall see each other again) (220).[8] Àkàrà-ògùn vanishes miraculously after saying the last word.

With this explicitly marked interchange of speakers, the story leads readers to note that Àkàrà-ògùn is not present for the words that the writer-editor addresses to readers on the last two pages of the book. The writer first instructs on the allegorical method appropriate for reading the fable:

Mo fẹ́ kí gbogbo ènìyàn fi í sí ọkàn pé kò sí ẹni tí kò ní Igbó Olódùmarè tirẹ̀ láti lọ nínú ayé, Igbó Olódùmarè ti ẹnì kan yàtọ̀ sí ti ẹnìkejì kí Olódùmaré jẹ́ kí olúkúlùkù ti Igbó Olódùmarè tirẹ̀ dé láìní ìpalára. (163) (I want all people to place it in their minds that there is no one who does not have its own Forest of Olódùmarè awaiting on earth, Igbó Olódùmarè of one person differs from the next—may God grant that the Forest of each and everyone be without injurious effects.) (221)

Given the positioning of females in the preceding story, it is very hard to believe that females can plot a Forest of Olódùmarè trip other than as self-sacrificing helpers who do not mind being abandoned. They could choose to be like Àjẹdìran, who serves as a causal agent for Olowo-aiye's journey but who dies a witch's brutal death later in life.[9]

As if the writer knows that something is wrong with the story handed down to him by the narrator, he then offers the following surprising prayer in the last paragraph of the book:

Kí Ọba Oníbúọrẹ bá abiyamọ tọ́jú ọmọ; kí Ó fún wúńdíá ni ọkọ àǹfàní; kí Ó fún ọmọkùnrin ní ìyàwó àlàáfíà; ọmọbínrin tí kò fẹ́ ní ọkọ àti ọmọkùnrin tí kò fẹ́ ní ìyàwó kí Olódùmarè fún wọn ní ìgbésí ayé rere. Kí Ó fi ìrẹ̀pọ́ sí àrin orogún. (164–165) (May the King of the Fount of Giving aid the mother in the child's upbringing, give the wife-seeker a wife that brings well-being; to the woman who chooses to avoid marriage and the man who prefers the single life, may Olodumare bless their existence on earth. Let him bring harmony in the midst of co-wives.) (222–223)

The wishes expressed in this strategically important part of textual closure contradict almost all the terms privileged in the fables spun by the hero and his son, none of which allow either unmarried bliss for mature adults or the peaceful habitation of co-wives.

The explanation of the writer-editor's interjecting commentary cannot come from the inscribed fable, and we should probe further into the circumstances surrounding the stories' publication, particularly the editorial exchanges that surround the release of each book. To begin that project, I want to suggest that we turn again to *Ìrìnkèrindò*'s dedication and preface. The honorees' list includes three Europeans identified specifically as females, and praised as such. One of them is Miss J. A. Mars, principal of Elementary Training Centre, in Akure, which is now Archbishop Vining College of Theology, and on whose website the following historical detail appears:

> Archbishop Vining College of Theology, Akure, dates back to 1917 when it was founded by the Church Missionary Society (CMS) and named Akure Training Centre (ATC). *It was founded mainly to train girls to become good house-wives. The first Principal was Miss Boyton and she was succeeded by Miss Mars* in whose time the centre had remarkable development and became a very popular Girls' Institution in the then Southern Nigeria. Many of the girls obtained the First School Leaving Certificates from the Centre. *The popular Government Certificate of Merit, then awarded to the students of the centre, formed the foundation stone of many successful women and house-wives in this country.* In 1958 the normal programme, run at the centre, came to an end. (emphases added)[10]

The second emphasis in Vining's summary history echoes the words Fágúnwà used in his 1954 tribute to Miss Mars, who he characterized as mother-in-law to many educated Yorùbá grooms:

> Miss J. A. Mars pẹ́ púpọ̀ ní ilẹ̀ wa, ó dúró gẹ́gẹ́ bí àna fún púpọ̀ nínú ọmọ Yorùbá nítorí ọ̀pọ̀lọpọ̀ àwọn obìnrin tí ó ti kọ́ ni nwọ́n ńpè é ní ìyá tí nwọ́n sì ti di ìyàwó ènìyàn pàtàkì káàkiri. Gbogbo agbára ni obìnrin náà fi ṣiṣẹ́ lọ́dọ̀ wa, bẹ́ẹ̀ ni ọ̀pọ̀lọpọ̀ ọmọ tí nwọ́n bí lójú rẹ̀ ti wọ ilé ọkọ láti ọjọ́ pípẹ́, a kò gbọdọ̀ gbàgbé obínrin yìí láíláí. (vi) (Miss J. A. Mars lived for a very long time in our country; she has stood like an in-law to many Yorùbá men because countless of the women she trained, who have become spouses of many an important people all over, call her mother. She worked with full energy in our land, and many young girls born during her time are long married now. We can never forget this woman.)

While the code-mixing in reference to her title may suggest that Miss Mars's unmarried status is an important identity factor to Fágúnwà, his praise of her motherly achievements decouples marriage and productive nurturing in a way that draws attention to the treatment of women in the heroic stories discussed in this chapter. The excellent wifely credentials praised as evidence of Miss Mars's great work in the education of Nigerian women saves neither Kàkó's fiancée, nor Ìrèké's mother, nor Àkàrà-ògùn's. It is equally revealing that the other woman singled out for particular honor in the same dedication, Dr. Margaret Read, former head of the Colonial Department of the University of London's Institute of Education, is famous for her work in teaching. Fágúnwà wrote that:

> Professor Margaret Read obìnrin ni, ó sì yẹ kí ọmọ Yorùbá kọ́ ọgbọ́n lára obìnrin yìí, púpọ̀ nínú wa ni ó sì ńwí pé kínni obìnrin lè ṣe, pẹ̀lú ìrọjú sì ni àwọn òbí mìíràn fi ńfi ọmọ wọn sí ilé ìwé bí ó bá sáà ti le jẹ́ obìnrin. (Preface to *Irinkerindo Ninu Igbo Elegbeje*, v) (Professor Margaret Read is a woman. Her life must serve as a lesson to every Yorùbá. Many among us are still mouthing the effete mantra about women's inherent lack, with many parents reluctant to educate their girls.)

Fágúnwà also praises the erudite ("obìnrin tí ó mọ iwé lọ́pọ̀lọpọ̀" [vi]) Miss J. V. Herklots, then the Diocesan Education Secretary-General of the Church Missionary Society (CMS) in southwestern Nigeria, for showing through her life that women can accomplish mighty things ("obìnrin lè ṣe nǹkan ńla"). He also draws attention to how many men of high standing serve under the direction of Miss Herklots. ("Nǹkan ńlá" [mighty things], it is also worth recalling, are what Olowo-aiye went out seeking in *Igbó Olódùmarè*.) I need not repeat that Fágúnwà's dedicatory exhortations in favor of high-achieving women and the potential ability of young girls do not correspond to the main lines of storytelling adopted in his famous novels, where the positive lesson readers can learn from the lives of women is that they should foster—better, if it is without regard for their own self-interest—a blissful domestic space for their spouses and children. It is also significant, I suggest, that the honor list filled with the names of a novelist and newspaper editor, top clergy, and teachers, includes no Yorùbá woman.

This is the quandary: in the preface, Fágúnwà is a modern man, a feminist of sorts, full of praise for men and women of achievement. In the fiction, his stories position women in the "traditional" adventure pattern. The author who commends independent, unattached European women in his preface mocks in his narrative proper the strong Èdìdàrẹ́ women who scold their men routinely, and lampoons the men who cannot control them. In the same story, there is the comical Aguntaninaki (Sheep-monkey) who, although male, indulges in wifely duties.[11] I am not able to conclude that Fágúnwà believes in the superiority of the independent ways of the European women praised in the dedication, because although the educational goals of the Akure women's training center led by Miss Mars for a long time are similar to the ethos that governs women's conduct in the novels, the latter are still doomed. It will not be a reckless speculation to conclude that the roles prescribed for men and women in the novels preponderantly follow the model promoted in schools like the one at Akure but which the unattached and highly praised Miss Mars did not quite practice.

Notes

1. Ogunsina (*The Development of the Yoruba Novel*) and Ilesanmi ("Naming Ceremony among the Yorùbá") both tease out the implications of this term in the popular understanding of masculinity in contemporary Yorùbá societies.

2. Falling into sudden wealth after being helped by a soon forgotten, selfless female to defeat a mortal enemy is a regular feature of Fágúnwà's plots. See Olowo-aiye's experience after overcoming Ojola-ibinu in *Igbo Olodumare*.

3. The discussion here adopts Mieke Bal's standard formulation: "Focalization is the relationship between the 'vision,' the agent that sees, and that which is seen" (*Narratology*, 146).

4. Under the pretext of sparing her mother unnecessary anguish, Àdììtú leaves home without readers having access to her immediate feelings. Akin Adesokan reminded me that Ìrìnkèrindò's mother, Eni-aye, shares her son's preference for wanting to go on the expedition to Oke Ironu.

5. The obvious reference is to Ecclesiastes 3:1–9: "There is a time for everything, and a season for every activity under the heavens."

6. The murder of Kàkó's wife comes back to haunt the Lángbòdó group when they are locked in by a mysterious, impenetrable bush (58). Kàkó, I should also note, did not return home. But the narration does not link the murder to his following the siren song of the seven women condemned to running around permanently.

7. The loyalty of the younger wife, who is typically portrayed as a fair-weather friend ("arírebánìjẹ"), is rarely steadfast in Yorùbá fiction.

8. These words mark the serialization cue that results in the sequel narrated in *Ògbójú Ọdẹ*, which was actually published before *Igbó Olódùmarè*.

9. After reading a draft of this chapter, Akin Adesokan advised that one should speak with less certainty about serial narratives and that the Àjẹ́dìran killed in the opening pages of *Ògbójú Ọdẹ* and the one mentioned in *Igbó Olódùmarè* could be different individuals. That notwithstanding, the unconventional audacity that binds the two women cannot be overlooked. In *Ògbójú Ọdẹ*, Àjẹ́dìran professes her love to Olowo-aiye before the man does.

10. http://www.viningcollegeakure.com/default_006.html.

11. We see in the terms used to characterize the poor fellow that a married man who performs domestic chores is exceedingly stupid. His cognomen, "dọ́ńgíṣọlá," is a neologism. It is perhaps not surprising that he failed to return home with the other hunters.

5 Akínwùmí Ìṣọ̀lá's *Ẹfúnṣetán Aníwúrà* and Yorùbá Woman-Being

ONE YORÙBÁ WOMAN seeks, finds, and wields mighty power in *Ẹfúnṣetán Aníwúrà*, Akínwùmí Ìṣọ̀lá's tragedy of the eponymous character's adventures in deadly power play. As with Fágúnwà's adventures, however, the play's reception is riven with conflicts regarding how construals of inscribed ways of proper female-being should be experienced in commentary-bound circulations of daily life: Is Ẹfúnṣetán's fate the result of what arises when females, against their predisposition, gain access to mighty power, or does it illustrate the truth of the basic disinterestedness of Yorùbá cultural inscriptions in sex and gender? The play's portrayal of Ẹfúnṣetán's self-representations on stage and film brings comfort to traditionalist viewpoints, which find in her tragic ending an appropriate treatment for the protagonist's violations of woman-being in the Yorùbá manner. Since her behaviors violate ways of being female transhistorically (ìwà obìnrin), her dying uncelebrated despite her high social attainments is judged satisfying. Against such traditionalisms, I argue in this chapter that the play's construction of Ẹfúnṣetán's alleged infractions of cultural violations could not be more Yorùbá, given the critical role of discourses of commentary—historiography, translation, and the intermediality of oral and literate traditions, theater, and video—in late twentieth-century textual depictions of her willful gender politics. At the most general level, the following amounts to an intervention in Yorùbá-denominated arguments about constructions of gender. In more specific terms, it proposes that skewed translations of discursive categories from, and rarely back into, the main languages of discovery, especially English, have shaped explanations of observed social phenomena regarding sex and gender relations that are classified as culturally Yorùbá. The primary evidence here will be the many ways in which known snippets of the life of Ìyálóde Ẹfúnṣetán Aníwúrà (c. 1825–1874), a high-ranking female chief in nineteenth-century Ìbàdàn, are deployed in written historical and literary accounts of the evolution of Yorùbá woman-being. I focus on the linguistic, cultural, and philosophical ramifications of the depiction of women in Akínwùmí Ìṣọ̀lá's play, *Ẹfúnṣetán Aníwúrà: Ìyálóde Ìbàdàn*, its two English translations, and its most recent video-film adaptation.

Translation problems I analyze in the chapter include how to render ordinarily gender neutral referents of Yorùbá texts into English. I also address textual inflections of how historical changes in Yorùbá gender constructs affect the intermedial translations that Akinwumi Ìṣọ̀lá must have faced while scripting the original play from sources in oral traditions and written, typically Christian, nationalist histories. Contrary to nationalist imaginations of cultural seamlessness, mid-nineteenth-century Ìbàdàn, a then imperial city-state, was not exactly like it was 1966, when the first version of the play was written. Within the century-long time span, the state lost its independence under British domination and regained a different kind of independence within the Nigerian state created by the British overlords that governed the space from the 1890s till 1960. The intervening century between Ẹfúnṣetán's time and the writing of Ìṣọ̀lá's play also witnessed vast changes that irreversibly reconfigured the social, political, and economic life of Ìbàdàn and made impossible a purely Yorùbá account of Ẹfúnṣetán Aníwúrà's life. Even if the facts of her life are somehow magically recovered, the inescapable use of technologies of representation that Ẹfúnṣetán never had the advantage of using to shape her life will intervene decisively in the form that the resultant product will take. Two significant influences on the argument of this chapter need to be acknowledged. The first is Oyèrónkẹ́ Oyěwùmí's analysis of the unexamined distortions that common English translations of Yorùbá kinship and social relations help produce in studies of gender in southwestern Nigeria (*The Invention of Women*). In parts of this chapter, I extend Oyěwùmí's trenchant critique of the glaring disparities between scholarly colloquialisms on gender, usually in English and French, and the living local languages of informing subjects on which the studies are ostensibly based. The second source of influence is Nkiru Nzegwu's criticism of the poverty of a truly comparatist temperament in transnational gender studies (*Family Matters*).

Ìyálóde Ẹfúnṣetán Aníwúrà in Power and Gender

The earliest written historical account describes Ẹfúnṣetán Aníwúrà's high office, Ìyálóde, as "queen of the ladies." According to Samuel Johnson, the Ìyálóde was "the most distinguished lady in the town," and representing women in "municipal and other affairs" (*The History of the Yorùbás*, 77) was her mandate. Bolanle Awe concurs: "The Iyalode became not only the voice of the women in government but also a kind of queen who coordinated all their activities. She settled their quarrels in her court and met with them to determine what should be the women's stand, for instance, on such questions as the declaration of war, the opening of new markets, or the administration of women at the local level" ("The Iyalode in the Traditional Yoruba Political System," 147). Another consensus in historical studies is that Ẹfúnṣetán Aníwúrà, the second person ever to hold that office in Ìbàdàn, fell out of favor with the city's principal leader, Látòòsà, who encouraged two of her slaves to assassinate her on June 30, 1874 (Johnson, *The History of the Yorùbás*,

392). After having been forced to confess to the killing, the slaves were publicly executed for murder on July 10, 1874 (393). Látòósà, in defiance of his council of chiefs, plotted Ẹfúnṣetán's murder because she refused to hide her displeasure at the general's unbridled warmongering, the most troubling expedition being the unprovoked assault against Ado in December 1873 and January 1874.[1] Ẹfúnṣetán's predecessor and pioneer Ìyálóde, Subúọ́lá, also came to a disastrous end when, after having been in office for about a decade, "she lost her wealth and was deposed from office in about 1867" (Denzer, *The Iyalode*, 9). Besides her name, Ìyáọlá, Ẹfúnṣetán's reluctant successor is largely unremembered in the traditional chronicles (13).

The first three Ìyálóde on record at Ìbàdàn were either disgraced or forced out of office. Historical studies have not explained why this was the case or why the steady rise of the influence of the office and the escalation of its definition as a "women's affair's" position over the next half a century after Ẹfúnṣetán's reign coincided with the establishment and growth of colonial rule. In 1893, the Ìyálóde's council had only three other official members, all female, bearing military titles, although their authority was mainly "civil"; it expanded to twelve members in 1965 and twenty-four in 1997 (Johnson, *The History of the Yorùbás*, 77; Denzer, *The Iyalode*, 45). It is likely that the earliest Ìyálóde in Ìbàdàn did not enjoy long chiefly tenure, because the office was a mid-nineteenth-century invention, although, as Awe argues, similar institutions existed in older Yorùbá kingdoms such as Iléṣà, Òndó, and Ìjẹbú ("The Ìyálóde in the Traditional Yorùbá Political System," 150–157). The stormy experiences of the first three Ìyálóde in Ìbàdàn could also have been a sign of the unsteady character of the political steps being taken to manage the socioeconomic inequities that were manifesting in gendered terms. After all, the state in nineteenth-century Ìbàdàn depended heavily on income from constant war making, and this meant that a disproportionate number of able-bodied males had to fight in distant lands over extended periods. Given that situation, women's participation in the city's internal affairs would have had to increase beyond the levels that had prevailed in prewar times, and the Ìyálóde office probably emerged to coordinate the increased level of influence. But because at Ẹfúnṣetán's time the Ìyálóde was the only member of her council that joined other male, principal chiefs in citywide high governance, female participation was still limited. Awe points out that "in theory she was acknowledged as the representative of all women and in all cases was free to comment on all policy matters. In practice, however, she suffered from one big disadvantage: she was always outnumbered as the only female in the crucial decision-making body" (148). While there must have been practical reasons for the institution of an exclusively female council of chiefs with titles of battle commander, although their duties are mainly civil, these have not been of major interest to historians. The main scholarly focus has been on the longevity and durability of political institutions that prosecute women-specific interests.

Literary drama stirred popular interest in the Ìyálóde office and in Ẹfúnṣetán Aníwúrà in 1970 with the publication of Akínwùmí Ìṣọlá's play, four years after the text won the top writing prize of the Yorùbá Studies Association (Ẹgbẹ́ Ìjìnlẹ̀ Yorùbá) and by which time the Ìyálóde council of chiefs, under Chief Olowode Adebisi Abeo, has almost tripled its original membership (Denzer, *The Iyalode*, 6, 45). The published play was soon widely adopted at all schooling levels and used as a required text in the literature curricula of various examination bodies. 1981 was a crucial year for the popular cultivation of Ẹfúnṣetán as an emblem of the perils of putting women in political office. That year, Bankole Bello made a feature-length movie based on the play, and the Isola Ogunsola (I-Show Pepper) Theater troupe organized a live production for a crowd of fourteen thousand spectators at a single performance at the Liberty Stadium in Ìbàdàn (Jeyifo, *The Yoruba Popular Travelling Theatre of Nigeria*, 115). The play's audience grew further in 1991 with Niyi Oladeji's English translation (*Two Contemporary African Plays*). In the intervening years, repeated television productions of the play were broadcast in the Yorùbá-speaking states of Nigeria. A French translation by Michka Sachnine (*Une Sombre Destinée*) was issued in 2003. When Pamela J. Olubunmi Smith's translation was released in 2005, *Ẹfúnṣetán Aníwúrà* became the first written secular text to have been translated twice from Yorùbá into English.

It is obvious from the language of repudiation often used even in feminist recuperations of the historical Ẹfúnṣetán Aníwúrà that the wide dissemination of Ìṣọlá's play to popular audiences and at different levels of the Nigerian school system might have encouraged the public to associate abuse of office with Ẹfúnṣetán's handling of the tragic power struggles she led as a female. A good part of Bolanle Awe's "Iyalode Efunsetan Aniwura" is devoted to disputing the claims of one tradition about Ẹfúnṣetán perpetuated "in a Yorùbá play" (69). Laray Denzer's rebuttal of the theatrics that surround the popular conception of Ẹfúnṣetán is not so subtle:

> The portrayal of Ẹfúnṣetán has tended to emphasize her more sinister, "unwomanly qualities." . . . Later generations, however, influenced by Christian values concerning the accumulation of wealth and perhaps sub-ethnic sentiments, clearly believe that her wickedness outweighs her positive woman-oriented leadership qualities. In some circles, there is even an attempt to downplay her contribution to the town's history. When two undergraduates attempted to interview a senior chief about her role, he told them pointblank that he did not wish to talk about such an evil woman. Newspaper reports show a penchant for using her as a negative example of female leadership. (*The Iyalode*, 12)

Foluke Ogunleye shows that the need to repudiate the idea of Ẹfúnṣetán fostered by Ìṣọlá's play becomes more urgent as time progresses: "We do not need to besmirch our past to be able to learn from it. There is a need for the self-definition of the African woman, and negative historical stereotypical portrayal such as that in Ìṣọ̀lá's *Ẹfúnṣetán Aníwúrà* erodes self-confidence. Gynecophobia of this type does not encourage young females of the species to have a sense of self-worth, nor does it provide positive models for emulation" (Ogunleye, "A Male-Centric Modification of History," 318). To these scholars, not only has literary drama mistranslated history and oral traditions, but intermedial reworkings of literature in film, theater, and television seem to have transmuted Ẹfúnṣetán the historical personage and recoded the meaning of her life to fit prevailing prejudices on gender relations as they have been nurtured by schooling, Islam and Christian monotheisms, ethnic slurring, and gender stereotypes.

In a revealing example of how deeply the negative estimation of Ẹfúnṣetán has percolated into popular thinking, a reporter, in 1994, put the then newly installed Ìyálóde, Wúràọlá Àkànkẹ́ Akíntọ́lá, on the defensive by reminding her that her most famous predecessor exemplified the incompatibility of women and high office. Ìyálóde Akíntọ́lá, probably having had no access to the scholarly nuances offered by Johnson, Akinyele, and Awe, responded thus: "That was her own choice in the way she wanted to exercise her powers. Even though the Ìyálóde had the power to take initiatives, this did not imply that she should misbehave. In Ẹfúnṣetán's case that was what she wanted to do. And it was not that there was nobody to put her under control, she had made up her mind not to listen" (qtd. in Denzer, *The Iyalode*, 12). Ìyálóde Akíntọ́lá was obviously referencing the popular culture view of her predecessor as it was circulated in the intermedial and interlingual translations of Ìṣọ̀lá's play. No historical record has established that Ẹfúnṣetán "misbehaved," as Ìyálóde Akíntọ́la conceded here. Only texts derived from Ìṣọ̀lá's play represent her as such. Reverend Johnson—an eyewitness to the execution of her assassins—and other historians agree that Ẹfúnṣetán fell victim to deadly power intrigues. Her exercising "initiatives"—a term that approximates the spirit of the divination quip recalled in chapter 1 to the effect that those who seek guidance in Ifá's counsel must also not neglect to consult their own intuitions—far more than not submitting to constitutional "control," caused Ẹfúnṣetán's fall.[2] The threat to order that the reporter and the newly installed, late twentieth-century Ìyálóde perpetrated about Ẹfúnṣetán is similar to the anachronic interpretation of sex and gender relations that Fágúnwà's male adventurer-narrator superimposes on the details of their experiences.

Ìyálóde in Translation

The two English translations of Ìṣọ̀lá's play landed in the minefield of writing about gendered life in Yorùbá culture and language, a field in which English-language discourse about Yorùbá sexual politics trips all because a noticeable semiotic gap separates the two languages, with gender terms that are generally free of prejudice, and sociolinguistic assumptions in Yorùbá that lack precise equivalents in English. The different word formation rules in the two languages place at a disadvantage every scholar writing in English but working with materials and situations primarily in the Yorùbá language. Writers who are not self-conscious about the difference in codes between the two linguistic and cultural domains often forget to qualify their conclusions as commentaries and not transcriptions of culture. For example, Yorùbá has no single-word, sex-specific denotations for son, daughter, niece, nephew, brother, or sister, a fact Oyěwùmí argues should be interpreted to mean that "anatomic categories are not used as social categories" in Yorùbá (*The Invention of Women*, 29). Conventions established through more than a century of practice should be not presumed to have eased the burden and, indeed, might have refashioned fundamentals of Yorùbá life and culture into less than desirous ends. English texts about Yorùbá societies are replete with "sons," "kings," "patriarchs," and "queens," although it is rarely acknowledged that the dictionary conceptions of these words derive from contexts that cannot accurately reflect the world they ostensibly translate (31–49, 157–179). Within the upside-down economy of Yorùbá–English translations involved in gender studies, the Yorùbá source code is disfigured and recomposed while the target language, English, is left unchanged.

Problems with incorrectly calibrated translations that complicate comprehension in English translations of *Efúnṣetán Aníwúrà* begin to show early in the different phrases used to translate "Ìyálóde Ìbàdàn," Ìṣọlá's descriptive subtitle for his play. Pamela J. Olubunmi Smith's translation of *Ìyálóde Ìbàdàn* tacitly acknowledges its untranslatability. Niyi Oladeji (*Two Contemporary African Plays*) interprets the play to be a portrayal of a woman's adventures in power, rewriting the subtitle as "A Portrait of an African Woman of Power." Given that Oladeji did most of the work on his translation, as well as premiering a stage presentation, while at Albany State College, a historically black college in Georgia, United States, his immediate audience might have been interested in a strong (even dictatorial), independent, traditional African womanhood. While Smith's minimal intervention sidesteps the muddled intelligibility that results from representing nineteenth-century Ìbàdàn political terminology in twenty-first-century English-language registers, Oladeji's rewrite, in making nineteenth-century Ìbàdàn into an emblematic African kingdom and in converting the exploits of a high-ranking female official of the city into a representative of African woman in power, refuses to resolve the difference between late twentieth-century English and mid-nineteenth-century Yorùbá political and cultural terminologies. Oladeji's explaining in his translator's notes that the Ìyálóde title means "mother in the streets" (vi) does not solve the problem of intelligibility because the phrasing makes no sense historically or colloquially in either language. When Smith, echoing Bolanle Awe, reports that she considered but rejected "mother of all or mother of external affairs" ("The Iyalode," 16), she affirms in effect the unique cultural provenance of the Ìyálóde's office.[3]

Older English definitions of "Ìyálóde" in both bilingual dictionaries and Johnson's history flounder around how much gender should count for. Johnson writes that the Ìyálóde represents the woman's viewpoints in the council of chiefs and could therefore be called "the queen of the ladies." But the phrasing of this observation is such that the office seems to merely confirm the social eminence already enjoyed by whoever holds it. According to Johnson, the title was typically "bestowed upon the most distinguished lady in town" (*The History of the Yorùbás*, 77). That is, the Ìyálóde office recognizes the city's most distinguished female and does not by itself makes a woman queen of the ladies. The Ìyálóde could only have been a queen in the figurative sense because Ìbàdàn was unique among historically significant nineteenth-century Yorùbá political formations in its rejection of hereditary nobility rights in its appointment of rulers. Perhaps more important, other parts of Johnson's book do not refer to high-ranking female officials as queens. Even in his beloved Ọ̀yọ́, which has a "king," Johnson identifies important "royal" spouses by their titles, simply calls them "wives," or refers to them derogatorily as members of the king's "harem." The *Dictionary of the Yoruba Language*, first published by the Church Missionary Society in 1913, also sheds more light on the attributes of the office holder than it does on the functions of the office: "a lady of high rank, the first lady in a town or village."[4] This description, too, fails to clarify whether the high social ranking results from the office or the office merely affirms an already acquired high social status. The *Dictionary*'s use of the "first lady" to indicate high social standing further blurs the picture when the meaning projected is transposed into the Yorùbá "source" society. The Ìyálóde is never conjugally related to the male holder of the highest political office, or the "first man." In other words, if the *Dictionary* is right, the Ìyálóde would have been a "first lady" without a first "man."

R. C. Abraham's newer Yorùbá–English dictionary defines the Ìyálóde as a "civic title" held by the leader of Ìyálóde society, who also doubles as "Head Woman" and the leader of a civic society in "every township" in "Ẹ̀gbá country." Her activities include gathering women "for public discussions about their concerns." The dictionary adds the following short narrative: "They formerly owned slaves. It was a woman's duty [in Ìyálóde society] to see that her husband was well provided with food, weapons and ammunitions. A rich Ìyálóde used to ensure that all the warriors of her township had the best guns Lagos [which at some point became the colonial capital] could produce." This definition translates into sexist English-language assumptions, whatever information Abraham gleaned from his Yorùbá-speaking collaborators: that the Ìyálóde's provisioning the township army with arms and ammunition is like a wife getting food ready for her husband. The connection between food, weapons, ammunition, and women's occupying a high office is left unexplained. In other respects, however, Abraham's dictionary raises two important questions: (1) Is the Ìyálóde a regional office rather than a pan-Yorùbá institution? and (2) Doesn't the arms supply association indicate that this institution was created during the long Yorùbá wars of the nineteenth century?

The definition offered in Isaac Delano's *Atúmọ̀ Ede Yoruba* is unencumbered by the pervasive metaphorization found in bilingual explanations straining to make intelligible in English an idea that is well outside its sociolinguistic parameters: "olóyè obìnrin ní ìlú tàbí láàrin ẹgbẹ́, olóri àwọn obìnrin" (a female chief in a town or a civic group, head of women). Delano seems to be of the view that there can be more than one type of Ìyálóde, some with town-wide authority that covers males and females, others controlling sections that could consist of females only or associations that are not gender exclusive.

The lexical items involved in the translation difficulties glossed above—a simple prepositional phrase made up of two nouns, ìyá (mother or older female), òde (outside, public, street), and one preposition, ní (at, on, in)—are not esoteric words. The translation problems pertain to the gender role connotations of the possible English equivalents of the main Yorùbá term, ìyá (mother or older female). As noted earlier, "Mother-in-the-streets" makes no sense in colloquial English, although that could be a correct, literal version of the Yorùbá words. "Mother-of-external-affairs" acknowledges the semantic extensions of "òde" (outside or public). The translation knots get really hard with the semantically nonsensical—in Yorùbá language, that is—result of associating motherhood (ìyá), outside-ness (òde), and gender spheres. Bilingual dictionary compilers, nationalist and feminist historians, and literary translators recognize that motherhood in traditional English speech connotes domesticity. These translators know also that it is possible to correlate domesticity with some spatialized Yorùbá kinship terms like ìyálé (the most senior wife of the household, lineage, or patrilineage [literally, "mother of/in the home"]) and baálé (the oldest male offspring of a patrilineage [literally "father of/in the home"]). In this line of thinking, the Ìyálóde is über-ìyálé or countrywide mother of/in the homeland. The correlation of social space and gender role breaks down, however, when it is realized that the ìyálé's obligations and allegiances extend to the entire patrilineage, not just to the wives and daughters of the household. That the Ìyálóde does not enlarge the ìyálé function is even clearer in the fact that while the latter, being a wife, is by definition from outside of the patrilineage where she "rules," the Ìyálóde could be a native of the city or an "immigrant" (typically by marriage) from another place. While the Ìyálóde need not have been an ìyálé, or the most senior wife in lineage, the leading male in the Ìbàdàn council of chiefs is required to have led a lineage and been recognized as worthy of leadership. We arrive at an impasse here because the Ìyálóde is not to the city (the public) as the ìyálé is to the household. This office is also not a female equivalent of the office held by the senior male chief. It is hard, even without the evidence in Delano's dictionary, to accept the normative translations that say the office serves women exclusively.[5]

The general meaning conundrums noted above are present in the English translations of *Ẹfúnṣetán Aníwúrà*. According to Oladeji, the Ìyálóde, in addition to their distinction in business and leadership, must be "high-strung and forceful individuals" and should be "tough, strict, and domineering because they are expected to monitor and control the activities of all females during all public occasions" (*Two Contemporary African Plays*, vi). Oladeji imagines the Ìyálóde to be a phallic female who needs a big stick to "lord" it over her women. Leadership in this model is repressive, autocratic, and androgynous, terms that make traditional sense in extended English literary and cultural idioms but miscarry when used to capture Ẹfúnṣetán's differently stratified society, where age, regardless of sex, denoted significant authority (Oyěwùmí, *The Invention of Women*, 110–112). What occurs here is that Oladeji's words, written about a decade after several television adaptations and the release of Bankole Bello's film of Ìṣọlá's play, retranslate the iconic visual theater and media characterization of Ẹfúnṣetán as gap-toothed, wiry, implacable, and deserving of a tragic ending, to mean an accurate representation of the historical personage.

Critics often state axiomatically that gender constructs vary across cultures, locations, economic strata, and historical periods but, in order to avoid the charge of essentialism, quickly proceed to make pronouncements that pay no heed to difference (Nzegwu, *Family Matters*, 20, 157–197). We rarely pause to consider how the language of theorizing and reporting discoveries overwrites observable colloquialisms of difference.[6] My extended discussion of the (un)translatability of "Ìyálóde" is meant to highlight the grossly inequitable, but inadequately interrogated, linguistic and discursive environments in which gender terms are constructed. As the examples discussed above illustrate, the translation decisions that scholars must make for the sake of intelligibility usually defer to the interests of socially dominant and intellectually prestigious target languages of reporting, such as English. In the hands of the most skillful and theoretically aware scholar, the sex "neutrality" of ordinary Yorùbá speech that subtends Ẹfúnṣetán Aníwúrà's legitimate claims in her fight against fellow chiefs has a very slim chance of moving across successfully into English, where cultural expressions drip with gendered calculations. This is the fraught reality that Ìṣọlá and his translators confront. Neither Ìṣọlá, nor the translators, nor the dictionary compilers have captured the essentially Yorùbá meaning of gender. Instead, they have all, like the Ifá divination, attached stories of meaning to the practices inscribed as Ìyálóde.

Gender and Thematic Framing in the Prologue to *Ẹfúnṣetán Aníwúrà*

Drama is ordinarily driven by direct discourse, with each event acted out for the most part, and with the plot unfolding in the interaction of character, place, and discrete actions. When a narrator appears outside of the proper drama to explain events, as in the prologue to *Ẹfúnṣetán Aníwúrà*, the intrusion works like a device of managing the play of chance in interpretation, to prevent meaning from flowing in whatever direction it pleases. Ìṣọ̀lá's original play begins with a prologue in which a character summarizes the political backstory of the events that are about to unfold, thus becoming an agent of cognitive oversight to pilot the audience and readers to a preferred perspective on the actions. That strategy succeeds in this play because the summary view of Ẹfúnṣetán promoted by this figure is the one that survives in popular perceptions of the protagonist.

The text stipulates that the prologue should be narrated by a female ("obìn-rin kan") (vii), a sex specificity that contrasts with sex-neutral terms used in the descriptions of social turbulence reported in the narrator's summary of communal anxieties regarding the uncertain existence caused by the ceaseless war making and high-handed abuses of power by city leaders. Oladeji's translation elides the narrator's sex but infuses masculinity into the political worries summarized by the prologue:

> Who installed the robber as market chief?
> Who employed a burglar as night-guard?
> No man can unravel the mysteries.
> Or do you know the answers?
> So let us sit and wait
> With patient expectation
> As God works his purpose out.
> I am going home now,
> A man does not expect to be strangled in his own bed
> Except if he lives next door to the Ìyálóde (3)

The self-references of the commoner who started as a gender-free speaker suddenly become general and male in the last two lines. Although Smith chooses sex-neutral terms in her translation of the narrator's perplexity—"These confusing mysteries defy pat answers" (63)—she too switches away from that track in the concluding lines and substitutes the English language's generic male terms ("man" and "he") for the second person plural used to voice the narrator's perspective in the Yorùbá original. Thus we have:

> Indeed, a man's house is his home; there
> He can expect not to break his neck in his own bed
> Except perhaps he happens to reside next door to Ìyálóde Ẹfúnṣetán. (64)

The Yorùbá statements in contention here are based on a proverb about the relative safety of one's homestead: "A kìí gbélé ẹni ká fọrùn rọ̀" (The chances are narrow for a domestic mishap to cause a spinal cord injury) (Ìṣọ̀lá, *Ẹfúnṣetán Aníwúrà*, viii). The translators' using male pronouns where the original text is sex neutral makes the female narrator sound unqualified to pronounce general, universal, proverbial statements. The gendered pronominal system of the English language clearly restricts the choices available to the translators. But merely acknowledging this fact does not explain the effect. The two languages' grammatical differences allocate values in incompatible ways. English's monosexual (Nzegwu, *Family Matters*, 20) usage rules allow for male gender pronouns to substitute for all. Yorùbá sociolinguistics, in contrast, permits the use of sex-neutral second-person honorific plural pronouns reserved for addressing elders. Thus the original play shows Ẹfúnṣetán's city to be full of power-intoxicated people occupying elders' positions (ipò àgbà). Their subjects mistrust each other because the conduct unbecoming of elders they observe all around them prevents them from knowing which neighbor spies for which chief. The Yorùbá text classifies neither power nor oppression as evils that only males perpetrate.

Motherhood and Empathy; Sexism and Self-Awareness

Women's childbearing and child-rearing experiences are critical to the play's tragic drama. The play joins activities relating to progeny, the pain of childbirth, empathy derived from motherhood, and fellow feeling for pregnant women to the protagonist's character flaws. Ẹfúnṣetán impugns family members' parental worries about their children, forbids her slaves from having children, and summarily executes any that flout the rule. The play's two explanations for these behaviors are witchcraft and childlessness. As the explanation goes, Ẹfúnṣetán repudiates all ethical obligations—except to her friend, Àjílé— because she is barren and refuses to take advantage of other opportunities that society affords her to fulfill the yearnings a normative adult is expected to have for nurturing young ones. Because she acts without feeling toward others, her community in the play interprets her antisocial behavior as a sure sign of her membership in the society of witches. In short, childlessness drives her into the cult of witches.

Thus Ìtáwuyì, Ẹfúnṣetán's leading male slave, says:

> Ẹni tí kò bá bí irú ẹni, kò lè fẹ́ràn ẹni
> Ẹni tí ó bá ti rí ìkúnlẹ̀ abiyamọ rí
> Kò ní fokùn dán ọmọ ẹ̀dá wò

> Certainly no woman who has experienced the pangs of childbirth
> Will ever tie a noose around the neck of another human being
> Certainly not around the neck of someone else's child (Smith's translation, 70)

These words effectively connect Ẹfúnṣetán's harsh dealings with her slaves to her not fulfilling a biologically destined female role. During the second meeting of the council of chiefs, at which, like the first, the Ìyálóde was not present, the leader of the assembled all male high chiefs, Látòósà, echoes the slave's sentiment: "Ẹfúnṣetán kò bímọ kò sì jẹ́ kí / Ẹni tí yóò bímọ bí" (55) (Ẹfúnṣetán has never had a child, and has vowed never to allow any woman in her household to have one) (Oladeji, 37). Ẹfúnṣetán corroborates both the chief and the slave when, early in the play, she ascribes her unconventional expression of political will to childlessness:

> Èmi kò mọ ohun tí mo fi ṣe Elédùwà
> Tí ó fi fọmọ lá mi lójú báyìí.
> Ṣùgbọ́n kò burú, ohun tí à á ṣe kù.
> Kí òun mú òkè Rẹ̀ lọ́wọ́ lọ́hun,
> Kí èmi náà mú ilẹ̀ lọ́wọ́ níhìn.

> I certainly do not know what terrible sin I have committed against God
> To be so punished with barrenness.
> But I am not yet beaten; I have my revenge figured out.
> Let God concern Himself with His heaven,
> I'll hold court here on earth. (Smith's translation, 73)

Here, Ẹfúnṣetán admits her guilt as charged and swears to give no thought to the consequences of her resolution.

The barrenness theme takes on a troubling, feminized dimension in the English translations in ways not expressed in the Yorùbá text. The English versions redirect, unintentionally perhaps, Látòósà's reiteration of Ẹfúnṣetán's edict against slaves' having children ("ẹni tí yóò bímọ" [whosoever will have a child]) to a rule meant for only female slaves ("any woman"). The Yorùbá terms in the original text reflect the gender neutrality of Ẹfúnṣetán's decree and its application. But the English translations render the rule as antiwoman, although in the play world Ẹfúnṣetán executes male and female slaves who attempt to have children. Pronoun choices in the translations reflect Látòósà's (and Ìtáwuyì's) malicious interpretation of events and, perhaps unintentionally, channel empathy against Ẹfúnṣetán. By casting the draconian law as targeting only women, as Látòósà does in the English versions, the translations affirm the accusation of unbridled and unnatural evil directed at Ẹfúnṣetán in other utterances. The English translations help Látòósà turn the audience and readers against his political enemy far beyond the facts stated in the original text, where sex is incidental and not essential to why Ẹfúnṣetán exercises power so wickedly.

In a revealing soliloquy toward the end of the play, Ẹfúnṣetán quotes a proverb on age, rank, and comportment to reiterate the correctness of her violent, improper, but not illegal, acts: "Bí ilẹ̀ bá ká àgbà mọ́, / Ó yẹ́ kí ó ṣẹ̀ṣe àgbà" (77). The sense portrayed by these words, uttered shortly before she kills herself, is that when an honorable, self-respecting ranking elder is trapped in an embarrassment, the concerned should obey the etiquette of age and rank without considerations for the pain or loss one would have to self-inflict. Oladeji translates the proverbial commentary thus: "An elder should know the path to honor when he is forced into a corner" (50); in Smith's words, "If an elder finds himself forced into a tight corner, / He should know how to extricate himself with dignity" (146). Pronoun choice in the English texts implies, once more, that the power to appropriate a general observation on worthwhile living belongs to the male sex only. It also recodes Ẹ́fúnṣetán's self-understanding of iron will as one more instance of her usurping men's prerogatives. In the Yorùbá text, not even the most determined of Ẹ́fúnṣetán's opponents deny her rank, age, and status as an elder. All her slaves call her "ìyá" (mother), the proper address for older women of childbearing age—whether or not they have biological offspring.[7]

The inherent sexism of word choice in the above episode reappears in the depiction of Ẹ́fúnṣetán's female slaves, who speak like pathetically unaware users of language at the beginning of the play. Adétutù and Àwẹ̀ró exchange thoughts about a slave's suffering in general and in Ẹ́fúnṣetán's household. These are not minor characters, their social status notwithstanding. The play founds the protagonist's moral culpability and readies her for a tragic fate with the depiction of her merciless execution of Adétutù, and Àwẹ̀ró's bold, but futile, daring to poison Ẹ́fúnṣetán and foment a slave revolt provides the popular basis for the military chiefs who later finish the job. Regarding her life as a slave, Adétutù says:

> Bẹ́ẹ̀ ni ìyà ní ó ńjẹ mí báyìì!
> Òṣìṣẹ́ wà lóòrùn, ẹní máa jẹ́ ẹ́ ńkọ́?
> Eléyìni wà ní bòoji tí ó ńgbéjú gbéré . . .
> A kì í háa wáyé ni mo wá bí?
> Ibi tí bàbá gbé yanrí, ọmọ ò mọ bẹ̀
> Bẹ́ẹ̀ ni àkúnlẹ̀yàn ni àdáyébá. (1)

Oladeji translates these thoughts into:

> The world is arranged so unfairly! Somebody labors his heart out in the sun. Afterwards a different person sits in the shade making derisive faces as he reaps all the fruits of the labour . . . Am I to blame that I was born? It is true one man's destiny is different from another's and a father's fate is different from his son's. Destinies are chosen in heaven by all men. (5)

This translation disrupts comprehension because Adétutù sounds as if she does not know that she is not a man. The passage is about Adétutù, the words are hers, and nowhere in the play do her male compatriots suffer a worse fate. Yet her proverb-laden generalizations are gendered male. In perhaps the most egregious instance, Adétutù observes that:

> Ayé ìyà mà ni ayé ẹrú o!
> Bí inú m̀bí ẹrú kò gbọdọ̀ fi hàn
> Bí inú ẹrú dùn àdùndẹ́hìn, èèwọ̀
> Ẹrú ko gbọdọ̀ rérìnín àsàsàmọ̀sì. (1–2)

Oladeji converts these into:

> A slave's life is a life of pain and sorrow! If he is happy he dares not show it. No matter how happy he may be, a slave dares not indulge in hearty laughter. (5)

Further in the passage, Adétutù compares necklaces to ropes used for tethering slaves: "Ẹrú kò lọ́rùn ìlẹ̀kẹ̀, àfi tokùn." Still, Oladeji abandons the sex of the self-referring character and the grammatically imposed gender neutrality of her words and translates her thoughts as "His neck is made for ropes and not for beads" (5). According to Smith,

> A slave's life is a life of pain and sorrow!
> If a slave feels anger, he dares not vent it
> If he is truly happy, he's forbidden any mirth whatsoever. (65–66)

But she translates the necklace line as "A slave's neck is made for tethers not for necklaces" (66). Word choice miscues in both English translations lump the female slave and her female owner as unaware users of proverbs. The language of the translation operates as if general observations, especially when they appear in proverbial forms, must bear male references. When Àwẹ̀ró recalls her freeborn past as "èmi ọmọ onílé, ọmọ ọlọ́nà, ọmọ onílẹ̀" (I, a worthy offspring of controllers of the land), Oladeji's translation calls her "heiress of a prosperous and wealthy man" (5) and attaches prosperous birth to a patrimony that is completely absent in her words. This contrasts with Smith's more attentive words: "well born heiress, descendant of a prosperous and wealthy clan" (66).

I do not intend to argue that the lack of gender marking in the Yorùbá pronominal system invalidates the use of all gendered rendering of Yorùbá references in English. My contention is that translations transport unintended ideological male dominance into situations that do not indicate them. In gender matters, translation between Yorùbá and English cannot but be commentary making; cultural transcription it is not. Monolingual readers of the English translations of *Ẹfúnṣetán Aníwúrà* cannot but see illegitimacy when an expression that ordinarily refers to a child born to unmarried partners ("ọmọ àlè") is converted to "bastards."[8] "Illustrious progeny" (ọmọ) is translated as "offspring" (and not "sons") in the praise poems of the male war chiefs and male slaves, but as "daughter" or "heiress" when female slaves speak of their proud birth. Thus Àwẹ̀ró is an "heiress," but Ọṣútúndé is an "offspring of Mogaji." The "whole world" ("gbogbo ayé") becomes "all men," and the Almighty (Elédùwà) is God. A person of royal birth (orí adé) is called a "prince"; an obstinate person (alágídí) is a "wicked man." The talkative Àwẹ̀ró is "the hag"[9] (Oladeji, 15). When Àwẹ̀ró expresses her well-founded suspicion that her friend might be pregnant, Adẹ́tutù playfully calls her "the [protective] mother" ("ìyá ọmọ"), but derides her in the English versions as a "nosy mother-hen." When, in another context, Ẹfúnṣetán dismisses her younger brother's parental worries for his son's health with an expression that means "the [protective] father" (bàbá ọmọ), neither English translation calls him cuckolded or a related sexist term.[10] Àwẹ̀ró appears as a meddler and gossip; Akínkúnlé is just unduly worried.

For a self-aware Yorùbá-English bilingual, the tendency to associate universality and generalizations with the masculine will provoke concerns about the truth value of the knowledge that English-speaking scholars produce about his or her society. In the English translations, more so in Oladeji's than in Smith's, masculinity approximates universality, and the gendered distribution of values strays close to systematic sexism. The word for "human" or "person" in the proverb that approximates how humans propose and the Almighty in heaven disposes ("ríró ni ti ènìyàn/ Ṣíṣe ńbẹ lọ́wọ́ Ọlọ́run Ọba") registers as man: "But though man can make his plans, it is God who makes things come to pass." When a male slave voices his doubts about Ẹfúnṣetán's humanity as he speculates on her ostensible pleasure in the summary execution of expectant slaves ("Ènìyàn ni ó sọ̀rọ̀ tàbí ẹbọra?" [42]), Oladeji uses a context-specific pronoun: "Was that a woman who spoke, or Lucifer?" (29).[11] But the reworking of "person" into "a woman," although the context seems to justify it, disregards the speaker's malice. The translation thereby colludes once more with Ẹfúnṣetán's textual antagonists, who have already concluded that she is an unfulfilled, barren woman who, left unchecked, will make all women childless.

The tendency of sexist language in English translations of this play to obstruct comprehension is further noticeable in other terms used to demonize Ẹfúnṣetán. The English versions of Ìyálóde's praising herself as an unfathomable, sublime entity (èèmọ̀) (62) after she rejects the warrior chiefs' demand that she should go on exile, depicts her as "Satan" (Oladeji, 41) and "the devil" (Smith, 132). But her chosen imagery of self-praise, "èèmọ̀," denotes not the unappeasable evil that "Satan" represents in Christianized English, but a source of profound "worry," an expression of "fancy," wonderment, extraordinariness (Abraham), or "strange occurrence" (*Dictionary of the Yoruba Language*).[12] The phrasing used in the English translation effectively advances the other chiefs' malicious understanding of Ẹfúnṣetán, whereas the original alludes to the underestimation of her considerable clout and capacious will. In other less obvious misdirected inflections, amorous friendship (yànrẹ́ [25]) becomes "choose a girl-friend;" the elder (àgbà

[35]) becomes "wise hunter" or "wise man"; the proverb that says an older or more powerful person is still below the Almighty (ajunilọ kò lè ju Ọlọ́run lọ [35]) is translated variously as "You can't terrorize men and bully God" (Oladeji, 25) and as "A man may play superior to his fellowman, but not with God" (Smith, 100). However, when Ẹfúnṣetán explicitly boasts that she is greater than men ("Èmi obìnrin tó ju ọkùnrin lọ" [77]), Oladeji compares her to other women: "the great-est of all women" (Oladeji, 50)!

Hubris and Two Concepts of Being in Yorùbá

Three years after the initial publication of *Ẹfúnṣetán Aníwúrà*, two professional philosophers, Barry Hallen and J. O. Sodipo, launched a research project aimed at understanding theory of knowledge as indigenous self-reflection encodes such in everyday Yorùbá language. They analyzed conversations with traditional male medicine makers (oníṣègùn), whose skills distinguish them as careful users of language and introspective observers of the reasoning patterns that govern life in their Yorùbá cultural environment. The university-based professional philoso-phers believed that these organic philosophers could help them understand the basis of Yorùbá thought and action through ordinary language exchanges on what constitutes knowledge (ìmọ̀) and belief (ìgbàgbọ́).

In the most systematic analysis of the conversations published thus far, Hal-len synthesizes the recorded responses of the oníṣègùn about being, knowing, believing, and acting into a "moral epistemology" in *The Good, the Bad, and the Beautiful*.[13] He gathers from his informers that the Yorùbá moral scale separates individuals into two large groups: bad humans (ènìyàn burúkú) and good humans (ènìyàn rere). Within this order, motivation for an utterance or action is assessed on the basis of how the presentation fits into the community's fund of perceptions about the individual speaker and the claims asserted. "Bad humans," for example, lie habitually, pick quarrels for no just reason or cause, steal, and are miserly. They "deliberately and consistently choose to prey upon others in an immoral manner in order to satisfy their own desires" (76). They pursue their needs monomania-cally without giving any thought to how their acts and utterances affect other people. Because they don't always choose their victims for cause, their malice can be "impersonal, or better, omnipersonal" (84). The "good human," however, will neither kill without cause nor lie persistently against the prompting of the con-science (ẹ̀rí ọkàn).

If we were to apply the language of Hallen's analysis to Ìṣọ̀lá's play, Ẹfúnṣetán is a "bad type" of human (ènìyàn burúkú). She declares a unilateral opposition to the Almighty, whom she accuses of having damned her with infertility. She re-jects all pleas for mercy from family, friends, and fellow chiefs when Adétutù is discovered pregnant. Till her end in a suicide, Ẹfúnṣetán holds on to absolute autonomy, regardless of prevailing rules. Her self-justifying words at the moment she kills herself,

> Èmi ni mo ni ẹrú mi
> Tí mo pá,
> Èmi náà ni mo sì ni ẹ̀mí mi
> Tí mo fẹ́ gbà
>
> I owned my slave
> That I executed,
> And I also own my life
> That I am about to take (77–78)

echo what she told the family members who came to plead for Adétutù's life under the pretext that she was impregnated by the Ìyálóde's younger brother:

> Gbogbo nǹkan le padà ní ayé
> Bí-n-ó-ti-ṣe-nǹkan-mi-nìyí, kò mà padà.
> Bí ó tilẹ̀ padà níbòmíràn,
> Kì í ṣe lọ́dọ̀ èmi Ẹfúnṣetán.
>
> Everything in the world might change
> I-am-going-to-dispose-my-property-in-any-manner-I-desire does not.
> Even if it changes elsewhere
> That will not be the case with me, Ẹfúnṣetán. (46)

Ẹfúnṣetán's radical autonomy can be reconciled neither with the "Yorùbá" account of normative being that Hallen distilled from conversations with oníṣẹ̀gùn, nor with what obtains in other parts of the play.[14] Within that Yorùbá "moral epistemology," Ẹfúnṣetán, the "bad human" (ènìyàn burúkú), deserves her tragic fate. Indeed Látòósà, her main political opponent, alleges "ìwà aburú" (abhorrent acts) against her at the last meeting held by the male chiefs before they attack her.

Hallen's very broad classifications of "Yorùbá" moral epistemology cannot justify the sexed distribution of virtues and vices highlighted in the English translations discussed above. If we agree to call Ẹfúnṣetán a female bad type (obìnrin burúkú) and the opposing chiefs as male bad types (ọkùnrin burúkú), the sex identifiers will be mere adjectives and would still not explain why even the Yorùbá original translates sex-neutral elements of daily life noted in written history and in oral traditions as fundamental features of woman-being. To understand that element of the play, we have to shift attention to how Ì ṣọlá codes observations about Ẹfúnṣetán's times in forms that reflect the gender environment of his play's production era.

Quiet agreement—or polite, good-natured disagreement—with menfolk define women in the play, including in the Yorùbá original: the pregnant Adétutù does not take any onstage initiative to save herself, leaving all intrigues to her lover, Ìtáwuyì, a male slave who cannot help himself either; Tòrò, Ẹfúnṣetán's sister-in-law, accepts all insults thrown at her by Ògúnníyì, a younger acquaintance and her husband's friend. Females who do not defer to men, beginning with the Ìyálóde, provoke unqualified resentment from their male compatriots: greed reportedly drives Mojí, Tòrò's friend and wife of the rude, though hilarious, Ògúnníyì, to abandon her husband; for the habit of expressing her mind freely, Àwẹ̀ró is distrusted by male slaves, who accuse her of talking too much, although when it comes time to poison the Ìyálóde, she strikes the first blow in the attempted slave mutiny while Ìtáwuyì, the alpha male slave, squirms in the wings; Àjílé, Ìyálóde's only friend, has no regard for her husband, who she derides as bound-to-ill-luck (olóríburúkú [10]) for not heeding her sound advice that he should stop game hunting at his advanced age; and Ẹfúnṣetán, of course, heads the pack of "undesirable" females, a cantankerous slave owner, veritable witch (ògbólògbó àjé), inexplicably wicked person (ìkà), profound cheat (arénijẹ), treasonous rabble-rouser (atúlùú), and reckless killer (apànìyàn).

The play contains other troubling translations of traditions that skew perception against women who will not ordinarily be in Hallen's class of bad humans. Men decide disputes with forceful, physical contests; favored women exchange insults and wound each other with innuendoes. According to Láwọyin, one of the warmongering chiefs, a woman should not dare to upset the political order in the city:

Kíni kí á ti gbọ́ pé obìnrin kanṣoṣo
Àní obìnrin lásánlàsàn,
Ni ó ńda gbogbo wa láàmú báyìí. (57)

How should it be told that one woman
That one ordinary female,
Troubles all of us so much.

Gender perversion allegation escalates in the next scene, when Ìtáwuyì and other slaves try to rouse themselves for insurgency:

Kíni àwa gan an tilẹ̀ ńṣe?
Bí ó ti wù kí ó lágbára tó,
Ṣebí obìnrin lásán ni?
Bí ó ti wù kí ọkùnrin kéré tó,
Kì í ṣe ẹgbẹ́ obìnrin mẹ́wàá. (57)

What actions are we [men] taking?
No matter how powerful this person might be,
Isn't she a mere female?

Regardless of how inconsequential one male might be,
Ten females added up are never up to a match.

Ìtáwuyì's words, mainly strung together from hackneyed sayings, assert ostensibly unassailable features of women's universal being (or lack thereof). In these words about the assured fate of women who, acting against their natural constitution, dare to defy men, both high-ranking male warrior chiefs and no-rank male slaves are in complete agreement. Since the take away from the textual closure of this historical play sides with the males, it is not surprising that "misbehavior" defines Ẹ̀fúnṣetán to one of her successors in 1994. Of course, Ìyálóde Akintola substituted late twentieth-century theatrical commentaries for the little that is known about the mid-nineteenth century. But the newer representation is all that she has.

To contest the validity of the commentaries masquerading as permanent cultural inscriptions about gender, we can call upon how the play's larger reality subverts the men's worldview privileged in the text. Ìtáwuyì's words, for example, are full of hollow and patently false observations. This character is a chattel holding of the person he denigrates as belonging to the effete female sex (obìnrin lásán), and his social status proves that sex does not naturally preclude aggressive repressiveness. His enslavement belies the facts of his thoughts and exposes outrightly the absurdity of his assertions about woman-being. Ìtáwuyì is so afraid of Ẹ̀fúnṣetán that he cannot summon enough "manly" nerve to claim his paternity of Adétutù's pregnancy while his lover still lives! Soon after making his empty boast about men's superiority, he proceeds to beg a slave of the allegedly inconsequential sex to poison the fearsome Ìyálóde, also of the effete sex. Since even Látòósà, Ẹ̀fúnṣetán's most powerful political opponent, never belittles her as "mere woman" when they battle each other, we have to dismiss Ìtáwuyì as insincere and classify him, too, as a bad type of human (ènìyàn burukú). The other male slave, Ọ̀ṣúntúndé, who spins the gender inferiority yarn during the short-lived slave uprising is not different from Ìtáwuyì. On the basis of sex alone, he casts doubts on Àwẹ̀ró's reliability for the task of leading the mutiny: "Gbogbo wa la mọ̀ pé àwọn obìnrin / Kò ní gògóńgò tí a ńfọ̀rọ̀ pamọ́ sí" (We all know that females / Lack the organ [the larynx] in which to hold secrets) (61).

It looks like there is a crisis of knowing here. On the one hand, the patterns noted above are consistent enough to support the view that despite the lack of gender-specific general references in the Yorùbá language, sex-related disparities are not strange to the play's "Yorùbá" context. It seems as if males follow certain ways, and females follow others. The patterns also suggest that only bad types like Ẹ̀fúnṣetán cross the bounds of propriety. The Ẹ̀fúnṣetán of this play, either in the Yorùbá original or in the English translations, is a bad person (ènìyàn burúkú).

On the other hand, the textual evidence is insufficient to prove that Ẹfúnṣetán's "Yorùbá" environment recognizes and treats her as if her "badness" emanates from her being female in the ways some of her clearly bad, male opponents have labeled her.

Tragic Badness: Ontological or Epistemological?

Sex makes a rare appearance in one of the statements offered by Hallen's "Yorùbá" philosophical interlocutors when the discussion shifts to morality and beauty:

> Tí ènìyàn bá ńlọ sí ilé ọkọ ní àtijọ́, a má ńsọ pé ìwà ni "kí o bá lọ, kí ó má bá ẹwà lọ." A máa ńkọ orin kan "iṣu ńmú àlùmọ̀n, ọ̀gẹ̀dẹ̀ ńmú àlùmọ̀n, obìnrin tí ó dára tí kò níwà asán ló jẹ́, tí ó ní ẹwà lójú tí kò ní ìwà asán ni." (*The Good, the Bad, and the Beautiful*, 170). (If someone [a woman getting married] is going to the husband's house in the olden days, they would way, "Go with character (*ìwà*) and not beauty (*ẹwà*)." We used to sing a song: "There are deceptive plantains [fruit that looks good on the outside but proves to be rotten on the inside]. A beautiful woman without a good [moral] character (*ìwà*) is of no real value. If she has beauty (*ẹwà*) of the face and has no character (*ìwà*)—it [her beauty] is of no real value." (116)

This passage is about different forms of human appearance, of human being, in society. One form relates to outer, proportional, preferably pleasant physique (ẹwà). The second form also concerns pleasantness (ìwà), but derives from how (or what) the interactions of a physically appearing body with another leads one to feel, beyond physical perception, about that other entity. Thus a human being who is abrasive is not desirable, even if his or her physical appearance (ẹwà) is pleasing to behold. Hence Hallen concludes that the "Yorùbá" found sociocultural being "on the basis of a pragmatic criterion—of the thing's utility to human society in general or to the individuals dealing with a specific situation" (*The Good, the Bad, and the Beautiful*, 119). In Hallen's system, the means to desirable, normative "being" in Yorùbá discourse involves exercising diligence about verifying claims shared with others. A normative "Yorùbá" individual preserves his or her usefulness and goodness (ìwà) by sharing only information verified by his or her sensory experience (ìmọ̀) or those believed (ìgbàgbọ́) to have been so experienced by credible others. However, because it is impractical for individuals in even the smallest communities to traffic only in direct experiences, the need for individuals to accumulate a large, credible fund of usefulness and goodness (ìwà) is critical for building a good society.

When, as quoted above, Látòósà alleges abhorrent acts (ìwà aburú) against Ẹfúnṣetán, he insinuates that her behavior is odious to the ruling norms of the city. Her estrangement from her larger family is very sharp. Her unprovoked challenge to the Almighty, and her defying the request of other chiefs for a change in behaviors, do not grant any regard to others. Nonetheless, it is one thing for Ẹfúnṣetán to deny the valid interests of others relentlessly; it is another for Ìtáwuyì to belittle her as "mere woman," as if hefty being is men's preserve. The actions and utterances of Ìtáwuyì and others, male and female, indicate that the anomalies imputed to Ẹfúnṣetán's being female do not derive from lived "Yorùbá" conduct in the play. In Hallen's system, abilities and inabilities that are beyond the individual's control, such as physical beauty or the alleged natural association of femaleness and effeteness in the play, constitute the less important form of being in society. The more important form concerns what is derived from estimations of individual usefulness and goodness. Dominant viewpoints articulated by male characters in *Ẹfúnṣetán Aníwúrà* correlate, against evidence, badness and femaleness, and bind Ẹfúnṣetán, Àjílé, Àwẹró, Adétutù, Tòrò, and the market women together as belonging to the inessential sex (obìnrin lásánlàsàn). No less striking is Hallen's leaving uninterrogated the implications of his oníṣègùn informant's use of women's appearance and ripe, inedible, but physically appealing, plantain to illustrate how deceptive physical appearance relates to socially desired ethical conduct. Hallen analyzes epistemic measures of what the oníṣègùn privileges as the more significant form of being and fails to consider systematically how those measures relate to the apprehensible, but ostensibly deceptive, outer form. That omission suggests, perhaps unintentionally, that physically appealing, pleasant appearances, like the rotten banana and charming females, cannot help but be deceptive.

In colloquial Yorùbá speech, humans exist in four forms: (1) as a subject of creation (ẹ̀dá), (2) as a phenomenon or ontological character (ìwà), (3) as an entity circumscribed by sociomoral character and perceived by other creations (ìhùwàsí), and (4) as an entity defined by peculiar physical acts and gestures (ìṣe). These forms of being or apprehension attach to a restricted series of grammatical predicators. Thus creating, inventing, or fabricating something tangible is phrased as "ṣe ẹ̀dá or dá ẹ̀dá"; for example, "Èdùmàrè ló ṣẹ̀dá gbogbo wa" (The Almighty created all of us) or "Òun ló dá wa" (It created our being). This predication extends in everyday speech to manufactures; for example, "Ìran wọn ló ńṣẹ̀dá aṣọ" (Their lineage manufactures textiles). Factual existence is predicated rather baldly with "wà"; for example, "Wọ́n wà" (They are/exist). Behavioral presentations that can be evaluated within the sociomoral scale are expressed with a verbal phrase that implies cultivation or initiating; for example, "Ṣọlá hu ìwà burúkú kan lánàá" (Ṣọlá grew a bad sociomoral character yesterday, or in colloquial English, Ṣọlá behaved badly yesterday). Physical actions and gestures are commonly predicated with "ṣe" (to do); for example, "Dáṣọfúnjó ṣe kísà lójú agbo" (Dáṣọfúnjó did [or performed] wonders in the arena).

It is ungrammatical to mix the predication usages sketched above. For example, Yorùbá syntax does not allow the equivalent of "They created their factual existence" (Wọ́n dá ara wọn). It is also ungrammatical in Yorùbá speech to assert the equivalent of "I made my child's factual [biological] existence" (Mo ṣẹ̀dá ọmọ mi). In other words, an individual can neither create, nor invent (dá), nor manufacture (ṣe) ontological character. This exclusion applies to all animate life. To attempt such a thing would amount to lying, dabbling in the occult, or, in this age and time, engaging in profoundly original scientific experiments. Individuals do initiate or cultivate (hù) their sociomoral character, as Hallen explains, by mediating truthfully to others what they know or have experienced through their senses. Semantically, this type of showing cannot be "made" or "manufactured" from nothing; it can only be cultured from other materials. Yorùbá grammar will not allow, for example, "Ṣọlá ṣe ìwà burúkú kan lánàá" (Ṣọlá manufactured a bad sociomoral character yesterday). It is permissible to say "Mo ṣe ẹdá bàtà kan" (I conjured the manufacture of a pair of shoes), but one cannot say "Mo hu ẹdá bàtà kan" (I grew/cultured the existence of a pair of shoes), because that would amount to saying one "behaved" a pair of shoes into existence.

Grammatically, a material creation or invention (ẹ̀dá) emanates from a will that is external to the existing object or person. Another will's motion (ìṣe) is necessary for its emergence. Surprisingly, the predicator of purposive, self-directed physical motions (ṣe) does not attach to either epistemic or ontological being (ìwà), although it serves as a very common root in forming many other verb phrases: ṣojú (represent), ṣẹ̀dá (invent), ṣèṣe (be injured), ṣìṣe (misact), ṣèlú (govern), ṣakin (act bravely), ṣojo (act cowardly), ṣèyí ṣọ̀hún (dillydally). But ṣèwà (manufacture conduct or existence) is barred in word formation rules. The other root morpheme for creation, dá, attaches to a lot of nouns to form verbs—dáre (absolve), dẹkun (limit), dálùú (found a polity), dábàá (propose), dáhùn (answer)—but not to ìwà. It seems as if ìwà—as factual existence or as something derived from conduct—exists by itself phonologically.

I conclude that the sexed terms of reference by which Ẹfúnṣetán is described in Ìṣọ̀lá's original play refer discursively to meaningful motions (ìṣe) that constitute her recognizable conduct (ìwà), which includes radical autonomy. Given the contradictions and inconsistencies of those making the allegations of "badness" against her, the motions (ìṣe) do not equate the permanently gendered, different ontology (ìwà) that is implied in the use of English pronominals in the translations. Ẹfúnṣetán's acts are behaviors (ìhùwàsí) that derive from her living in Ìbàdàn at a point in time. They are not features of femaleness, the quasi-genetic and unalterable features of human existence described in colloquial Yorùbá speech as àdámọ́ and referred to by Hallen's informants as ìpín (primordial allotment).[15] After all, women are not supposed to floor men in a fight, but Ẹfúnṣetán enslaves them. When confronted by Ìtáwuyì, she mesmerizes him with superior spell casting and kills him off with only a little further effort. At the last meeting of the council of chiefs, Láwọyin feigns perplexity over Ẹfúnṣetán's repudiation of a woman's inherent softness or calmness (ẹ̀rọ̀). In reality, however, the complaint is about her acts and epistemic behaviors (ìṣe and ìhùwàsí). The warrior chiefs and the slaves, both vested antagonists of Ẹfúnṣetán, blame her for incorrigible unwomanlike actions (ìṣe) but exaggerate these as violations of woman's inherent nature (ìwà). In short, malice drives Ẹfúnṣetán's antagonists to translate features of epistemic character into ontologically determined conduct.

Correcting Mistranslations

For the 2005 adaptation filmed by Tunde Kelani, who is also the cinematographer of the 1981 celluloid version, Akínwùmí Ìṣọ̀lá wrote a new screenplay that mitigates the popular demonization of Ìyálóde Ẹfúnṣetán Aníwúrà and responds to the concerns of feminist historians about the original play's role in how she is perceived. The seriousness of purpose that went into the revision could be estimated in the very high caliber of stars who acted minor roles in the video: Kàrímù Adépọ̀jù (aka Bàbá Wándé), a top echelon star in Yorùbá language theater and film, plays Akínkúnlé; Tóyọ̀sí Arígbábuwó, an eminent actor in literary and popular dramas, acts as a war chief; Adébáyọ̀ Fálétí, a denizen of Yorùbá high literary arts, acts the role of Akíngbadé; and Àlàbí Ògúndépò, a highly esteemed poet, is the Praise Singer.

The new movie provides a fuller context for Ìyálóde's acts. The playwright himself serves as the conarrator of the prologue, which now places Ìbàdàn within a larger nineteenth-century Yorùbá history and emphasizes its being a slave state: "Ìbàdàn ńmẹ́rú, ẹrú rẹ̀ náà ńmẹ́rú" (Ìbàdàn captures slaves, and its slaves also capture slaves), it is reported. The female conarrator reminds the playwright to speak of important female political actors, including warriors, like Ọmọ́ṣá and Ìyá Ọ̀fà. Civil unrest defines Ìbàdàn in the new prologue, and Ẹfúnṣetán is not an anomaly but a fitting emblem of her times. She does not unleash death on her people indiscriminately, but is just another belligerent leader among many in a state prone to war. The narrated prologue segues into the protagonist's confident, calm, and business-like strides among a retinue of women, members of Ìyálóde-in-council, with her complaining about Látòósà's warmongering. She sits in council with co-chiefs and is present when the vendetta against Fọ̀kọ̀, a chief who has fallen out of favor, is engineered by Látòósà, the supreme leader.

The opening sequence includes Ẹfúnṣetán telling her followers that she is tired of contributing to war efforts. The new Ẹfúnṣetán has a married daughter, Ọmọ́tóyọ̀sí, who dies at childbirth. She is a doting mother to all, including her slaves, one of whom gives birth to a set of twins and with whom she rejoices heartily, giving her a sack of money in congratulations.

Ọmọ́tóyọ̀sí's death devastates Ẹfúnṣetán. She develops insomnia and migraines and will not take medicines for the ailments; she is so profoundly depressed, she wants to die. Her decree against slaves having children comes to her on a whim when she hears a baby crying during her mourning period. Even Ìtáwuyì confirms in a conversation with his friend that "Ìwà ìyá ṣẹ̀ṣẹ̀ yí padà ni" (The old woman's behaviors changed only recently). According to Ọ̀ṣúntúndé, her sadness is understandable because Ọmọ́tóyọ̀sí's death is like a twilight loss (òfò alẹ́) that is bound to induce nightmares. The heinousness of the alleged misdeeds in the original play is thus significantly reduced. Adétutù and Àwẹ̀ró behave like true friends toward each other, and both consider running away after Adétutù becomes pregnant. The Tòrò-Ògúnníyì comic interlude that berates women generally, and Ògúnníyì's wife specifically, has been removed. While Ìtáwuyì contracts Akinkule's help to save Adétutù, as in the published play, Àwẹ̀ró also approaches Àjílé, Ẹfúnṣetán's only friend, for intervention too. In the new film, women make efforts to aid each other.

Perhaps most significantly, Ẹfúnṣetán dies in her home and is not disgraced as a captive at Látòósà's court. She walks calmly into her boudoir and poisons herself, as any person of her status, historically speaking, would have done after suffering a political disgrace. Látòósà frees her slaves but decrees, as history relates, that the household otherwise be left intact for the family. The new film repudiates insinuations of Ẹfúnṣetán's fate being the result of her having violated women's inherent nature. The tragedy's emphasis now rests unmistakably on political treacheries aggravated by the behavioral peculiarities (ìwà) of a major historical figure. With the new film, Ì ṣọlá seems to want to reiterate that gender, at least in Ẹfúnṣetán's Ìbàdàn, is epistemic, historical, and malleable. No sex in the most recent incarnation of Ẹfúnṣetán Aníwúrà's story is effete just for being female.

Notes

1. See also Akinyele, *Iwe Itan Ibadan*, 281.

2. The act closest to a "misbehavior" that Johnson records, and which Awe ("Iyalode Efunsetan Aniwura") has challenged, is her mistreatment of slaves. According to Johnson, Ìyálóde Ẹfúnṣetán "had an only daughter who died in childbirth in 1860 and since that sad event took place she became strangely cruel to all her female slaves found in an interesting condition, using all cruel means to cause forcible abortion, most of which ended in death" (*The History of the Yorubas*, 393). See Adéẹ̀kọ́'s *Slave's Rebellion* (145–156) for a fuller discussion of how Awe's defense of Ẹfúnṣetán overlooks the plight of her slaves.

3. Evidence about Ìyálóde's activities also indicates that the term could be "'mother or all or mother of external affairs' or, in practical terms, the mother 'in charge of dealings between members of the society and outsiders'" (Denzer, *The Ìyálóde*, 145). According to Denzer, Ìyálóde is the title of the "most senior" office in the "female hierarchies of chief" (1) in Ìbàdàn. Anna Hinderer gives an eyewitness account of how the Ìyálóde settled women's problems in 1854 (*Seventeen Years in the Yoruba Country*, 110–111).

4. Awe ("Iyalode Efunsetan Aniwura") also lists superior material wealth as a qualification. Other attributes of typical Ìyálóde in Ìbàdàn are advanced trading skills learned from close female relatives, few children, and generally obscure spouses.

5. This discussion has benefitted heavily from conversations with Oyèrónkẹ́ Oyěwùmí. See also Oyěwùmí's *The Invention of Women*, 109–112. In any case, no "civil" chieftaincy is dedicated to controlling men's affairs exclusively.

6. How, for example, should the necessarily convoluted self-understanding of a male believed by his grandmother to be an incarnation of her own mother (i.e., the man's great grandmother), and thus addressed as "mother" by this woman, be depicted in English? Should a translator refer to this character with the male pronoun or allow for a female pronoun when the grandmother talks about her "mother" who is also her "grandson"?

7. That is also the one gender-related term about which the two English translators disagree most obviously. While While Oladeji chooses a literal equivalent, "mother," Smith code-switches, keeps the Yorùbá word, and explains it in an endnote.

8. See Oladeji's translation, 6 and 10; Smith's translation, 75. Smith seems to be uncomfortable with that English term, though, and when Ẹfúnṣetán first uses it to put down her slaves verbally, Smith renders it as "imbeciles" (68).

9. This is the most egregiously sexist term used in the Oladeji text. In the *Oxford English Dictionary*, a hag is "an evil spirit, daemon, or infernal being, in female form: applied in early use to the Furies, Harpies, etc. of Graeco-Latin mythology; also to malicious female sprites or 'fairies' of Teutonic mythology."

10. Smith: "acting the fool as if he's the only father the world has ever known" (73); Oladeji: "the only father in the world! Wretched father of a worthless son" (9).

11. Smith is again more observant of the gender implications of her word choice: "Was that a human that just spoke or was it a demon?" (106).

12. Although colloquial usage sometimes imply monstrosity, here it is in the sense of a bold violation of precedence and not the irremediable malevolence implied by "Satan" or "evil." Moreover, the original play does not use the often translated deity of chance, Èṣù, permanently mistranslated as "Satan" in Christianity. Of course, both translators write Èṣù as "Satan."

13. See also Hallen and Sodipo, *Knowledge, Belief, and Witchcraft*, and part 3 of Hallen's *African Philosophy*.

14. Fẹ́mi Táíwò commented on an earlier draft of this chapter that radical autonomy allegation, even if it were true, need not be a tragic flaw, because it does not contradict any tenet that could be called Yorùbá.

15. Hallen does not distinguish well enough the difference between epistemic ìwà (being) and ontological ìwà. He presents the latter more or less as an aesthetic, art history, sociological problem. Hallen also accepts his informants' ideas on knowledge (ìmọ̀) at face value. But ìmọ̀ is never evident as such—that is, as things experienced and cognized directly; it emerges after applying considered processes of interpretation (ìtúmọ̀). The meaning of meaning was not pursued at all in the dialogues. That meaning, and therefore knowledge, is a function of mediation appears starkly in the insights offered by the oníṣègùn when they stress the importance of inú (inside, inner wisdom) and speak about the centrality of orí and ìpín (destiny), two deductions that cannot be experienced directly but are central to ìmọ̀ about individuals.

6 Photography and the Panegyric in Contemporary Yorùbá Culture

With a title that proclaims a throaty dedication to praise, predominantly red glossy covers, and every page filled with compilations of adulatory, colored photographs taken on festive occasions, *Ovation* magazine works very hard to put its subjects in the best light. Its many clones based in Lagos—*Accolade, Crystals, Empire, The Entertainer, Events International, Fame Weekly, Gallery, Global Excellence, Reality, Society Celebration,* and *Vintage,* to name a few—proclaim their devotion to the valorization of objects, persons, and status. Encomium Ventures, also located in Lagos, houses a stable of magazines—*National Encomium, Encomium Weekly, E[ncomium] Lifestyle*—devoted entirely to the *Ovation* model.[1] In the United States, out of the Washington, DC, area comes *Prudence;* from Indianapolis, *Applause;* and from Houston, *International Socialites Connection. Agoo, Ancorra,* and *Sankofa* are published in Accra and distributed all over the Ghanaian diaspora. Some of these titles have copied *Ovation*'s layout down to the color and measurements of the cover margins. The magazines are also adapting quickly to new technologies. The now defunct web-based *Trendy Africa,* published by Tosan Aduayi, *Ovation*'s former US representative, devised a means by which subjects photographed at parties can purchase printed copies for their own records. *Ovation* itself is developing a robust internet platform.

At its inception, *Ovation* sought to work within the image restitution discourse about Africa: the continent suffers from rampant negative depictions of its situation in global media; such representations do not resemble the wide variety of life on the ground; sympathetic media leaders, even more so if they have African roots, are duty-bound to correct the distortion. By using a glamorous depiction of the activities of Africa's wealthy as its main strategy of polishing Africa's image, *Ovation* aims to recondition the popular perception of the continent's being by extolling the ways of its high-achievers (see Figure 6.1). In the magazine's approach to contemporary life, it is held implicitly that a society's comparative global standing is best measured not by the existential problems of its weakest but by the deeds of its affluent. The ambition of the magazine, as envisioned by the publisher, also includes connecting Africa to black America: "African-Americans were looking at an alternative to *Ebony.* They wanted to link

Figure 6.1. *Ovation Igbinedion*. Courtesy of Ovation International Magazine.

up with Africa, and we have that platform. So, we are working very hard to make sure that wherever blacks are, whether they are Americans, aborigines in Australia, anyone who is interested in Black issues, we will go there. And give them popular coverage" (Bakare, "At Home in London," 62). The cover of the inaugural issue demonstrated the magazine's worldwide conception of Africa with a generous coverage of the person then adjudged to be the wealthiest African anywhere in the universe, Mohammed Al-Fayed, the Egyptian émigré in England and owner of Harrods, the London department store.

The editor's Africanist proclamations notwithstanding, and despite its sporadic coverage of events in Ghana, Gambia, and Jamaica, *Ovation*'s core market is in Nigeria and the Nigerian diaspora. The magazine's Nigeria focus is obvious in the overwhelming presence of that country's wealthy on the inside pages and the always prominent placement of Nigerians on its covers. If—as the publisher reiterates in his statements about the magazine's goal of projecting Africa—signs of wealth alone were to determine the magazine's contents, South Africans and Egyptians should, given their comparatively large economies, also feature prominently in *Ovation*. For reasons of culture, I believe, the Maghrebi and South African markets are yet to be cracked. The main proposition of this chapter is that the magazine audience in Nigeria has embraced *Ovation* because it translates into photography the panegyric tendency that pervades popular self-projection arts in the Yorùbá cultural environment of southwestern Nigeria. The subgenre of Yorùbá panegyric that *Ovation* translates into the photographic medium is oríkì bòròkìnní (chants in praise of the eminent). The magazine's title, Òkìkí in Yorùbá, barely disguises the intent to quote the oríkì praise poetry tradition, the preferred verbal art form of proclaiming status within Yorùbá and non-Yorùbá hegemonic circles in southwestern Nigeria.[2] In this chapter, I attempt to show clearly the latent process by which constantly shape-shifting traditions get crosshatched with features of historically emergent media. I also propose that a "poetic" construal of images—and not "theatricality" or "melancholy" as they are conventionally presented in theories of media and culture—animates the intermedial practices that recommend *Ovation* to its audience.

A cursory survey of any issue of *Ovation* will confirm that the extramural activities of politicians, businesspeople, and sports stars represent for *Ovation* the traits and ideals most useful for culturally intelligible self-projections. The magazine's photographs of its subjects focus on the consumption of the fruits of achievement: elegant homes, exquisite-looking spouses, well-connected friends, adequately fed and peaceable children, and sumptuous parties. The photo spreads and brief accompanying stories say very little about biographical peculiarities and uncommon gifts that produce the apparently uncommon success to which the glamorous photographs attest.[3] Many "serious" journalists worry that this manner of covering the wealthy resembles praise singing too closely.[4] Several editors lamented to me in interviews the ill effect they believe *Ovation*'s coziness with its subjects imposes on its journalism. The magazine was also derided for its fawning, thoroughly unironic misuse of its access to the high and mighty. "Soft sell" is the common term that all the "serious" editors used to put down the magazine and, sometimes, the publisher. To my literary and cultural criticism–oriented suggestion that the magazine might be reworking the oral panegyric tradition, one editor responded that praise singing is precisely the problem because the world no longer operates within the face-to-face moral milieu of oral traditions. Confronted with these issues during an undated interview published in a defunct Nigerian celebrity gossip website, *Ovation*'s publisher, Délé Mòmódù, affirmed that:

> It is a photo album. Every magazine must have a concept and its target audience. There are various magazines on different topics and issues like cars, motorcycles, health and beauty and fashion fair. So why is *Ovation* different? It is a photo album magazine that covers weddings, funeral and chieftaincy title ceremonies, house-warming, and so on. If you want to read about serious news, go and buy magazines like *Tell* and *Time*. If you want a photo album, go and buy *Ovation*. *Ovation* is out to celebrate people's successes and achievements. We do not cover just the rich, but also the poor who have risen through the ranks and become successful.[5]

At face value, Mòmódú's repeating the phrase "photo album" three times and reiterating the professional correctness of choosing and serving a market niche suggests that he feels no need to be unduly defensive; the magazine's reporting style is superficial by design. Readers hungering for the details of how the magazine's subjects rose to eminence must have mistaken it for *Tell* and *Time*.[6]

Mòmódù maintained this stance when I recounted the professional concerns of his colleagues to him in an interview in August 2008:

> I don't judge people. They say, "No, you should judge people." No. I'm not carrying out any investigation, hearsay upon hearsay. "I hear say Abacha stole money." But what happened I present to you. They had a wedding in the family. And when I got there, I told my photographer that I am interested in this building. Nobody saw where Abacha was buried, the mausoleum, until *Ovation* published it. And then other papers started lifting our pictures. (Délé Mòmódú, interview with the author)

Mòmódù declares here that nothing is illegitimate or otherwise untoward about praise singing, if that is the best style of speaking to a consciously selected market. Praise singing, Mòmódù insists, facilitates the gathering and dissemination of some types of information that are foreclosed in the high-minded assumptions and styles of other types of journalism.[7] Because *Ovation* does not peer too closely into the sources of its subjects' wealth, members of the Abacha family did, for example, lower their guard and unwittingly expose signs of their fortune, without prejudice as to how this is acquired, to the photographer.

Kúnlé Bákàrè, a graduate of one of Nigeria's premier journalism colleges, the University of Lagos, and owner of the *Encomium* publications, proudly carries himself as an avatar of "praise" journalism. Bákàrè believes that magazines like his are popular because they speak the language of their audience, who appreciate the photographic representation of the tangible results of achievements. Asked how he selects events and people to cover in his magazine, Bákàrè gave two criteria: (1) the status of the event and (2) the number of celebrities ("big people") expected. Prompted for his reactions to criticisms of "praise" journalism, he responded without flinching that his allegedly serious colleagues wished that they, like him, owned their publications and exercised the kind of editorial control he enjoys.[8] Bákàrè's words echo the answer Délé Mọ̀mọ́dù gave to the same question in the profile published in *Encomium* in December 2002. To the question "What do you think is responsible for [critical] views about what you are doing?" Mọ̀mọ́dù replied, "Sometimes it could be envy, or just an act of wickedness."[9]

Their stout defenses notwithstanding, Bákàrè and Mọ̀mọ́dù are probably concerned by the doubts cast on the social value of their work. The hurried tone of Mọ̀mọ́dù's mea culpa of "If you want to read about serious news, go and buy magazines like *Tell* and *Time*" implies a dissatisfaction that could only be expressed as an unsolicited endorsement of other magazines. Bákàrè's defensiveness seeps through in his stressing that his magazines do not feature fraudulent characters or people with "untraceable income." To quell anxieties about the moral standards of his editorial decisions, Bákàrè recounted to me the names of many unglamorous intellectuals and scientists who have been profiled in his magazines: the famous mathematician Chike Obi, the literary giant Wole Soyinka, the well-known historian of education Babs Fafunwa, and the playwright Femi Osofisan. As Bákàrè explained, glamorized depictions of successful scholars and artists, even when they are neither powerful nor rich in the ordinary sense, provide relief and release for the population, who are bombarded daily with stories of seemingly permanent national adversities. In this chapter, praise "singing" is a serious subject. Its critique of repudiators of the *Ovation* genre will be obvious in the long history of the use of the panegyric in West African print culture. It is hoped as well that the deep contextualizations offered will show the chapter's dissatisfaction with the easy capitulations of the maligned contemporary practitioners of photographic panegyric today. Publishing and editing photographic panegyrics, I will demonstrate, repositions an art form of Yorùbá cultural being.

Ovation's Immediate Contexts

It is easy for gatekeepers of cultural and professional propriety, such as newspaper editors, to dismiss the *Ovation* genre as a Nigerian domestication of gossip publications in Europe and America. The bases for such a comparison are undeniable: the foregrounded stories and pictures of the rich and famous, for instance, join *Ovation* to *People* (American) and *Hello!* (British) magazines. Kúnlé Bákàrè said he fell in love with America's *National Enquirer* when he first encountered the format during his journalism studies at the University of Lagos (Interview with author, June 2006). The magazine's unusual ways greatly appealed to him, and after graduating he sought employment at *Prime People*, the oldest celebrity gossip newspaper in Lagos. Zina Saro-Wiwa's positive portrayal of *Ovation* in her documentary "Hello Nigeria!" also follows the line of reasoning that endures on its showing that the Nigerian magazine's similarities to the British *Hello!* are too numerous to be coincidental. *Ovation*, my studies show, is neither the *National Enquirer* nor even Nigeria's *Prime People*, and the difference is not just in naming. First, Lagos-based magazines with "people" in their title follow the *National Enquirer* scandal-mongering model, not *Ovation*'s model of praising high celebrity. Furthermore, from its inception, *Ovation* has distinguished itself by emphasizing pictures over words. It does not report gossip, it carries few interviews, and it minimizes verbal narratives. None of the ostensibly American and British antecedents focus on pictures of well-coiffed individuals in well-choreographed circumstances as overwhelmingly as *Ovation* does. Unlike the popular American and British celebrity publications, images that can embarrass or expose character flaws in the rich and powerful do not get published in *Ovation*. The typical *Ovation* picture exudes controlled authority in all circumstances, even at parties.

Ovation's publisher, Délé Mòmódù, earned a baccalaureate degree in Yorùbá Studies at the Obafemi Awolowo University, Ilé-Ifè, and is therefore well-schooled in elements of high Yorùbá culture and arts. His graduate degree in Literature in English from the same university included a rigorous study of the artistic and social dimensions of oral traditions. It stands to reason that both Mòmódù's advanced training in the workings of Yorùbá culture and art and the pervasive Yorùbá cultural presence in southwestern Nigeria are foundational elements in the success of the pictorial magazine pack that *Ovation* leads. A clear awareness of the traditional panegyric style shows in *Encomium*'s depiction of Mòmódù as "the first and only Nigerian to hold a first degree in Yorùbá and Masters in Literature in English."[10] Hyperbolic phrasing in this revealing, self-reflexive instance of the *Ovation* style of the arts of reporting the eminent represents the common act of switching the focus of university studies from one literary tradition to another as a mark of genius. In Yorùbá praise-singing traditions emulated in the report, setting precedence is a quality of arduous founding figures to whom progenies must forever be grateful.[11] When Mọ̀mọ́dù defends his publication as "a photo album magazine that covers weddings, funeral and chieftaincy title ceremonies, house-warming, and so on," the illustrative rites are not selected randomly; they are, in the oral traditions, occasions for celebrating life's milestones.

Variants of the Yorùbá panegyric tradition have long been the staple of southwestern Nigerian verbal popular culture. In music, popular lyrics in Yorùbá very frequently rely on effusive commemoration of persons, social groups, ideals, events, objects, aspirations, and divinities. Even non-Yorùbá but Lagos-based singers have developed forms of praise epithets to match the rhythms of their ordinarily nonpanegyric musical forms and idioms. Oliver de Coque, a Highlife music great who performed in Igbo, incorporated a formulaic Yorùbá epithet into his praise song for the predominantly Igbo members of the Peoples Club of Nigeria, at the end of which he sang two Yorùbá lines in praise of the Aláàfin of Ọ̀yọ́, Làmídì Adéyẹmí, as a gesture of gratitude for the honor that the king had bestowed on a member of the club.[12] The reverse happens when the jùjú music superstar, Sir Shina Peters, praised in Yorùbá language a wealthy Igbo man, Maurice Ibekwe, partly by converting Igbo rallying phrases into an appellative panegyric.[13] In contemporary Lagos, the urge to praise has crossed ethnic particularities.

Praise singing has infiltrated popular culture in Lagos not because some inexplicable dynamism directs Yorùbá verbal arts but because the Yorùbá panegyric is a supple and versatile form that has always been open to reinterpretation and improvisation. In Yorùbá oral traditions outside of Lagos, for example, oríkì (appellative poetry) is the popular form. Its performance is not restricted to particular divinities, professional groups, festivals, or communities. Lineage praise poetry, for instance, can be performed in the sedate style of itinerary chanters or in the more frenzied style of the hunters' guild recitations. Lines about the peculiar attributes of the deities, about the great divination priests of the past, and even about the divination God himself are found in Ifá verses chanted during consultation proceedings. Ògúndáre Fóyánmu has done a praise chant of the Christianized Almighty God in ìjálá, a performance mode traditionally reserved for the worship of Ògún, the hunters' patron deity. The praise form is so responsive to new usage that Karin Barber calls it the basic intertext of Yorùbá poetry ("Yorùbá Oríkì and Deconstructive Criticism"). Further underlining the openness of Yorùbá panegyric, the form could be used for mock heroic purposes when well-known epithetic formulas are turned around to praise ordinarily undesirable traits such as accomplished indolence and pickpocketing.

In Ọ̀yọ́ Yorùbá societies, every individual acquires at least one name that expresses his or her parents' wishes and aspirations—for example, auspicious

luck, beauty, bravery, or great wealth. As individuals grow, they acquire appellative attributes to commemorate their skills, physical appearance, professional
acumen, individual predisposition, or fulfilling relationships. The greater an
individual's achievements, the more extensive the attributions he or she acquires.
As Adébóyè Babalọlá puts it, "Àkànpọ̀ àwọn ẹyọ-oríkì báwọ̀nyí . . . ló ńdi oríkì
jántìrẹrẹ, oríkì bọ̀rọ̀kìnní" (Such attributes accumulated over time become the
substantial oríkì by which the eminent is hailed) (*Àwọn Oríkì Bọ̀rọ̀kìnní*, 5). On
festive occasions, entertainers and praise chanters throw the accreted pride-
inducing phrases at those kings, village heads, war chiefs, and civil society leaders
judged to be deserving. According to Babalọlá, the truly eminent are those who,
having been favored by the deity of commerce, have accumulated more than adequate wealth to fulfill all obligations, including the call of glamour.[14] In their
proper contexts, the words of an effective poetic recognition should swell the
listener's head and tangibly affirm the eminent subject's honorable position. To
paraphrase Babalọlá, the praise poem becomes a thing (ohun) whose successful
production confers prestige (iyì) and honor (ẹ̀yẹ) and provokes pride (ìwúrí).
Praise chants stoke euphoria and put the addressed self in the best sociocultural
light because they conjure through verbal imageries the extraordinary achievements (iṣẹ́), pedigree (ìbánitan), peculiar physique (ìrísí), and uncommon acts
(ìhùwásí) of the subject of praise. The poems exaggerate abilities, understate deficiencies, and deflect weaknesses with flattering word pictures.

Ovation, like traditional orature and contemporary popular music, adulates
individual achievements. Both in traditional oral poetry and in *Ovation*'s printed
photographs, wealth—or its large-scale manifestation at social gatherings and in
tangible consumer products—plays a decisive role in the content and form of the
panegyric. In *Ovation*, those who receive the greatest attention include wealthy
merchants, manufacturers, charismatic preachers, bankers, doctors, lawyers,
entertainment and show business stars, and prominent politicians. Nonparodic
depictions of teachers, researchers, university professors, diviners, or farmers,
professional acclaim notwithstanding, are rare. Those who work with the mysteries of physics, mathematics, and engineering may be glamorous in folk imagination; however, their hardy ways do not respond favorably to panegyrics.[15]

How Does *Ovation* Celebrate?

The degree to which photographed sumptuousness can exemplify the celebrants' achievement is the primary measure of eminence in *Ovation*. Indicators
of abundance include a crowd of well-appointed guests of high social and political ranking, expensive body adornments, exclusive venues like elegant hotels and
exotic islands, and best-selling entertainers. The more of these indicators that are
photographed at an event, the more eminent the gathering and the higher the

celebrant's place on the social ladder. When the celebrant is yet to rise to the top of the ladder, the pictures are presented, mainly through suggestive captions, as prefigurations of great achievements: a young man's wedding presupposes a bounteous progeny and a developing manhood; a birthday connotes gratitude. A funeral of an old person is depicted as the culmination of a high-achieving individual; the rare representation of the death of a young person often laments the unfortunate abbreviation of an unfolding greatness.

The *Ovation* photo spread processes material acquisition and consumption patterns into an overpowering visual energy that compels viewers to bind conspicuous consumption to the reward of ambition. The photographed size and scale of what has been accumulated and consumed project the size and scale of the celebrant's leisurely expenditure and invite the reader/viewer to imagine what is unspent. Repeated poses of different celebrants and guests in numerous variations of 4″ × 3″ prints, especially when they appear in designated event colors or specially selected fabrics, create visual vastness.[16] The magazine gestures toward representing individual distinction with intimate portraits of principal celebrants wearing recognizably expensive clothing and jewelry and also with full-length shots of celebrants with well-connected persons like state governors, business leaders, politicians, and neotraditional chiefs. For the superrich, a whole issue might be created and named for the individual celebrating some new achievement.[17] Whatever the occasion, the *Ovation* celebrant occupies the symmetrical center of the frame in different pictures taken with other affluent-looking people. Subjects in the group photograph are usually standing, arranged to form a semicircle around an empty foreground. Except for occasions that involve well-known personalities, the captions omit individual names, identifying the group either with the celebrant's name or with the name of a relative or friend who invited them and in whose honor they have bought their common attire. A caption might say "Friends of the Bride" or mimic the titling style of artistic portraits, as in "Men in Blue." In the *Ovation* coverage, the celebrant's retinue need not be known by name; their showing up in numbers to honor the celebrant is enough as a sign of eminence.

I have selected three *Ovation* events for close reading. The first celebration covers the wedding ceremony of an information technology businessman, Basil Iredia of Benin City, Nigeria. The second event concerns two reports about retired general Buba Marwa, onetime military governor of Lagos State (1996–1999) and later presidential aspirant in 2005. The third event covers the representation of the professional lives of young people. For each discussion, I have chosen epithets drawn from Yorùbá praise poetry as subtitles.

Basil Iredia's Wedding

Aṣọ là ńkí, a à kí'nìyàn (Salutations hail the adornment; not the body): Basil Iredia and Winifred Garland in *Ovation* issue 66

The groom is Basil Iredia, the CEO of Gold Computer Ltd. in Benin City. His bride, Winifred Garland, is an economics undergraduate at the University of Benin. The short narrative that accompanies the pictures says nothing about the bride's family background except that they live in the largely middle-class Satellite Town near Lagos. The groom's parents, however, are mentioned by name as Sir and Lady Raphael Asakome, the titles indicating an important knighthood from either the Catholic Church or a European country. Most of the eminent people identified by name in photo captions belong to the groom's side of the bridal party: an ex-governor of the groom's home state, two heads of traditional kingdoms from the same state, and one Benin traditional chief. The celebrants are photographed with all these personalities through who they, in effect, announce their affiliation with the well known.

The full-color photograph is the magazine's main draw, not the verbal narratives; even captions seem to be a grudging concession. The Iredia/Garland spread—the only *Ovation* wedding in which the bride is not given the groom's last name—consists of eight pages of forty-five glossy color photos. The couple appears on the cover page with two royal guests fully dressed in traditional official regalia, one of them wearing a beaded crown and a large necklace made of ivory links, and the other a red hat. The man with the beaded crown is identified in a photo captioned on an inside page as "the paramount ruler of Onne clan" (*Ovation* no. 66, 78). The red-hatted man is Chief N. Isekhure of Benin Kingdom. Also in the picture is the Edo Aidenojie II of Uromi in Esan Kingdom. These are traditional royalty. Of the eight-page spread, a picture of the couple cutting the wedding cake occupies one full page (see figure 6.2). They appear alone in three other pictures, one showing them cutting the cake in another set of clothes.

The couple appear in twenty-four other pictures with a variety of guests. The groom, without his wife, is in three group pictures: one with his sisters, one with Sir Asakome and his wife, and one with a group of seven guests, six of them women. There is a group picture of eleven women identified as "friends of the bride," each one wearing a pink-colored blouse and long skirt and a silver-grey headgear (see figure 6.3). That the bride, Winifred Garland, is not in this picture and that no other picture in the spread attaches any guests, including her parents, to her indicates that she is not the primary eminence being celebrated in the coverage. We may even say she is another sign of the groom's achievements. Guests in seventeen other pictures wear the same damask traditional outfit the groom wears for the couple's portraits.

Figure 6.2. Basil Iredia and Winifred Garland with wedding cake. Courtesy of Ovation International Magazine.

Figure 6.3. Friends of the bride. Courtesy of Ovation International Magazine.

Eminence shows in the spread on both micro and macro levels. The macro scale of representation speaks for itself: the wedding coverage takes up eight of the magazine's one hundred pages; thirty-four of the forty-five pictures contain at least one person or object in blue, apparently the color chosen for the day; and numbered among the guests are a former state governor, two kings, several un-named chiefs, the wife of the Ministry of Solid Minerals, and guests whose names and outfits suggest they are from different parts of the country. Largeness shows in the pictures, too, and not just in the captions: one cake-cutting picture covers a full page (9.5" × 13.25"), and two intimate portraits of the couple take up half a page. The couple's eminent social standing and/or aspiration could also be seen at the smaller level of composition, especially in tightly cropped portraits that detail and enlarge the expensive adornments worn by the newlyweds.

In the full-page cake-cutting photo (see figure 6.2), the cake and the instru-ments of displaying it fill up about two-thirds of the frame. The upright section of an arched plastic green floral vine dotted with three bright pink, plastic fruits outlines the left limit of the frame. The floral theme is repeated in the lower sec-tion of the picture, where a vine of assorted colors trims both the picture and the white table covering on which sits the triple-level vanilla cake, a little off center to the left of the frame, each layer topped with a setting of white hibiscus. The couple, placed to the right of the frame, is in white lace for the groom's kaftan and a damask wrapper from the bosom to the ankle for the bride. The groom's dog-ear-style cap is of the same damask fabric used for the bride's wrapper. Sharply contrasting with the white adornment and decorations are the heavy, bright reddish coral beads hanging on the couple's necks and wrists. The groom wears a pair of necklaces; the bride, three necklaces of different sizes, two wristbands on each hand, and several in different shapes to decorate her hair. The three circles of bead that ring the bride's head suggest a queenly presentation. The beads eclipse the gold necklace, the prominent hairpieces overshadow the gold earrings, and the gold wristwatch recedes into the background in contrast to the coral wristbands. Although they are at slightly different angles, the prominent necklaces, the green floral vine, the spiraling cake pedestal, and the celebrants' upright bodies approximate some symmetry that suggests loftiness. The caption announces that "Culture and Splendor Mix at the Glamorous Traditional Wedding" of Basil Iredia and Winifred Garland. The obvious indices of splendid glamour are the triple-decker cake and the costly beads and clothes, especially the bride's white damask. Culture shows in the styling of the clothes and the beads. The couple's eminence, more properly the groom's, shows unmistakably in the presentation of what he can afford in abundance: a tall cake, yards of expensive clothing, and many pieces of costly body adornments. Mr. Iredia and Ms. Garland may not be chiefs yet, but if *Ovation* readers were to judge from the similarity between the number of beads they could afford and the ones worn by true chiefs present at their wedding, they are well on their way.

There can be no doubt about the intent to project eminence in the semitight portrait of the couple (see figure 6.4). Clothing and jewelry show that these are not ordinary bodies. The couple almost completely fills the frame. The groom's hat and the bride's headgear extend the limits of their heads and shape a balance of color to the lower part of the frame. The faces—distinct markers of individuality—occupy less than a third of the frame; body adornment takes up the rest of the picture. The groom's blue damask agbádá outfit, dotted by many gold floral appliqués, fills a good part of the frame, suggesting the reality of yards of expensive fabric cropped out of the picture. The focus on the bride's body, fully nested in her groom's loving arms, is a little better because her blue blouse and skirt hug her form. Her bright blue outfit contrasts with her husband's more subdued darker hue of the same color. Even so, the parts visible in the picture are framed for wealth: the oval-shaped gold and coral bead necklaces replicate the shape of her face, and her diadem-shaped headpiece completes the obvious queenly showing. In this intimate portrait, as in the cake-cutting piece, expensive adornments invite the viewer to recognize and salute eminence. The individuals wearing the adornments are mere placeholders. To paraphrase the proverbial

Figure 6.4. Basil Iredia and Winifred Garland wedding portrait. Courtesy of
Ovation International Magazine.

metacommentary about body adornment cited at the beginning of this section, the picture hails the significance of the expensive apparel worn by the couple, not Mr. Iredia or Ms. Garland. The couple's faces, as they show in the picture, bear no distinctive marks that the magazine's cameras intend to "capture" for the public's pleasure; the person is not the object of record. This particular couple brings to the reader little that is uniquely Iredia or Garland. The pictures steady the viewers' gaze by emphasizing objects and features that denote high expense: yards of embroidered damask, expensive coral beads that only the regally endowed wallet can buy, and, perhaps most important, a multipage coverage in *Ovation* magazine, the avowed documenter of eminence.

The Businessperson/Politician: Retired General Buba Marwa

The year 2003 was particularly good to the Pittsburgh- and Harvard-educated Buba Marwa because "within those twelve glory-filled months, he commemorated his fiftieth birthday, and honors kept flying at him from all over the world" (*Ovation* no. 70, 22). In 2003, the former military governor of Lagos State and, later, owner of Albarka Airlines and presidential candidate, received an honorary doctorate degree from the University of Nigeria, Nsukka, and the "Outstanding Leadership Award" from the Center for Multicultural Leadership at the University of Kansas, where he endowed the Marwa Africana Lecture Series. He was also decorated with a Nigerian national high honor, Officer of the Federal Republic. Any one of these events—a golden jubilee birthday, a national honor, birth of a child, tenth wedding anniversary, business success, university honors—is a good ground for one great *Ovation* celebration. All of them occurring within one year creates a perfect season.

Although Marwa celebrated all these achievements in 2003, only the two covered in *Ovation* will be discussed here. The cover picture for the end-of-a-glorious-year coverage in issue 70 shows Buba Marwa with his wife and four young children (see figure 6.5). The portrait places the patriarch, the main celebrant, in the middle of the frame. Unlike southern Nigerian men who pose in colorful outfits for family portraits, Marwa wears, as his northern Nigerian compatriots tend to do, a simple black caftan with white stripes. The patriarch's subdued appearance contrasts with his youthful wife's bright complexion and clothing. The children's placement anchors symmetry in the frame. Two girls in matching skirt and blouse outfits are at extreme ends. One of their younger siblings, a boy, stands at the center of the frame behind the parents, placing one hand each on the father and the mother. An infant, placed symmetrically below a male sibling, is held on the father's lap. In the inside spread, two women, identified as Mariam Buba Marwa and Rahmat A. Marwa, are at the end-of-year party. If these are the celebrant's conjugal relations, their relaxed and amicable presence at the celebration further enhances Buba Marwa's stature as an honorable person and affirms the ex-governor's credentials as an excellent manager of his domestic affairs.

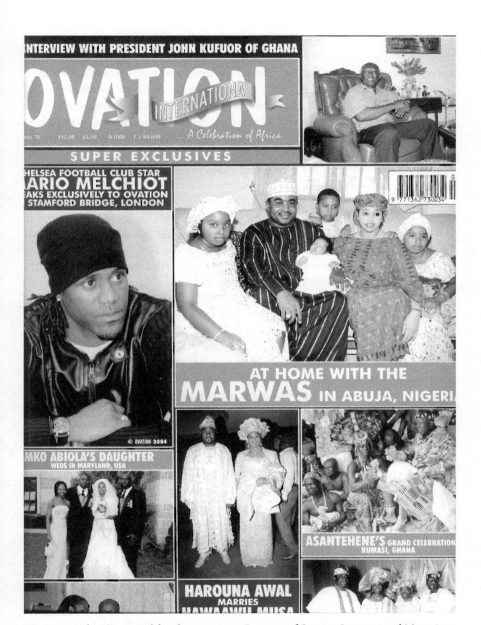

Figure 6.5. Buba Marwa and family cover page. Courtesy of Ovation International Magazine.

Five issues earlier, in *Ovation* issue 65, General Marwa celebrated a 2003 University of Nigeria, Nsukka, honorary doctorate degree and a chieftaincy title from a nearby eastern Nigeria community with friends and well-wishers drawn from many sectors of Nigerian high society. The two honors conferred by the proverbial "gown" and "town" make Marwa into a person of considerable appeal to both high academic and civil systems of recognizing merit. Besides a few snapshots taken at the university's formal ceremony, academics are not featured in the coverage. Unlike in his dull showing in the cover family portrait described above, Marwa puts on bright colors at both the university and community awards. Both events took place in southeastern Nigeria.

The coverage of the university event would have been an ordinary *Ovation* report about an important "Big Man," except that something odd stands out in the half-page lead picture (see figure 6.6). Although not agitated, the celebrant is "active" in a way that does not match the staid repose of *Ovation* high celebrity. Marwa's puzzling, perhaps flippant, pouted lips depict that rare moment in which an *Ovation* subject exhibits a remotely ironic emotion. Of course, Marwa may be squirming pleasantly at the exaggerations and other unduly officious gracefulness the university orator is spouting about him in the formal citation. Nonetheless, within the magazine's conventions, the governor's bemused demeanor surprises. No other picture taken at the university ceremony shows anybody smiling. Other pictures that show Marwa smiling while wearing an academic gown were taken aboard his Albarka Airlines jet. The celebrant's pout is thus remarkable. On one level, Marwa's "un-*Ovation*" behavior at the graduation ceremony belongs to the university, the natural home of pouting, where individuals routinely thump their noses at authorities. In this regard, Marwa is no different from Professor G. F. Mbanefoh, the university vice-chancellor and his official host. The honoree even wears a studious pair of eyeglasses like other academics at the occasion. He stares in the same direction as Mbanefoh. On another level, the depiction is utterly ironic in that the characteristic behavior of university folks that the camera catches Marwa mimicking here is usually severely punished by the celebrant and his military cohorts when they hold public office. These similarities notwithstanding, Mbanefoh's watchful look suggests that he is simply going through the motions. It is also not quite certain that Marwa wants to be at the event; nor does it appear that Mbanefoh, looking away from his honored guest, wants Marwa there.

There are good reasons for the two prominent subjects in this picture not to want to be together in the same frame. Mbanefoh is probably wondering why the university is throwing away its highest honors to a prominent leader of one of the many military juntas that ruined the Nigerian university system. As if to explain Mbanefoh's sour look, the short narrative that accompanies the picture notes the dilapidation of the university—"One hopes that the crumbling physical structures of the university are not symbolic of a more significant deterioration in the

Figure 6.6. G. F. Mbanefoh and Buba Marwa. Courtesy of Ovation International Magazine.

intellectual and academic sophistication that this great university was once known for" (*Ovation*, no 65, 190)—but fails to link the acts of people like the honoree to the deplorable situation. Since *Ovation* is neither *Time* nor *Tell*, the uncritical note cannot rile the reader. Relevant for the current analysis is that this praise picture represents a crack in the magazine's carefully curated depictions of eminence. While it would have been more satisfying to know whether the eminent is having a good time or is dying to get out of the stuffy gown, it cannot but be noticed that Professor Mbanefoh's un-*Ovation* showing in shaggy beard and unglamorous thick and wide glasses constitutes a pictorial warning to anyone aspiring to eminence to not follow him. The professor's face models almost perfectly the stereotypical academic whose unsmiling ways Ebenezer Obey depicted in a very popular song in 1971 with a phrase that later became an epithetic formula for characterizing academic-minded persons: "alákòrí akádá to ńrojú kóíkóí" (the relentlessly sour-looking, hardheaded, studious one). In the cultural narrative that subtends this picture, the individual who follows Mbanefoh will only end up handing out emblems of achievement to those who own airlines and become military governors.

Outside the university, *Ovation*'s typical mannerisms return and all nuanced quibbling is abandoned. At the community ceremony at which Marwa is installed as the first Ochi Oha (Father of the Poor [or People]) of Umuozzi and his wife as the first "Mother of the Poor/People" or Nne Oha, the pictures are unambiguously cheerful.[18] The emblematic portrait of the event transforms Marwa into a modern, eminent southern Nigerian at home in "indigenous" traditions (see figure 6.7). The image contrasts sharply in its colorfulness, massiveness, and pose with the one projected in the "northern" Nigerian family portrait (figure 6.5), depicting the eminent one by himself, not quite disdainful, but definitely not showing much interest in the photographer. Unlike the homely persona projected in the family picture, the chiefly body presented here does not carry a child on its lap. The eminent subject of this portrait sits as if he knows what is required for a "Yorùbá," southwestern Nigerian, photographic preservation of an occasion like this, although the event takes place in the southeast. Marwa is a northern Nigerian Muslim, honored with a "traditional" office in southeastern Nigeria, and appears for his official chieftaincy title in a southwestern Nigerian pose. The magazine thus helps the aspiring president construct a pan-Nigerian public persona. Its management of Marwa's "lofty, famed, and mighty pose" establishes the candidate's credentials for the highest national office, which he was seeking at that time (Trachtenberg, "Brady's Portraits," 250). The key to that presentation is the "Yorùbá traditional pose," which, according to Sprague, requires the photographed person to present him or herself in the

> best traditional dress . . . squarely facing the camera. Both hands are placed on the lap or on top of the knees, and the legs are well apart to spread the garments and display the fabrics. The face has a dignified but distant expression as the eyes look directly at and through the camera. Symbols of the subject's position in Yorùbá society are worn, held, or placed conspicuously near by. The photographer enhances the sense of dignified stateliness by a camera viewpoint either level with the subject's waist or looking slightly upward, as if from the position of one paying homage. ("Yoruba Photography," 54)

Marwa's picture obviously quotes these conventions: his legs are spread wide apart; he sits on an ornately decorated throne-like chair with his title carved on the back; the intricately beaded cane he holds in his right hand is part of the official insignia that include three coral bead necklaces, the toga embroidered in gold, and the red hat also trimmed with gold embroidery; the subject confronts the camera from high above; and his face, although small in comparison to the abundant signs of office, commands the viewer to salute and applaud.

To acknowledge that the photographic presentation I have, after Sprague, called the "Yorùbá pose" here has been in use in West Africa throughout the twentieth century and that it is not reserved for the use of the already eminent but is a compositional convention of respectful self-projection, I would like to draw attention to three other portraits: (1) an early twentieth-century postcard picture of Kwabene Wiafe II, the Omanhene of Ofinsu, Ghana (see figure 6.8); (2) the picture of the king of Ìlá Òràngún taken by Stephen Sprague in the 1970s

Figure 6.7. Buba Marwa, Father of the Poor. Courtesy of Ovation International Magazine.

Figure 6.8. Nana Kwabene Wiafe II, Omanhene of Ofinsu, c. 1900–1915.
Photographer unknown.

Figure 6.9. Ọ̀ràngún of Ìlá. In Stephen F. Sprague, "Yoruba Photography: How the Yoruba See Themselves," *African Arts* 12, no. 1 (November 1978): 52–59. Courtesy of The MIT Press.

(see figure 6.9); and (3) formal portraits of a nonroyal "Yorùbá" female and male also taken by Sprague (see figure 6.10). Except for the beads, each chiefly item of adornment—footrest, footwear, voluminous robes, some headdress item, and a wrist ornament—is repeated in the portraits of General Marwa, the Omanhene, and the Ọ̀ràngún, although the earliest picture is separated from the latest by eighty-eight years. Both the Omanhene and the Ọ̀ràngún, like Marwa, seem pleased with themselves. Unlike Marwa's, their offices are truly "traditional." Neither king has a higher civil office to seek; the Ọ̀ràngún is, by tradition, already "second" only to the Gods. Their sedate, but slightly anxious, showing suggests people with civic responsibilities and contrasts with Marwa's entitled pose.

The Young at Work in Ovation

Funfun niyì eyín
Ẹ̀gùn gàgà*à*gà niyì ọrùn,
Ọmú ṣíkí ṣìkì ṣíkí niyì obìnrin.

Being white enriches the teeth
Stimulating gracefulness makes the neck desirable,
Fulsome bouncy breasts make a woman desirable.
   (Abimbola, *Ìjìnlẹ̀ Ohùn Ẹnu Ifá: Apá Kinní*, 54)

Figure 6.10. Two Subjects in Yorùbá Pose. In Stephen F. Sprague, "Yoruba Photography: How the Yoruba See Themselves," *African Arts* 12, no. 1 (November 1978): 52–59. Courtesy of The MIT Press.

Each issue of *Ovation* magazine is almost always evenly divided between the wealthy old and the aspiring young, with the latter set usually depicted as getting married, graduating from college, busy at work in some entrepreneurial venture—typically fashion, charismatic Christianity, and real estate—at rest in their palatial homes, and, on rare occasions, at funerals. Except for celebrity preachers and sports stars, many of the young are relatives of the old and wealthy. Events that are anchored by young persons and do not involve sociocultural rites of passage are often accompanied by short interviews—that usually read like paid advertorials—about their motivation for getting into a particular business, the risks and rewards of entrepreneurship, and advice for others who might want to follow similar paths to success. Pictorially, *Ovation*'s celebration of the rising young depicts agile bodies at work or at play. In intimate close-ups, youths tend to stare into the lens more directly than older people. Because they frequently wear form-fitting, "Westernized" outfits that one rarely finds on *Ovation*'s older subjects, it is not difficult to conclude that the presentation of younger women's bodies signals some sensual, sometimes understated, erotic attraction that is lacking in pictures of older males.

Figure 6.11. Modupe Ozolua. Courtesy of Ovation International Magazine.

The front-page coverage of Modupe Ozolua's body enhancement business in issue 34 presents the magazine's quintessential story of the young (see figure 6.11). Pictures that emphasize conspicuously stylized means of breast presentation, all modeled by Ms. Ozolua, constitute half of the coverage. The cover picture emphasizes Ms. Ozolua's breasts as the main body part at the center of the frame.[19] In the inside spread, ornate couches and revealing formal wear made out of lace and velvet worn in suggestive poses create an ambience of seductive attraction. Every pose in the Ozolua spread points back at the breast. While erotic responses cannot be ruled out completely, overt sexuality is not the object. There is no mistaking in these pictures a photographic translation of the epithetic enthusiasm for the fulsome bouncy breast cited above. The social good served by Ms. Ozolua's body enhancement business dominates the spread. In the accompanying inter-view, Ms. Ozolua restates her business plan and the satisfaction it has brought her: "Before, my breasts were a B-cup, but today thanks to cosmetic surgery I have full C-Cup/Small D size boobs! I am extremely proud and pleased with them!" (*Ovation* no. 34, 19). She appeals directly to the older, justly eminent, fe-male readers of the magazine who might otherwise think that the lines about the desirability of firm breasts do not apply to them: "Do you see a young, hot 18-year old girl, instantly hate her guts and then think to yourself, 'That girl thinks she is hot, she should have seen me when I was younger!'" According to Ozolua, who-ever wants a hot body can get it at her shop.[20] In short, fulsome bouncy breasts (ọmú ṣíkí ṣìkì ṣíkí) are available to any woman who wants them. Daring to com-bat signs of age, she seems to be telling rich and powerful women, should be a new sign of eminence.

Consciously designed or not, the magazine's presentation of Ozolua extends and revises "traditional" conceptions of the woman's breasts. Ozolua herself connects working for, and profiting from, the woman's beautiful and eroticized body to the task of motherhood and attributes her motivation to succeed to her strong desire for her son's comfort. She says: "I am a woman who is set on build-ing an empire for my son to rule and control when he gets big" (*Ovation* no. 34, 21). In other words, her devotion to the profitable business of reversing the effects of childbearing on the woman's body is driven by motherhood. In the character-istic *Ovation* form, the spread praises youthful Ozolua's leisure and work in ways that argue that one cannot be divorced from the other: the woman who desires a great body—the type "hot" enough to appear in the magazine—and works for it in a certain way, is bound to profit from it.

Other emblematic pictures of young females fill every issue of the magazine. Like Modupe Ozolua, the women are often pictured in their places of business or shown modeling their products, which often have to do with body adornment. For *Ovation*'s younger women, pleasure is work, and work is pleasant. They all look contented, appear to be in motion, headed somewhere, radiating confidence. They are always in top shape and, by implication, in good health. While these may be clichéd poses of fashion photography, in *Ovation* they signify the burgeoning entrepreneur.

The picture of the upwardly mobile, thirty-one-year-old Ayo Ojo, a London-based securities trader who is said to have been instrumental in starting the Gambian stock exchange, presents in issue 53 the *Ovation* young man par excel-lence (see figure 6.12). His dark suit bespeaks success and modernization. The open-neck shirt alludes to someone not yet given to stuffiness. The face is clean-shaven and the hair is closely cropped; the fashionable rimless eyewear suggests a studiousness that is not quite academic. The trophy in the blurry background alludes to a triumph of some sort. Ojo looks down and slightly away from the

Figure 6.12. Ayo Ojo. Courtesy of Ovation International Magazine.

lens to suggest that the camera is not that consequential. He looks prosperous but not in Marwa's office-seeking ways. The image of quiet achievement and understated elegance that Ojo intends to portray can be gleaned in this exchange with the magazine:

QUESTION: You look very prosperous. Have you made a lot of money from this business?

ANSWER: Prosperity can be defined in various ways. Intellectually I have gained. Relationships wise I have gained. In terms of traveling widely, I have also gained. The bottom line that people want to know is how much I have made. But if you know my strength, then I'll be unable to bargain with you. I can say it is a situation where I am able to make a good living and maintain my standard of living but more important I am able to live my dream which is making impact on mankind. If I tell you exactly how much I have made, I might not be able to sleep anymore. My phone would ring several times. So, it's better left to the imagination. (*Ovation* no. 53, 158)

If they are read as a sort of self-captioning to the picture, Ojo's words seem to be baiting the reader with a promise to take the young to where they have not been but should desire to be.

The Portrait of the Publisher as an Eminent Person

The profitable pictorial chronicling of the ways of the eminent (or those aspiring to that status) has made *Ovation*'s publisher and editor-in-chief one of the high, and possibly, mighty. Délé Mọmọdù is photographed so frequently as an eminent guest at events covered in his magazine that it is safe to surmise that his name and person are extensions of the brand. It looks like the best way to announce high social standing in southwestern Nigeria is to be seen in Délé Mọmọdù's magazine with Délé Mọmọdù. The best way to show the Nigerian world that your event is truly eminent is to invite Délé Mọmọdù, photograph his appearance, and ensure that the picture is published in Mọmọdù's magazine. At some events, the publisher wears the event outfit, aṣọ ẹbí, and makes himself part of the event he is reporting. In the magazine's coverage of the government's reception held in honor of Queen Elizabeth II's official trip to Nigeria in December 2003, Mọmọdù, wearing attire made in Nigeria's national colors of green and white, was photographed chatting with the queen. The publisher also appears very frequently on the cover, usually in the top right corner, after receiving an achievement recognition award. Mọmọdù's face, it seems, has become a valuable part of the social successes his magazine vends. The publisher's photographed appearances at the events covered in his magazines subliminally indicates his intimacy with eminence.

But Mọmọdù, once described by another editor and publisher as "one of the best dressed men in Nigeria" (Bakare, "At Home in London," 63), would have appeared in a magazine like *Ovation* if he did not publish one. Like those celebrated in his magazine, Mọmọdù describes himself as a "risk taker": "I like to gamble in the sense that I take risks. Like *Ovation*. It is a big risk . . . Life itself is a risk" (64). Like his patrons, he proudly displays his tangible signs of success. He told Bákàrè, *Encomium*'s editor:

I'm dying to have a Bentley. I've refused to drive a car in this town [London] because all I want is a Bentley. At 42, I've seen people drive such cars when they're much younger. In Ife, we used to see the then Prince Okunade Sijuwade, before he became the king, driving a Bentley. I am hoping that soon I'll be able to afford a Bentley whether old or new. (Bakare, "At Home in London,"64)

Between the time the interview was granted and publication, Mọmọdù achieved his dream. Inserted in parentheses is the following editorial statement: "And he has bought one" (64). These words reveal the operating assumption of *Ovation*: distributing positive images of the eminent, especially representations of the good life they purchase with money, can inspire readers to desire to be like them. Eminence is not an abstraction; it consists of the recognition that tangible acquisitions compel. *Ovation*'s pictures, like Matthew Brady's portraits in nineteenth-century New York, procure and dispense "vicarious excitement, a glimpse into the lives that seem magical, glamorous, and mysterious" (Trachtenberg, "Brady's Portraits," 231).

Ovation's editor acts like a self-conscious panegyrist. Like the traditional poet, Mọmọdù places himself at the center of his operations, fully involved in sourcing events to be covered and supervising how the product will be delivered. In striving to be like his patrons, Mọmọdù illustrates a profound difference between the oral poet and the magazine entrepreneur. In the traditional hierarchy, the panegyrist is by definition uneminent; he or she is not a bọrọkìnní. Whereas the praise singer of the past—often called alágbe (or, beggar) in Yorùbá—was a maker and seller of other people's eminent "aura," the contemporary photo praise portraitist sells reproducible, tangible items that can, independent of the patron's presence, be multiplied, packaged, and sold (or exhibited) many times over. The portraits are intellectual properties of the publication and not the subject of praise. Unlike the traditional praise singer, the editor controls an image brokerage. All that a traditional poet can sell is a poetic reputation that cannot transform into the type of eminence that underwrites his or her work. Although the traditional praise singer manufactures verbal images solely for others to consume, the contemporary editor sells as part of his trade his own tangible image as a high achiever whose praiseworthiness is not tied to his expertise but what he has acquired with his profits. Whereas chanting appellative poetry connotes the performer's lack of signal eminence in the traditional model, the modern commodity system enables the magazine editor and publisher to convert images into wealth-yielding products such that editorship of a successful praise-singing vehicle itself unequivocally signifies eminence.

Visuality in Orality

Whether they are construed as a historical unconscious amenable to modifications, or as a deliberately chosen approach to recording historical experience, orality-to-literacy paradigms, as I noted in chapter 2, have enabled theorists of

African culture to create unified accounts of African cultures from premodernity to postmodernity. However, my presenting the use of photographs in contemporary southwestern Nigerian magazine culture as an extension of the traditional panegyric form is not meant to add another layer of evidence to the perpetuation of oral traditions in Yorùbá consciousness, but to describe the workings of intermediality in contemporary southwestern Nigerian culture (Belting, "Image, Medium, Body"). I do not think of the historically antecedent appellative tradition of praising the eminent in Yorùbá oríkì as lurking deep in the cultural psyche of readers and publishers until Délé Mọ̀mọ́dù enlivens and brings it into consciousness in the print magazine business. To the contrary, I seek to clarify that visual sensibility is a major resource in oral traditions. What the "mouth" proclaimed in traditional appellative poems, particularly those composed about the eminent, relied on what the "eyes" passed on to it. Vision, as it were, serves as the basis of poetics in Yorùbá praise chants of the eminent (oríkì bọ̀rọ̀kìnní).

In Babalọlá's *Àwọn Oríkì Bọ̀rọ̀kìnní*, figures of representation derived from sight are the most frequently used means of establishing characteristic qualities of poetic subjects of praise, even when the distinctions are abstractions like grace, kindness, mirthfulness, and so forth. To highlight the diminutive physical stature of a socially eminent person, for instance, the praise singer speaks about the advantages of a hawk's light weight to its visibly dexterous flight maneuvers, and describes the praised as "pẹ́ńpẹ́ bí àṣá" (weightless like a swift hawk in motion). By presenting swiftness and smallness as essential to the eminent being of a hawk, the simile naturalizes remarkable predation and decouples social distinction from large physique. A tall person is likened to the broad side of a bolt of textile ("namu bí ọwọ́ aṣọ"). A full-bodied man is said to be rotund like a gaboon viper ("kọ́rọ́bọ́tọ́ bí ọká"). Like the hawk imagery noted above, this simile ties predatory, remarkable eminence to visibility. Two common epithets for highlighting sincerity as a praiseworthy attribute liken the subject to unblemished whiteness: "abínú ífunfun bí ẹmu" (one whose inside is white like palm-wine foam) or "abìsàlẹ̀ ikùn bíi tákàdá" (one whose inside is like a plain sheet of [white] writing paper). A brave warrior is "àdá ńlá b'èèkù yàmù" (hefty cutlass with a mighty handle); someone who can hold his or her drink is "olójú iná" (one with fire in the eyes). A cunning individual is said to be "kọ́í bi igun ilé" (caution prone like the edge of a house). In performance contexts, these epithets are used as if they were proper names. Thus the sincere person is not merely compared to palm-wine froth; with the epithet expressed grammatically as a nominative, the sincere person is addressed directly as if his or her name is one who has converted his or her inside into some palm-wine-froth-whiteness that all can see. The drinkard is not a fiery-eyed person but one whose eyes are made of fire's redness. The nominalization processes convert visual observations into evocative peculiarities that turn on specular perception.

In a poem dedicated to Prince Afọlábí (Babalọlá, *Àwọn Oríkì Bọ̀rọ̀kìnní*, 17–20), three physical attributes, all drawn from sight seeing, are used to define the man: pitch dark complexion, bulky physique, and short height. It is obvious in the poem that the prince is noticeably short, maybe darker than average, and a little paunchy. Two epithets, repeated every fifteen lines on average, remark on his complexion: one whose darkness crowns his eminence ("dúdúparíọlá") (lines 4, 50, 71); one whose darkness rivals that of sought after blue beads ("adúdúbás-ẹ̀gìṣọ̀gbà") (lines 20, 26, 61). Both terms conjoin the visible pitch of Prince Afọlábí's complexion and the extent of his wealth in a single semantic cluster such that the ratio of his wealth to others' matches that of his dark complexion to others'. The depth of skin complexion, in short, projects vast wealth. Because the short prince—"kúkúrú bí ikú" (stumpy like death)—probably has to look up during conversations with taller people, the poet shifts focus away from Afọlábí's clear physical disadvantage to his visible, confident strides ("kọ́únkí ọmọ"). Although of a slight physique ("igi jẹ́gẹ́dẹ́" [unremarkable sapling]), no one dares to cheat him ("akérémáṣeíyànjẹ" [tiny, but impossible to fit on the tip of a skewer]) (lines 22, 55). His roundness—"kọ́rọ́bọ́tọ́ bí ọká" (lines 12, 31)—neither implies softness nor invites a caress but, because it is like that of a viper, conceals the ability to strike the unaware who misconstrue the short height and contemplate denying him his due. Prince Afọlábí confronts his adversaries and stands his ground ("aríwọnmásàá") (lines 26, 41, 62, 72) and never betrays fear ("aríwọnmáṣojo") (lines 45, 66). As it is in other epithets, sight or vision (rí) is the active verb in these two descriptions. The unnamed enemies that Prince Afọlábí stares down are probably not the poet's phantom creations but most likely his business rivals, political opponents, other palace position seekers, litigation adversaries, or even those competing with him for a lover's attention. The identities of these persons can be determined through interviews with either the chanter or other members of the community. But these details are circumstantial to the formulaic epithet and not essential to the defining activities that those not familiar with Prince Afọlábí can still visualize and appreciate.

Prince Afọlábí's visibly large retinue of followers seems to have awed the praise singer who made this attribute the second main sign of his eminence. Besides the five bald references to his royal birth ("ọmọ ọba") (lines 14, 21, 41, 46, 60), his being a favorite son comes up nearly every five lines. Sometimes, especially when he is hailed as one who ordered a king for a father ("abibabáijọba") (lines 4, 16, 55, 64), the description portrays Prince Afọlábí as if his being born to a king is something he made to happen willfully. The most effective epithet of Prince Afọlábí's royal birth involves a keen visual sensibility and feeling ("ajírinníbi") (lines 18, 65, 74), or one who rises every morning dripping auspicious birth. Prince Afọlábí cannot be mistaken here for a sponge passively swollen by an inflow of water; he is instead a visible center of a largesse-dispensing ("dripping") system.

The poetic characterizations summarized above simultaneously describe individuals and inscribe, like portrait photographs, social identity. Static qualities like height and complexion are conjured in visually pleasing ways, and imageries of visible movements—a hawk's preying on hapless animals and a slow motion dispensation of favors—animate the characterization.

The traditional poets use visual contrasts to order attributes and to convert prosaic signs of high status—money, big house, and royal parentage—into depictions of eminence. The physically challenged Prince Afọlábí is obviously well-endowed materially. But stating the bare facts of wealth and royal birth alone does not constitute praise poetry. The poet makes memorable texts out of the facts by creating verbal pictures out of visual contrasts and juxtaposition. The tall and long-necked Fágbèmókùn, a king of Ìpetumodù, is "ajígalọ́rùn bí ìyàwó" (he that is long-necked like a nubile bride) (Babalọlá, *Àwọn Oríkì Bọ̀rọ̀kìnní*, 32); the curvature of his back is compared to a mountain peak ("tẹ́ lẹ́hìn bí òkè") (32). The poet associates Rùfáí Àjàní Adégoróyè's tallness with the volume of textile needed for adorning his body ("agùntáṣọílò") (tall enough to use swathes of textile) (46). In the Prince Afọlábí text, the poet invents a causal link between the prince's sparse physical presence, dark skin (dúdú), and social eminence (ọlá)—dúdúparíọlá—as if the skin complexion is deliberately acquired to frame the upper limits of (ìparí) of wealth. All who can see should have noticed Prince Afọlábí's dark skin. What they would never have known until told by the poet is that the prince orders the complexion to polish his eminence. The phrasing turns the prince's exceptional skin shade into an index of exceptional wealth. When the poet hails Prince Afọlábí as handsome and monied ("ọ̀lẹ́wàlówó") (17), both the beautiful dark skin and money are used to denominate eminence in a complementary fashion. A similar logic is evident in the description of the fleet-footed Àbá-nikán-ńdá-Àmìdá as "Igbó fi dúdú ṣọlá" (The dense wood's eminence shows in its darkness) (49) and Sèèdùn Olúwòó as "adúbíàrán" (dark-skinned like a bolt of shimmering velvet) (53). Prince Afọlábí's magnanimity is also constructed with a visual contrast: "atóbi-má-rànán-ró" (hefty but not vengeful) (18). The heftiness of this phrase refers to his social standing, not to his physical stature. The epithet juxtaposes a "naturally" intimidating visual proportion to an equally noticeable social largeness, but softens the intimidating appearance with adorable moderate behaviors.

Praise poems of the eminent always place the subject of adulation, usually with a large retinue of admirers, at the center of a set of activities that confirm eminence. A large group of associates drawn from the whole town fills the verbal space that portrays Àbá-nikán-ńdá-Àmìdá as one who has a whole town of cohorts to accompany him for a glamorous showing-off ("ò-ré-gbé-ìlú-ṣe-fújà") (Babalọlá, *Àwọn Oríkì Bọ̀rọ̀kìnní*, 49). Rùfáí Adégoróyè is praised as fit for picking and sustenance like a vast piece of hide ("ató ìti bí awọ") (46) in an epithet that characterizes its subject not by his own acts but by those of his admirers. The adulated, by analogy, is the skin on which the retinue works continuously for sustenance and the central factor in the observation of the activities that only eminence can underwrite.

Countless Yorùbá proverbs urge individuals to give due attention to visual self-presentation as a means of controlling how they will like to be perceived by others. Going by the letter of some of the sayings, visual self-presentation and self-composition are not unlike names about which one must show the utmost care. The proverb "Ìrínisí nìsọnilójọ̀" (How one is viewed circumscribes the esteem one garners) blatantly associates projected self-worth to visual bodily presentation, particularly physique and adornment; abundant midriff in a male still suggests well-being in some quarters, and opulent buttocks in a female might indicate a comfortable marriage. Necklaces of deep-blue glass beads (sègi) imply opulence. Body art, clothing, headgear, and footwear, the estimation of whose social worth depends heavily on sight, are deemed to be reliable markers of achieved or aspired social status in men and women; hence the beaded crown shows a king, and the variety of necklace worn depicts the type of chief ("adé orí la fi í mọba, ìlèkè la fi í mọ̀ 'jòyè' "). The shape of headgear can indicate age, social status, and vocation that the wearer wants to project at a particular time. As noted earlier, one remarkably counterintuitive proverb ties the concept of the person as socially cognized— progeny, wealth, profession—to visual presentation and self-showing by flatly declaring that "Aṣọ là ńkí, a à kí'nìyàn" (Verbal pleasantries acknowledge the clothing and not the person). In the following lines, the cotton plant is praised for the honor it does to the human body, even at interment:

> Òwú là bá gbìn; a à gbin'dẹ (We should plant cotton; brass is not virile)
> Òwú là bá gbìn; a à gbìn'lèkè (We should plant cotton; beads are not virile)
> Àtidẹ, àtì lèkè, kò séyìí tíí bá ni í dé horo òkú (Neither brass nor bead follows the dead to the grave)
> Aṣọ nìkàn níí bá ní i lọ (Only cotton is that loyal)[21]

These lines connect appearance and clothing adornment to organic planting and harvesting. The most loyal acquisition, as far as the body's social life is concerned, is clothing, the epitome of bodily adornment that accompanies the dead to the grave. The lines rank perishable, organic cotton higher than materially more durable brass and beads, probably because clothes define social existence in inimitable ways. Systems of clothing obey nature and culture and follow a life trajectory. Brass and beads, although subject to the wearers' caprices too, are products of mere technical know-how.[22]

Yorùbá oral traditions bind the mouth to what the eye has seen ("Ohun tójú bá rí ló yẹ kẹ́nu ó sọ") and never the other way around. Within this logic, only a lying mouth speaks first and then hunts for a confirming sight. Of course, a "sweet" mouth can embellish figures of sight. If, however, the mouth's "sweetness" intrudes as much as to be suspect, the speaker's integrity and intent are usually the problem and not spiced speech as such. Why is the mouth subjected to the rule of the eye, given that the mouth produces something "tangible" but the eye does not? The simple answer is that the eyes' work passes through other organs like the mouth, the hand (drawing, sculpting), or the foot (drawing, dancing, movements, etc.) in order for other seeing people to share in the reproduction. Results of the eyes' observations are preserved and materially realized only in the movement of manufacturing organs that cannot on their own completely make things up. Every instance of painting, poetry, and so forth, accounts, as it were, for some funds earlier drawn from the eyes. Imageries make the debts tangible and re-present to the eye what the eye made possible in the first place. Thus Yorùbá idioms express accomplished stylization in fashion, sculpting, painting, architecture, and so forth, as debts repaid to the eyes ("jẹ ojú nígbèsè"). Poetry, oratory, and music are never represented analogously as owing the ears or mouth a debt. In the Prince Afọlábí text discussed above, the poet's eyes saw a short man, but the debt recorded by the praise poem describes a person who cannot be cheated by taller people despite his height challenges. That is, poetic words do not exactly replicate what the eyes saw because the proportional scaling demanded, even in stylized distortions, in sculpture and other grossly visual arts, does not apply in poetry. In the poet's mouth, Prince Afọlábí's diminutiveness signals his invulnerability to maneuvers of the physically tall; his exceedingly dark complexion enters the verbal/poetic "studio" as the equivalent of expensive glass beads. In short, the poetic mouth always says something different from what the eyes see.

A comparative analysis of the situation in another West African society, even if brief, might be helpful here. When André Magnin asked the celebrated Malian photographer Malick Sidibé to confirm the critical consensus that he distinguished himself artistically in postindependence Malian portrait photography by recording without prejudice the processes of rapid modernization embodied in the lives of the youths, the theory of practice he offered defies the modernity and tradition dichotomy pursued in standard critical commentaries on African photography:

> I always photographed with the intention of satisfying the customer. All my photographs were done with perspective. I wanted and felt obliged to give my clients their very best image. As in my drawings I looked for beauty in my photographic images. A client who poses any old how will not be satisfied with his picture, it will not please him and he will not return to the studio. So it is up to the photographer to look for a good position, a good angle, to limit the faults so that the portrait shows him to his best advantage. That is in his

interest and my interest. That is why *I say that the photographer, the portraitist and reporter that I am, must be like a "griot." I must flatter and beautify the client as does a "griot."* (Magnin and Sidibé, "In My Life," 79; emphasis added)

Probably surprised by this "poetic" view of portraiture, which joins a quintessentially modern machine of ego projection to a "traditional" verbal practice, Magnin pushes for further clarification: "The 'griots' form a caste; they are considered to be genealogists, historians. They have a social function which the photographer does not" (Magnin and Sidibé, "In My Life," 79). But Sidibé insists on the similarities between his vocation and those of the traditional raconteur: "The 'griots' can allow themselves everything because they know the history of the families. It is true, a photographer does not achieve this dimension, only producing an image. If the client is satisfied the photograph is published and I am a good photographic 'griot'" (79). In the rest of the interview, Sidibé discloses nothing more about his aesthetics despite Magnin's prodding for how the photographer "revealed" the youths' "expression and well-being" (79). When further pressed to "speak of the technical aspects of photography," Sidibé responds with an account of his favorite cameras, films, and lens (80).[23]

I find Sidibé's words striking because they suggest that photography, like praise poems, traffics in egos and selves[24] without concealing its own material, commodity status. Photographic portraits and appellative poetry, many times driven by the profit motive, both position bodily adornments, fashion sense, professional calling, fame, notoriety, and other measures of desire and achievement as self-projection validators. Portraits, verbal or photographic, present themselves as fulfillers of self-yearning and aspirational needs, perhaps the most important of which is the urge to have a portrait taken or a few praise lines chanted.[25] Although Tagg is writing about portrait photography's origin in painting, the following words apply as well to the verbal panegyric: "To 'have one's portrait done' was one of the symbolic acts by which individuals from the rising social classes made their ascent visible to themselves and others and classed themselves among those who enjoyed social status" (Tagg, *The Burden of Representation*, 37). In Sidibé's Mali, at least to the photographer, the progression from praise poetry to the studio portrait is undeniable.[26]

After Tradition, before *Ovation*

Verbal imaginings did not leap in one clean jump from the raconteur's lips onto either Sidibé's portraits or the pages of Mọ̀mọ́dù's *Ovation*. It is undeniable, for example, that *Drum* magazine, which originated in South Africa and had such a successful run in West Africa that it spurned self-sustaining versions in Nigeria and Ghana early in the 1960s, is a crucial predecessor for *Ovation*. The Nigerian edition of *Drum* continued until the mid-1980s, when adverse economic conditions rendered glamour magazine publishing unprofitable for a long while. Fleming and Falola credit *Drum*'s privileging of pictures over written text for its success in West Africa. They argue that generous photo layouts and the limited use of written texts enabled the magazine "to attract both literate and illiterate readers" ("Africa's Media Empire," 153). According to Graeme Addison, *Drum*'s written contents were of three parts: "panegyrics, probes, and prose" ("Drum Beat," 1464). *Drum*, like *Ovation*, used photographs to celebrate the achievements of musicians, political activists, and trade union leaders. Given the difficult conditions faced by black populations in mid-twentieth-century South Africa, these categories about exhaust achievement avenues that were open to black people. *Drum*'s probes of the appalling conditions of black laborers in the mines, and of the underhanded ways apartheid was rapidly consolidating itself, created a sort of "reverse panegyric" in which telling photographic depictions provide undeniable evidence of the sordid state of African affairs. The lives of the urban lumpen also commanded attention both in prose and photographic illustrations of the lives of the poor in Johannesburg shebeens. The documented wedding ceremonies, drinking, and even murders serve as corollaries of the protests and violent state victimizations, which included imprisonment and savage killing. In essence, the distinction between *Drum*'s "probes" and its panegyrics may not be as sharp as Addison suggests.

One other magazine that probably influenced the content and format of *Ovation* is the short-lived *Root*, launched in London in 1979 with the financial backing of Nigerians and intended to be the black British equivalent of the American *Ebony*. As Hal Austin, its original editor, recalls, *Root* wanted to showcase "the increasing number of young people who were succeeding in their professional and business lives" and whose "lifestyle . . . was neither middle class nor bourgeois but, rather, reflected their achievement" ("The Launch of *Root*," 1473). To use the language of African cultural criticism, *Root* aimed to praise and hail black eminence. Like *Drum*, *Root* suffered political criticisms that its pages were irrelevant to the lives of the majority of its audience and that it was "the chronicle of a hedonistic lifestyle assumed by a growing number of young people who, for whatever reason, did not want to face the harsh realities of being black in Britain," had somehow "'betrayed' the cause," and had "sold out to the white man for a safe job and the sham of respectability" (1473). Austin argued that the hostility misperceived *Root*'s purpose and misread profound changes within black Britain.[27] The magazine focused intensely, as *Ovation* would do decades later, on "the social scene: fashion shows, dances, parties, foreign holidays, a renewed interest in clothes" (1474).

Austin's retrospective response to *Root*'s critics reveals a very useful Nigerian connection. He says that he was able to contain criticisms from "ill-informed and vindictive" black Britons with his steadfast belief that the magazine's reading of the social pulse was accurate, although the magazine's inadequate income could not sustain for long its "basic conceit" of "the pretense of a thriving, young organization of dynamic, go-getting people" ("The Launch of *Root*," 1474). The editors were confident that, given time, they could nurture to profitability the new, black, and wealthy brand they wanted to sell. Unanticipated was the meddling of their unnamed Nigerian financiers, who sought to use the magazine to advocate unspecified "dubious" politics. Believing that the funds they were spending were a "'gift' from one of the Nigerian benefactors," the editors held in August 1982 a party whose grandeur belied the magazine's precarious finances. While owing printers and typesetters, *Root* hosted an £18,000 anniversary celebration that it then went on to cover in its pages "with accompanying photographs of the guests at play" (1474).[28] Austin's frustratingly muted descriptions of developments thereafter goes thus: "In the October issue, as usual, I did a report of the party with accompanying photographs of the guests at play. However, a number of those photographs were of Nigerian politicians and businessmen, many of them married and almost all Muslims. At the time the directors were in Nigeria, and only saw the contents of that issue when they returned to Britain. Then all hell broke loose" (1474). Although "none of the Nigerians had complained about their pictures being included in the issue," the board resolved that "in future all copy to be included in the magazine to be vetted by the three directors before the finished artwork went to the studio" (1474). The details of *Root*'s short life span show that rich Nigerians got involved in a celebrity vehicle far from their homeland at a time when nothing like that existed in their country. It is also important that the disagreements that, according to Austin, destroyed the magazine revolve around the proper control of images as Nigerian financiers, rightly or wrongly, construed it.

Ovation appeared seventeen years later in London with a Nigerian focus and a Nigerian editor, publisher, and financiers. Its editors did not have to accommodate the political reckonings of a British racial minority. Being a political exile, *Ovation*'s publisher and editor had a contingent relationship with London. His chosen subjects were high achievers of the newer black diaspora, most of whom did not reside permanently in London. Like *Root*, *Ovation* did not enjoy the support of large advertising agencies; unlike *Root*, it had the support of wealthy and well-connected Nigerians to whom praise singing was a cultural given.

It is worth noting, of course, that profiting from widely circulated photographs has a long history in Africa. N. Walwin Holm opened the first studio in Accra in 1883, and in 1897 became "the first African photographer" to be granted membership in the Royal Photographic Society of Great Britain. George Da Costa opened shop in Lagos in 1895. F. R. C. Lutterodt, who also operated in Cameroon and Gabon, and Fernando Po, owned a studio in Accra. The precocious Alphonse Lisk-Carew, at eighteen years of age, started a photo shop in Freetown in 1905.

Malick Sidibé, who started in the mid-twentieth century in Bamako, captures the commercial inspiration for popular photography in Africa with these apt words: "it wasn't the love of the camera that first drew Africans to photography, it was the promise of financial gain and respectable employment" (Lamunierè, *You Look Beautiful Like That*, 22).

African Photography in High Theory

Until very recently, cultural commentators generally neglected African photographic practice, mainly because the ethnographic route through which other arts like music and the plastic forms gained academic attention faced peculiar difficulties in photography.[29] It was assumed that the mechanical nature of the relationship of the camera to the photographed subject is so direct and impersonal that it leaves no room for the insertion of any aesthetically significant differences that can be attributed to culture. The situation began to change gradually toward the end of the twentieth century, with African photographers gaining prestigious attention in European and American museums and galleries. Even then, creating an African photographic criticism is somewhat tricky. Writing about the Africanness of a photograph for no reason other than the historical contingency of the photographer and the subject living in Bamako, for example, is bound to trigger the suspicion of essentialism, that inordinately feared term whose virtues have been rendered ambiguous in postmodern critiques of nationalism. The absence of precolonial practices of mechanized "light writing," which critics could argue are cultural antecedents for Seydou Keita and Malick Sidibé (Bamako), Alphonso Lisk-Carew (Freetown), Sunmi Smart-Cole (Lagos), and others, creates a historiographic hardship that other historians of Africanist art and culture do not suffer. These are the historical conditions pressing on the following statement:

> For photographs to have any meaning beyond their functions as memento mori and as instruments of evidence and record, we must acknowledge another stabilizing factor: the gaze, that which Gordon Bleach has aptly termed "the negotiated space of viewing." When we take on Africa as the subject and African photographers as the interlocutors in this "negotiated space of viewing," the difficulty of interpreting what has been encoded as visual truth arises. Because there is now no prior existence of a language per se with which to discuss photographic activity in Africa (although photography in Africa is no different from that in any region of the world), what is revealed in interpreting the gaze or the field of vision is its implicit contest for the power of ownership. (Enwezor and Zaya, "Colonial Imagery," 21)

Enwezor and Zaya are trying to manage a paradox: If the photographic phenomenon has no peculiarity in Africa—since the mechanical processes need not be tropicalized to produce the necessary effect—why should, and how can, the critic speak of African photography? They argue their way out of the contradiction by recommending that photographic practices should be seen not as completely natural chemical reactions but as the result of the immersion of chemical and optical machineries in local sociocultural conditions. While, on the one hand, local history is not a precondition for photographs to form physically, on the other hand, subjects presenting themselves to the camera, and the circulation of photographs as objects of reflection, subsist almost completely on cultural (and historical) contingencies. But as Batchen argues, in iterative motions like "camera placement, the position of the photographer in relationship to the subject, and the 'natural' environment selected by the photographer to enact the subject's authenticity," it is obvious that capturing difference is inherent to photography (*Burning with Desire*, 25–26).[30]

Enwezor and Zaya make sense of mid-twentieth-century African photographic aesthetics by appealing to terms broadly drawn from Francophone postcolonial thought. They contrast representative Malian photographers with Négritude poets and adjudge the photographers liberated from the need to evoke "tradition" to justify their aesthetic choices.[31] Photo portraitists, unlike the poets, constructed anxiety-free, modern Africans:

> Nowhere in their works do we detect the sitters' desires to live in that so-called Negro-African museum. In fact, what we see is their reluctance to be confined in such a natural-history or ethnographic setting. Looking at the majestic portraits of the worldly men and sophisticated men and women who frequented the studios of these photographers, we find the unique intersection and cross-referencing of notions of tradition and modernity. Even Senghor himself sat for a portrait by Salla Casset. These photographs produced just before World War II and thereafter contest Senghor's Africanité, an ideal rooted in almost incontestable, primal authenticity, which has drawn from the powerful residues of oratory and represented by the griot and traditional folklore. (Enwezor and Zaya, "Colonial Imaginary, Tropes of Disruption," 28)

"External" factors of intellectual milieu and "internal" close reading considerations do not quite support this historiography. The combative response of Anglophone writers and critics of Senghor's Négritude would not unfold until after 1960, the closing year of Enwezor and Zaya's historical period. Moreover, the work of the alleged anti-Négritudists does not oppose Senghor's as it is starkly presented here.[32] Furthermore, the claim that Négritude is "rooted in an almost incontestable, primal authenticity" grossly distorts the true shape of the archive, at least in poetry.

One can easily dismiss the notion that post–World War II African photography approaches modernization without tradition's baggage, as if the camera magically robbed the photographed subjects of their facility of received codes of self-presentation. A glance at the pictures reveals that the subjects these artists photographed constructed majesty mainly in traditional attire: bellbottom pants, ill-fitting suits, and the use of electronic gadgets as signs of affluence mainly speak of youthfulness, daring, risk, and sometimes mockery. In the Malian portraits, grandly showing does not seem to be the aim of subjects in oddly fitting jackets. Loftiness comes from codes lifted from tradition: flowing robes for men, elegant boubous for women, ample physique and healthy children for both genders. Beyond the youths' donning nonnative casual wear like swimsuits, plastic flowers, garish sunglasses, and so forth, one cannot find "textual" evidence for the submission that there is a "vehement cultural and ideological" dispute between the photos and the nationalist intellectuals. Enwezor and Zaya overplay the evidence when they interpret the casualness of some of the youths in the portraits as confirmation of their supreme comfort in the forms of appearance that history had willed to them and not at all concerned "by the questionable episteme of ethnographic delectation and otherization" ("Colonial Imaginary, Tropes of Disruption," 28).

The city-dwelling youths photographed by Keita, Sidibé, and Fosse indeed constructed, with their clearly uneasy, playful wearing of modernization on the body, an otherness against their compatriots left in the village. Wearing suits and ties is not enough evidence to say that the photographed youths are not Africans in the Senghorian way. One does not lose his/her lineage appellation just because one lives in the city, wears a suit, or has been to Paris or London. Senghor, wearing a dark suit, well fitted, of course, posed for a studio portrait for Salla Casset. That the anti-authenticity paradigm they adopted motivates the contentious claims made by Enwezor and Zaya's pioneering analysis is clear in the following statement: "What we seek to reveal is a whole transactional flow that refutes both Senghorian négritude's salvage paradigms and a complacent Western historicity or morbidly inscribed ethnographic yearnings, lusts, prejudices, appropriations, and corrosive violence" ("Colonial Imaginary, Tropes of Disruption," 29).

Enwezor and Zaya's application of the tradition of theatricality in portraiture, especially the predominance of the spirit of contingency, in their understanding of African popular photography may be useful for repudiating some elements of cultural nationalist thinking. It is clear, for example, that conventions of mid-twentieth-century-Malian commercial portrait photography might have enabled individuals to inventory elements of their urbanized existence with self-selected props and gestures from the corpus historically available to them. Contingency and theatricality fail, however, when they lead to the conclusion that playful individuals somehow enthusiastically "witness their own transformation as well as the disappearance over time of customs and cultural symbols" ("Colonial Imaginary, Tropes of Disruption," 34). This view extends too far the melancholic (mourning) concept of the photographic image. As

Enwezor and Zaya construe it, the African photographic text "has deposited in our care, for our gaze to linger upon, the traces and imprints of vanished moments, while it leaves unaccounted the motivations behind the making of individual photographs" (20). But neither "mourning" nor "identity," per se, explains, for example, the *Ovation* photographic artifact whose ego-supplementing motivation is prominently advertised in images and captions. It does not look like *Ovation* photographs want to function like lifeless memorials; they blare their goals like social heralds and announce an eminence that is either directly here or about to appear.

In "Photography and the Substance of the Image," Olu Oguibe proposes a deeply engaging historicist-functionalist framework for understanding the life of photographic images in Africa. Working primarily with the evidence of "verisimilar representation" in àkó funeral effigies among the Ọ̀wọ̀ people in southwestern Nigeria, Oguibe, following Rowland Abiodun, argues that àkó funerary woodcarvings record the essential identity marks and proportions of the deceased but eschew "photographic realism" because they are invocation aids used by descendants to hail the dead. "The eyes of the effigies are always wide open," for instance, "because the deceased to which they refer must keep awake on the other side, watchful over the living" (240). In other words, the imagistic showing not only extends existence but tangibly manifests the survivor's wish fulfillment. Hence, Oguibe concludes that in àkó figures:

> We find a different kind of portraiture: representation as anticipation. The verisimilitude we are introduced to is a meditated gesture between faithfulness and faith, between reflection and projection; it is a configuration of representation as both reflection and invocation beyond the limitations of transparency. For that which projects, that which anticipates and conjures, though faithful it may yet be to appearance, cannot be transparent since to be transparent is to convey that which already exists, that which precedes rather than supersedes the agency of its representation: to remain, as it were, within the reaches of death. The essence of verisimilitude here is not transparency but efficacy, the fulfillment of an intent beyond the materiality of the image. ("Photography and the Substance of the Image," 240)

Portraiture here is not a memorial, because it does not approximate the really departed. The dead has become something else that is not visible to the "naked" eye. The departed cannot by itself be represented. The loss cannot rise to the level of a pathology. The àkó figure helps speculate about the departed.

The àkó model of figuration could be found in other invocatory artifacts like the twin (ìbejì) carvings and Gẹ̀lẹ̀dẹ́ masques, both in southwestern Nigeria. When a twin dies, it is not uncommon for parents to sustain an appearance of togetherness, despite death, by commissioning portraits that duplicate the surviving person in a single frame. Carrying photographs of the deceased during funeral processions in Ethiopia and southwestern Nigeria also falls into the same class of picturing. In Oguibe's propositions, photography is rapidly assimilated into ritual practices mainly because mechanical reproduction "offers the unique ease of combining possibilities of fidelity not readily available to the human agent with those of manipulability requisite to the fulfillment of the essence of the image" ("Photography and the Substance of the Image," 247).

Oguibe's central argument is that the assimilation of photographs into a special occasion like the funeral betrays a general attitude: regardless of stylistic and technological differences between wood carving and "light writing," in the African milieu, continuous "making" and remaking is more important than "taking" in the creation of visuals. Construing images as products of a "making" imagination rather than as "taken" constructs, Oguibe suggests, better reflects the life of the photograph in African societies. In other words, neither the medium, nor the subject depicted, nor the artist's technique—all processes of "taking"—expresses the essence of the image. The "making" of the object, which includes the specific manner the consumer materializes it in use, carries more weight. The scandalous thought Roland Barthes once pondered aloud presents Oguibe's point in clearer relief. Barthes says:

> I may well worship an Image, a Painting, a Statue, but a photograph? I cannot place it in a ritual (on my desk, in an album) unless, somehow, I avoid looking at it (or avoid its looking at me), deliberately disappointing its unendurable plenitude and, by my very inattention, attaching it to an entirely different class of fetishes: the icons which are kissed in the Greek churches without being seen—on their shiny glass surface. (*Camera Lucida*, 90–91)

Nigerians and Ethiopians, Christians included, place pictures in funeral rituals not as substitutions for a source of melancholy but as instruments of agential invocations. The photograph does not immobilize the irremediably past presence of the dead but reminds the living of transition's perpetuity. No particular presence is unsurpassable. Living, after all, does not end at the cessation of breath. The image is not a lifeless reproduction of the living but a testimony to the existence of the departed somewhere else, as something else, interacting with the living-here-now in another form. Oguibe's sense of the image is not anything like Barthes's "that-has-been" (*Camera Lucida*, 77). It is not a reproduction of an unrepeatable eventuality that took place in front of a specific camera. The presence that stood in front of the machine that recorded the paraded image of the deceased is "out" there, but in a changed form, a palpable variant of which might be the photographic image itself. The existence in the image has passed on. The photograph presents not the person that stood in front of the camera but the trace made by that body in the life of the user or consumer.[33]

While Oguibe's thesis represents a great advancement over the one that constitutes mid-twentieth-century West African photographic practices of self-
showing as a radical counterdiscourse to nationalist ideologies, the long history of
"taking" practices in Africa he asks historians to rethink poses a difficult limit.
Ovation, like *Drum* and *Roots*, distributes secular, worldly, "taken" images. "Taken"
images of the politically important are also found in monumental sculptures that
dot African public spaces. To explain these images, we have, as I believe I have
done in this chapter, to go to panegyric poetry, a form in which the end product
is not meant to preserve the dead in life but to rally the prompt commemoration
of a still living ego.

In the forum I am configuring, theatricality does not capture the essence of
image making. Because the panegyric abhors death as permanent disappearance,
one can conclude that adulatory image making—verbal portraits, wood (àkó)
carvings, and photographic images—commemorates the living. In its ideal form,
the panegyric portrait hails the "living" consumer into conformity by adoring the
eminent. The *Ovation* image enchants not because of the theatrical antics of its
subject but by its quoting the panegyric impulse. Except for the aspiring young, the
eminent is always still in the magazine.[34] The pictures do not "inform," and readers
do not look for journalistic accuracy in the event. For that we go to *Time* and *Tell*.
Ovation does not inform, because its pictures look alike. This could be due to the
similarity of the formal celebrations covered. More important, the *Ovation* picture
cannot "inform," because it deliberately elides historical cognition—for instance,
the magazine is numbered but not dated. Surprises seldom occur, because the photographer lacks an intention toward specific subjects and events covered. *Ovation*,
like the verbal panegyric, only works at unretractable consent.

The cultural and historical contextualizations proposed above are meant
to show that self-projection practices grew exponentially in late twentieth-
century southwestern Nigeria. It is also intended to allude to the advantages of
Ovation's format over other means of culturally acceptable self-projection. The
magazine's mass distribution platform and the relatively affordable cost of accessing its pages open up the print panegyric form and democratize the self-
projection market even for the moderately rich, who can pay for the number of
pages they can afford. As much as the analysis exposes the Yorùbá roots of the
practices that sustain *Ovation*, it is obvious that the magazine's clientele could
not be exclusively Yorùbá. Publisher, readers, and patrons all participate in the
visual panegyrics that *Ovation* curates for everyone's delight. The magazine, if
not all its consumers, translates culture in a thoroughly contemporary medium
by "quoting" from oral practices and from social journalism that originated in
South Africa, England, and the United States. Meanwhile, its offices are in Accra,
Ghana. The analysis here does not speak of some cultural resilience peculiar to

an ethnic group but demonstrates how the Yorùbá oral panegyric, as a system of "inscribing" praise and eminence, lives on.

Notes

1. *Encomium* magazine's December 2002 profile of Dele Momodu describes *Ovation* as "the reference point" for its type (*Encomium Special*, December 2002, 61).

2. The proprietor, Dele Momodu, said he considered alternative titles: "In the thesaurus we saw different names. We saw glitterati, we saw encomium, and so along the line we saw ovation, I just jumped and said, 'Yeah, that is the name, that is the one I want.' You know, a standing ovation: loud, something loud, loud for a purpose. We even thought of calling the magazine *Loud*. Then I said, 'No ovation, loud for a purpose' " (Dele Momodu, interview with the author, Accra, Ghana, August 12, 2008).

3. There are a few exceptions: (1) the coverage of Philip Emeagwali, the American software engineer of Nigerian descent, whose peculiar ways with numbers since childhood are said to have culminated in his devising novel equations for predicting the volume of oil deposits in an exploratory area; and (2) stories about the life, times, and legacy of M. K. O. Abiola, the publisher's mentor and erstwhile employer.

4. Momodu has "returned" to the ranks of "serious" journalism with a weekly column in *This Day*, a Lagos-based daily newspaper with bias toward business activities.

5. http://www.gisters.com/profiles/bob_q_a.html (accessed November 7, 2004).

6. *Tell*, in the mold of the New York-based *Time*, is a Lagos weekly "hard" news magazine.

7. "If you are paying Sunny Ade to come and perform at your party, so why should I come and do it for free? Sunny Ade is a praise-singer; what *Ovation* would do for you is also praise singing. So why should you pay one and not pay the other?" (Délé Mòmòdú, interview with the author).

8. Kúnlé Bákàrè, interview with the author, Lagos, Nigeria, June 19, 2006.

9. *Encomium Special* (December 2002), 62. In my August 2008 interview with him, Momodu attributed the criticisms to biliousness; "ẹtanú" is his exact Yorùbá term.

10. *Encomium Special* (December 2002), 62.

11. In Yorùbá, the formulaic epithet would be: "Àràbà ni bàbá; / Ẹni a bá lábà ni baba" (Àràbà is the father [of trees]; The original homesteader is prior and superior in all things).

12. "Kó máa ró/ ṣèkèrè Aláàfin" (Let it shake / the Aláàfin's beaded gourds).

13. The phrases are "igbo kwenu" and "zobu, zobu." Since Peters, the popular Yorùbá fújì musician Wasiu Ayinde has used the "kwenu" formula to denote the Igbó ethnicity of his subjects of praise. The late àpàlà maestro Ayinla Omowura sang in Yorùbá the praise of Alhaji Danjuma, the wealthy Hausa cinema operator in Agege, a Lagos suburb.

14. "Ẹni t'ó ṣoríire dé'bi pé ajé bá a sòrẹ́; ó rí owó lò dáadáa, lati gbọ́ bùkátà, ó rí jẹ, ó rí mu, ó sì rí ṣe fújà" (Babalọlá, *Àwọn Oríkì Bòròkinní*, 5).

15. The few professors who might have appeared in *Ovation* did so for their material wealth in other concerns, not for innovative teaching or discovery.

16. The Yorùbá term for the practice of ordering a common outfit for a party, "aṣọ ẹbí" (family outfit), is used all over southern Nigeria.

17. For example, *Ovation Igbinedion* (see figure 6.1) contains portraits of family members of Chief Gabriel Osawaru Igbinedion of Benin City and pictures of events related to his seventieth birthday celebrations and associated ceremonies at Okada University, founded by Igbinedion.

18. I thank Anthonia Kalu and Chiji Akoma for the translations.

19. A devilish irony that associates glamorous body enhancement and commerce comes into play in the printer's placement of the magazine's barcodes in the Ozolua frame.

20. Ozolua's company is a cosmetic surgery brokerage firm that flies in doctors from the United States to do the jobs in Nigeria. She is not a medical practitioner (*Ovation* no. 34, 19–20). Her description of her business resembles that of the high couture boutiques that advertise in the magazine.

21. These lines are from a response Professor Rowland Abiodun gave to an initial version of this paper when it was read at the 2004 meeting of the African Studies Association in New Orleans.

22. Another poetic fragment makes a special plea that the cotton plant be treated with care in appreciation of the generosity of clothes to the human body, even after death: "Igi mẹ́ta là bá ṣe lóore /Ẹ jẹ́ á ṣe 'gi òwú lóore / Ènìyàn tó bá rè gbọ̀nsè / Kó má fewé òwú nùdìí / Ọjọ́ a bá kú / Aṣọ ní í sin ni . . . aṣọ lèdídí ènìyàn" (Three plants deserve special favors / We should be kind to the cotton plant / The person who visits the outhouse / Should not clean up with the cotton leaf / Because at death / Only clothes will accompany us to the grave) (qtd. in Oyètádé, "Body Beautification," 402).

23. In a different context and language, Rowland Abiodun ("Understanding Yorùbá Art and Aesthetics") argues for the validity of Sidibé's perspective of visual processes. The visual artist uses his or her ojú-inú (inner eye) and ojú-ọnà (design consciousness) to select, combine, and represent specific colors, patterns, motifs, and aspects of the subject matter in order to communicates its aṣẹ with the maximum visual impact." Although he is a fan of Malian popular photography, Manthia Diawara expresses misgivings about the social value of the griot's projections ("The Song of the Griot," 26–27.)

24. In the same interview, Sidibé points out the hypocrisy of religious leaders who condemn portrait photography as idolatry but do not hesitate to obtain passport photographs for travel documents when it's time to prepare for the hajj (pilgrimage to Mecca).

25. See, for an example, Diawara's "The Song of the Griot," 29–30.

26. Sidibé's photographs work like *Ovation*'s layout in some respects. As in *Ovation*, a considerable part of Sidibé's work documents youth culture. Like *Ovation* magazine reporters, Sidibé followed his clients to their chosen locations and events, including "family celebrations (weddings, baptisms) or to bare-earth dances" (Magnin and Sidibé, "In My Life," 77) and "added prestige to the occasion." Although Sidibé's clients had very modest acquisitions to show for their lives in the city, they still "came to the studio with their latest riches. They came because of them." They yearned for their portraits to say, as *Ovation*'s subjects do with much grander acquisitions, "look at me with my bag, my watch, my spectacles, my shoes, and my clothes, look at me with my moped" (78).

27. The criticism is very similar to the charges of unseriousness leveled against *Ovation*.

28. These details are not irrelevant to understanding *Ovation*'s story. In my August 2008 interview with him, Dele Momodu said that although he had only £15,000 to start the magazine, he spent £14,000 on leasing an elegant office in Dockland, and that this scared off an investor who did not like the spending.

29. Of course, there are exceptions. See Sprague's "Yoruba Photography" and "How I See the Yoruba," for example.

30. See chapter 1 of Batchen, *Burning with Desire,* for a discussion of the intractable troubles that photography's peculiarities have created for thinking about photography and the writing of its history.

31. They start at the interwar years because archival storage beyond that point is unavailable.

32. Wole Soyinka, for example, is not uniformly anti-Négritude. Very few texts are as trenchantly Africanist as the philosophical defense of Yorùbá viewpoints (or what Soyinka presents as such) in *Myth, Literature and the African World*.

33. Even Barthes admits that a person that presents a body to be photographed "makes another body" for himself and "transform[s]" himself "in advance into an image" (*Camera Lucida*).

34. Of course, this is not to say that theatricality is strange to the panegyric; after all, Nigerians love to speak of verbal gymnastics!

Conclusion

Book Launches as Cultural Affirmation

Practical aspirations—as to schooling success, professional advancement, and rewarding spiritual favors, for example—drive publishing and reading practices in contemporary southwestern Nigeria, going by the dominant patterns of titles on the shelves of the few notable bookshops that remain open in Lagos, Ìbàdàn, and Ìlọrin, three major cities with very large Yorùbá-speaking populations. College textbooks, manuals on shortcuts to magnificent wealth, voluminous professional examination preparation paperbacks, and how-to titles regarding attaining high spirituality that guarantees earthly well-being fill rows and rows of shelf space in the bookstores. One not so practical genre that could not be missed by even an inattentive visitor to the bookshops is the prominently displayed autobiography, usually stocked in the general reading interest sections, where one will find life accounts of politicians, traditional kings and chiefs, modern professionals, retired top-level civil servants, senior military men (and sometimes their spouses), and leaders of industry and commerce. Festschrifts dedicated to retiring and retired university professors, typically in the humanities and social sciences, recently joined this company. The conspicuous display of biographies in the bookshops reiterates the growing importance of print-centered, self-fashioning, self-presentation projects in contemporary Yorùbá-dominated southwestern Nigerian culture. The more curious and perhaps more culturally significant dimension of the life-writing projects is that more titles than displayed are actually published and celebrated at elaborately and carefully structured launch ceremonies that, if fully realized, ought to get the books into the hands of the number of people that should want to own them for reasons other than disinterested intellectual or cultural enrichment.

The discussion below focuses on the deeply embedded cultural unconscious that makes the book launch the successful form it has attained in southwestern Nigeria. I conclude that the southwestern Nigeria book launch, which is not a book-signing event, abstracts elements of Yorùbá naming and/or outing gatherings, usually for a newborn, and joins these to protocols of affirming social ties consolidated in the panegyric traditions, variants of which I discussed in chapter 6.[1] If one were to draw on the formulaic proclamation launchers make at book events—"I launch this book (title inserted) in the amount of so, so, and so"—exclude the monetary part, and substitute "child" for book, the idea stands out clearly that the originators of the book launch as it is currently practiced intend an allusion to the Yorùbá-naming ceremonial. At both the newborn's naming (ìkómọjáde) and the book launch (ìkówèéjáde, as it were), the central verbal convention announces and names a presence that cannot yet speak for itself and has emanated from a cherished acquaintance of the launcher or namer. While proceedings at both events are presented as honors to the newborn and the new book, as will be seen below, a book launch commemorates the author's person, not the book that it purports to out and name.

Ovation blazed a popular trail into printed page self-projection on a path that was first cut in biographies of senior military officers who played leading roles either in the Nigerian Civil War (1967–1970) or in the military regimes that ruled the country from the end of the civil war until 1999. The trend began with General Olusegun Obasanjo's *My Command*. Bola Ige, Obasanjo's personal friend, political adversary, and then governor of Ọ̀yọ́ State, generated widespread interest with his scathing review of the book at its public launch in Ìbàdàn in 1981. Until as late as 2013, when General Alabi-Isama published his *Tragedy of Victory*, other military leaders and political leaders who had witnessed either the civil war or the events that had led to it, had been refuting Obasanjo's heroic self-projection in that memoir.[2] However, the cultural development with which I want to close *Arts of Being Yorùbá* has little to do with the contents of the biographical selves of the earliest set of post-independence Nigerian military leadership. My focus here is the character of the elaborate ceremony orchestrated to launch the book, the one regard in which the public presentation of Olusegun Obasanjo's *My Command* marks a turning point.

In their ever-growing pursuit of self-commemoration, eminent Nigerians now commission and pay for the publication of books about their lives, launching the books to great fanfare attended by their equally eminent friends. Being a self-projection event that needs some stimulus to materialize, the book launch is usually tied to landmark rites of passage such as birthdays, retirements, the acquisition of a chieftaincy title, or memorials. An adulatory reviewer participates in the event by reading a summary of its high points, discussing the national significance of the life celebrated in the book. The usually festive launch climaxes with the announcement by the biographical subject's friends and well-wishers of huge purchases and cash donations. If the celebrant is a former senior government official, it is not uncommon for representatives of state agencies to donate large sums of money in appreciation of the services the person being honored has rendered or is believed to have rendered society.[3]

The following description of two events involving Professor Tóyìn Fálọlá, one in Lagos and one in Ìbàdàn, during the first week of July 2012—augmented with brief observations about an event involving Alhaji, Chief, Kọ́lá Anímáṣaun in Lagos—is meant to affirm the observation that the contemporary south-western Nigeria book launch has thrived as well as it has because it makes cultural sense in an environment that valorizes the panegyric as Yorùbá traditions do. Anímáṣaun is retired from politics, and writes columns for *Vanguard* in Lagos. Dr. Tóyìn Fálọlá, a historian, is the Jacob and Frances Sanger Mossiker Professor in the Humanities, University of Texas at Austin. For each author, as it is almost always, the book launch is tied to a significant life event or professional attainment. The two books launched at the Anímáṣaun event, an autobiography (*1Thousand 9hundred and Thirty9: An Autobiography*) and an anthology of select articles from his newspaper columns (*The Voice of Reason 2, the Obasanjo Years: The Best of His Journalism*), marked his seventy-third birthday. Dr. Fálọlá launched a voluminous history of the city of Ìbàdàn (*Ìbàdàn: Foundation, Growth, and Change, 1830–1960*) on the occasion of his giving the fifth Adegoke Adelabu Lecture, an annual event sponsored by the Ìbàdàn Foundation. Neither event gave notable consideration to the arts of biography, newspaper writing, or historiography, the substantive grounds of each author's contribution to culture and knowledge. Because the Ìbàdàn event is about a professional historian, it is more noteworthy that little at the event was observable regarding the intellectual difference that was to be made by the thousand-page book. In both cases, the author guided the activities. The sidelining of the book at the book launching events should not be ignored but, as I propose in this concluding chapter, be interpreted for what it says about processes of self-cultivation in contemporary Yorùbá societies.

I will argue that the book launch is a culturally palatable, aspiration-inducing institution at which men and women of power in Yorùbá spheres of influence register and consolidate the reality of their eminence. The discussion is grounded in the pride-inducing (literally "head-swelling" [ìwúrí]) theory of praise culture, an apt phrasing which, as discussed in chapter 6, Adébóyè Babalọlá formulated to characterize a listener/reader response overview of Yorùbá panegyrics, written and oral. While the book launch does not address the cultural past explicitly, as traditional praise does, the structure of events stokes achievement thrills associated with public celebrations of individuals in traditional poetic adulation. The book launch creates a forum for the eminent to be hailed directly (see Figure C.1) and also for those who are gathered, even if they are not yet eminent, to feel honored for appearing as relations, no matter how remote or thin, of those who have blazed trails worthy to be written about in a book, self-authored or not, that can be publicly launched. The eminent in contemporary southwestern Nigeria enthusiastically embrace the book launch both because it repurposes inherited encomiastic practices and also because its most pronounced conventions quote and rechannel gestures associated with the culturally familiar processes of naming newborns and introducing them to the community.

Figure C.1. Tóyìn Fáḷọlá listening to citation. Photo by the author.

Tóyìn Fálọlá, the Historian as an Eminent Person

Summer 2012 was a remarkable time for Professor Tóyìn Fálọlá. On July 4, at the city's Civic Center, he gave the fifth Ìbàdàn Foundation's annual Adegoke Adelabu Lecture and launched his thousand-page history of the city. Two days earlier in Lagos, Professor Fálọlá had bagged another honor when he became the first (and perhaps only) African scholar for whom a yearly academic conference was to be publicly named. I am stressing precedence setting and quick aggregation about the events in order to reiterate the time-honored parameter of recognizing repeated, remarkable, pioneering endeavors as sure signs of true eminence in traditional processes of praise. On July 2, some prominent individuals, several of them powerful, former students of Tóyìn Fálọlá, and one major cultural institution, the Center for Black Arts and Culture, founded in 1977 by the Culture Department of the Nigerian government when it hosted the second World Black and African Festival of Arts and Culture (FESTAC) in Lagos, publicly launched the Toyin Falola Annual Conference on Africa and the African Diaspora (TOFAC).[4] The inauguration was a grand cultural and academic affair about book-based knowledge.

In academic terms, TOFAC 2012 was not about Professor Fálọlá's intellectual achievements, although a few papers listed on the program addressed his award-winning autobiography, *A Mouth Sweeter than Salt*, and his books of poems. No participant examined Fálọlá's formidable and, to say the obvious, praiseworthy bibliography on Yorùbá history, the locus of his academic reputation. These omissions, I suggest, are not accidental. Within the Lagos cultural milieu of TOFAC 2012, gatherings in the name of books typically celebrated the named authors who often doubled as the subject of the book. Outside of universities, activities that test and debate the ideas and thoughts in the text rarely appear in the program.[5] Capturing the essence of the early twenty-first-century Yorùbá-based southwestern Nigerian culture of self-projection, the public launch of TOFAC 2012 brought together diverse peoples of the book, in the name of a person of the book who had acquired his fame inside institutions of the book while pursuing the cause of knowledge gathered from and disseminated preferably in book form. It could be stated right away that the countless references, both at TOFAC 2012 and at the Adelabu Lecture, to the very large number of books that Fálọlá has written speaks to the metacritical import of the two gatherings. In Lagos, academics created a conference around a totemic figure who had written many books and whose stellar achievements many others at the gathering aspired to attain, partly by contributing to a conference book that would increase their fund of professional credentials and move them a step closer to becoming eminent. Celebrating the already eminent Tóyìn Fálọlá at TOFAC, I am saying, extends the reach of eminence available to the already eminent and, because those aspiring to the celebrated status present themselves as working hard to be in the book version of conference proceedings, the gathering validates the main ground of Fálọlá's fame as a tireless author of books and further legitimizes the aspiration of the adulating participants.

The multimodal, multilingual, and multicultural opening ceremony at TOFAC 2012 amounts to a pride-stoking performance that could cohere and therefore make sense culturally only in southwestern Nigeria and related societies. There were prayers, academic keynotes, and speeches given by the convener, Adémọ́lá DaSylva, Professor of English at the University of Ìbàdàn and leader of the Ìbàdàn Cultural Studies Group, and by representatives of the major funders of the conference (Professor Tunde Babawale, Director of Center for Black Arts and Culture; and Chief Edem Duke, then Nigeria's Minister of Culture and Tourism). Cultural performances were staged—mainly southwestern Nigerian drumming and a Zulu-inspired choreography—that could have been viewed as providing mere relief because they bore no direct relation to the substance of the conference.

However, two entertainment agenda items call for closer attention because of the Yorùbá sensibilities they insinuated, especially in relation to the conference titular eponym, Professor Tóyìn Fálọlá. The first was a ten-minute oríkì praise poetry chant rendered in Yorùbá and dedicated to Professor Fálọlá; the second, a peculiar variation of the eulogistic mode called "citation" performed in English. The poet, Adéọlá Fálẹ́yẹ, is on the Faculty of Arts at Obafemi Awolowo University, Ilé-Ifẹ̀, where Professor Fálọlá earned all his academic degrees and taught for many years before relocating to North America. The excerpts Fálẹ́yẹ chanted at the opening ceremony were taken from her audio CD compilation, "Ìbàdàn Ọmọ Ajòrosùn," a celebration of Yorùbá heroes that highlights the centrality of historical Ìbàdàn leaders in the survival of modern Yorùbá as a people. A nineteen-minute track in the CD locates Fálọlá squarely within that arduous progeny. (Fálẹ́yẹ's album was on sale at the lecture venue in Ìbàdàn when Fálọlá gave the Adegoke Adelabu Lecture.) In the live performance at TOFAC 2012, Fálẹ́yẹ praised Fálọlá's remarkable erudition, recounted his wife's names and hometown, extolled Fálọlá's friends, and commented on their fortuitous association with such eminence. Notable members of the audience, several of whom do not identify culturally as Yorùbá and perhaps do not understand the language, found Fálẹ́yẹ's words and gestures pleasant, rising up to paste money on her brow in appreciation. Professor Fálọlá walked down from the podium to paste currency notes on the poet's brow when Fálẹ́yẹ declaimed:

Ọkọ Lábísí
ọkọ apọ́nbéporẹ́
baba Dọlápọ̀ oò
ìwọ lọmọ ajísunwọ̀n

ọmọ wọn nílé Agbo
Tóyìn Fálọlá ò
Tóyìn Fálọlá
tí nbá ńpè ọ́
dákun dá mi lóhùn
ìwọ nì ǹńké sí
ọkùnrin takun, takun, takun
nílé Agbo

Labisi's husband
husband of the fair-skinned one
the father of Dọlápọ̀
you, offspring of the ever radiant
descendant of the Agbo household
oh, Tóyìn Fálọlá
one and only Tóyìn Fálọlá
as I am calling out to you
please answer me
you are the one I am hailing
a solid, solid, solid gentleman
of the Agbo household

When she chanted, "Ìwọ lọmọ Adéṣínà o ò / ọmọ Fálọlá / ẹ dákun kẹ́ẹ pàtẹ́wọ́ fún Tóyìn Fálọlá" (You are the son of Adéṣínà / the one born by Fálọlá / please rise up and clap for Fálọlá), the audience stood up in unison and did as she instructed. She also saluted Fálọlá for his marrying a worthy woman from Ìlawẹ̀-Èkìtì:

Tóyìn Fálọlá lọkọ Lábísí
ọmọ ọ̀rín awẹ̀ ní'lawẹ̀-Èkìtì
Lábísí, aya rere
Filọ́rẹ́ǹsì, aya gidi

Tóyìn Fálọlá is married to Lábísí
the one who hails from Ìlawẹ̀-Èkìtì
Lábísí, the good wife
Florence, the genuine wife

At this point, Mrs. Fálọlá, hitherto reluctant to come down from the stage, rose to show her appreciation. Fálẹ́yẹ rounded off her presentation by singing:

Ọmọ ò lè jọ baba
ká máa bínú ọmọ
Toyín Fálọlá jọ bàbá ẹ̀ jù
ọmọ ò lè jọ baba
ká máa bínú ọmọ

When a child resembles the father
We should not begrudge the child
Tóyìn Fálọlá resembles his father exceedingly
When a child resembles the father
We should not begrudge the child

Both the Lagos performance and the nineteen-minute CD recording praise Fálọlá's global fame, attribute his success to his Ìbàdàn birth, and acknowledge his friends and academic collaborators. Although the city (mentioned twenty-seven times in the CD track) and Fálọlá's person (repeated twenty-three times) are the dominant organizing items in Fáléyẹ's poems, the listener is not afforded any specific information either about Ìbàdàn or about its celebrated famous son and his Ìbàdàn-born associates. In the CD, Fáléyẹ announces twice that Fálọlá's prestige is global (aníyìkáríayé), identifies him twice in two succeeding lines as a historian ("òpìtàn" [story-auteur]; "onímọ̀ ìtàn" [historiographer; one knowledgeable in the arts of history and storytelling]). The audio recording calls him the wisdom-filled moon that illuminates the entire universe ("òṣùpá ajírànmọ́ fáyé rí nínú ọgbọ́n") and a bright star that is visible in all corners ("ìràwọ̀ ojú ọrun tó lé téńté níbi gbogbo"), and likens him to a needle that mends torn clothes ("abẹ́rẹ́ ni ọ́ tíí táṣọ́ọ̀ ṣe"). The poem does not disclose Mrs. Fálọlá's profession. It is reported that the younger Tóyìn (Professor Fálọlá's son), like the older Tóyìn (Professor Fálọlá) does his own father (the late Adéṣìnà Fálọlá), resembles the senior Tóyìn (Professor Fálọlá) tremendously, but we are not told as to how.

The remainder of the nineteen-minute recording contains repeated lines of praise for Fálọlá's lineage and those of his named associates: businessman, mogul, and Ìbàdàn chieftain, Alhaji Aríṣekọ́lá Àlàó; and notable novelist, playwright, and movie director, Professor Akínwùmí Ìṣọ̀lá (also born in Ìbàdàn, the hometown of Professor Akin Àlàó, a historian at Obafemi Awolowo University, and former student of Fálọlá). A few lines each are also devoted to Professors Akin Ògúndìran (University of North Carolina) and Philip Ògúndèjì (University of Ìbàdàn), both of Ìbàdàn origin. Except for Professors Túndé Babáwálé and Adémọ́lá Dasylva, names of non-Ìbàdàn indigenes are rattled out in quick succession.

The poem's focus on Fálọlá's birth city could be explained as a contingent acknowledgment of the occasion of the Ìbàdàn Foundation's honoring Fálọlá with the Adegoke Adelabu Lecture and the launching of the hefty history Fálọlá has written about Ìbàdàn. However, this explanation is not without difficulty because the official lecture program, an event totally devoted to Ìbàdàn's continuing significance in time and place, gives no room for Fáléyẹ to perform although copies of the recording are, along with the printed text of the lecture, available at the entrance to the hall. This disjuncture is worth recalling because numerous, less formally orchestrated types of praise singers and chanters performed inside the hall.

Fálẹ́yẹ's recording lists three causes for Fálọlá's success, and all will make full sense only to those educated in the panegyric arts of being Yorùbá. The first is an account of the place of birth in the opening lines of the recording. Fálẹ́yẹ sings:

Mo bojú wolé
Nílẹ̀ Ìbadan
Mo tún rẹ́ni rere
Ọ̀jọ̀gbọ́n Tóyìn Fálọlá
Ìsọ̀lá ni ọ́ o
Ọmọ Adéṣínà Fálọlá
Nílé Agbo l'Ọ́jàagbó
Aníyìkáyé ni ọ́
Abẹ́rẹ́ ni ọ́
Tíí táṣọ ọ́ ṣe
Ọmọ núulé ni ọ́
Tí ọ̀ gbọdọ̀ balé jẹ́
Abájọ tọ́rọ̀ Ìbàdàn yìí fi jẹ́ ọ́ lógún

I cast my eyes all over the homestead
All over Ìbàdàn-land
And I found one genuine citizen
Professor Tóyìn Fálọlá
You, also called Ìṣọ̀lá
Son of Adéṣínà Fálọlá
of the Agbo compound at Ọjàagbó
Prestigious all over the world are you
You are the needle
That mends torn clothes
You are a freeborn of the household
Who must not destroy the household
No surprise Ìbàdàn heritage matters to you

Within the logic of these lines, Fálọlá owes his professional prominence to the preparation that his Ìbàdàn birth and upbringing gave him. The poem offers two other factors of causation. One insinuates that the family's association with Ifá, the most dominant Yorùbá discourse of intellectual prognostication, whose inscription and writing processes I discuss in chapter 1, plays a significant role in the celebrant's achievement:

Ifá ò tẹ́ rí o
Bẹ́ẹ̀ nifá ò tẹ́ rí láéláé
Abájọ tórúkọ fíí ro
Tóyìn Ìṣọ̀lá ọmọ Adéṣínà Fálọlá
Ó jọ bàbá ẹ̀ bí ìmumu

Ifá never fails
Exactly. Ifá never, never fails
That is the reason the family name stirs you so
Tóyìn Ìṣọ̀lá, son of Adéṣínà Fálọlá
One who takes after his father like a tiger-nut

These lines appeal to deeply held Yorùbá beliefs about names and naming: eminence (ọlá) and intellectual discernment came to Professor Fálọlá through the family's appropriately selected belief affiliation. Finally, Fáléyẹ thanks Fálọlá's native predisposition, expressed in Yorùbá cultural convention of orí (the inner head):[6]

Wọ́n ti lóríburúkú ò ní wú tùùlù
Orí tí ó gbe ni ò rí dùngbẹ̀ dungbẹ
Ẹnì tó bá yanrí ọlà látọrun
Dandan ní kó lọ́lá láyé

An ill-disposed head does not advertise its misfortune
The fortunate one need not be outsized
Whosoever chooses a honor bound head before birth
Fortune will be his or her lot on earth

In increasing order of importance, Fálọlá's city of birth, his family's totemic deity, and essential predisposition conspire to help the historian achieve his irresistible charisma (àpésìn) and global recognition and fame. The recording, as in the live performance, does not educate listeners regarding Fálọlá's skills as a historical researcher or writer, and the many accolades he has won for his academic achievements are left unremembered. Fálọlá's Ìbàdàn birth is heavily emphasized, as if everything the historian does derives from the singular factor of birth. More than once, the poet thanks the heavens for Ìbàdàn's gifting of Fálọlá to the world.

As noted above, Fáléyẹ did not perform live at the lecture or book launch. But other forms of homage to eminence, all unofficial, dominated the lecture hall's soundscape. Besides the reading of citations and commissioned reviews, which will be discussed below, were male and female itinerant praise singers, several with musical accompaniments, who could not get inside the hall but vigorously hailed high-ranking individuals as the individuals stepped out of their cars. Among the few that managed to enter the hall was a fairly well-dressed old man who simply chanted, without care, in freestyle, praise lines not addressed to any particular person. Among the stray lines the man spoke in the state governor's direction during his official procession to the podium was "Àìmèsì ni ó pẹni ọ́ pọ̀ jù" (Indecorous speech will be the death of many). In the same vein, as the state governor was about to mount the stage, a group of women stepped in front, ready to spread pieces of cloth in his path, on which he was expected to throw money in appreciation. The women were gently shooed away by plainclothes security officers.

The honoree's "citation" is one other eulogistic feature of both the TOFAC 2012 opening and the endowed Adelabu Lecture at which Fálọlá's book was launched. The southwestern Nigerian "citation" hybridizes what in other places are known as guest speaker's introduction and special honoree's profile read at academic convocations. In Ìbàdàn and Lagos, Professor Akin Àlàó delivered lengthy citations that spoke about the achievements that recommend Fálọlá for both the lecture and conference honors. The text, part of which is reproduced as the guest speaker's introduction in the printed version of the Adelabu Lecture, is a distended compilation of schools attended, professional training received, travels undertaken, and offices held. It includes Fálọlá's publications, an approximation of the number of advanced degrees earned under Fálọlá's tutelage, and much academic ephemera. The citation reader asks, "Who then is Toyin Falola and what manner of teacher, scholar leader is this legendary personality, who has assumed a larger than life image in scholarship and society?" He answers the question with some descriptive terms that echo those used by Adéọlá Fáléyẹ: "Prof. Toyin Falola is a proud son of Ibadan land and whose love for his home city, Ibadan is exemplary, never in doubt and encompassing. He is ever committed to the greater glory of Ibadan and relentless in his philanthropy to deserving sons and daughters of Ibadan" ("Professor Toyin Omoyeni Falola," 9). Professor Àlàó expands:

> Tóyìn Falola is a distinguished alumnus of the University of Ife, now Obafemi Awolowo University, Ile-Ife, Nigeria and an accomplished author, engaging speaker, organizer of no mean standing and passionate public intellectual whose primary concern is the engagement of knowledge for public good, progress and development. As at the last count last year, Professor Falola has authored, co-authored, edited and co-edited over 110 books excluding journal articles, essays in books and such other writings. He is the recipient of the much coveted University of Texas at Austin Outstanding Graduate Teaching Award for 2010 and the Career Research Excellence Award 2011. Professor Tóyìn Falola has recently been appointed, on personal merit and based on his unequalled academic productivity, to the Scholars Council of the Library of Congress of the United States of America, and he is also the 2012 recipient of the Dean's Scholarship and Leadership Award, Office of Women's Affairs, Indiana University Bloomington, USA. (9–10)

Because the southwestern Nigerian citation is not a review essay, although it could be as long, patterns of either themes or methodology in Fálọlá's oeuvre are not highlighted or appraised. The text emphasizes quantity, specifically the prodigious number of book titles edited or authored by Fálọlá, in addition to his tireless work on countless journals and academic publications. Professor Àlàó does not isolate for reference any distinguishing elements of the historiographic significance of Fálolá's vast bibliography. Regarding the significance of Fálolá's academic work, curious listeners would have had to assume that this had been evaluated and affirmed at the academic forum recounted in the citation. Just as the traditional panegyrist's main task is to enrich the social worth of the praised subject by highlighting accumulated emblems of heroic achievements, the citation author or reader focuses mostly on embodiments of accolades, registered in this instance with a long list. In Professor Àlàó's presentation, the intimidating number of books that Fálolá has published speaks eloquently of his achievement in nineteenth-century precolonial African or, more specifically, Ìbàdàn history. Like its largely oral, traditional counterpart, the Nigerian citation's main purpose is to nurture the dissemination and perception of respectful regard for its subject.

Very close to the citation, but originating from a completely different tradition, is the book launch review. Typically, one or two well-known individuals (usually newspaper columnists, university academics,[7] editors, or senior members of the commentariat) are commissioned to extol the merits of the book being launched and explain its weaknesses. In the version published for the record by the Ìbàdàn Foundation, Professor Akin Ògúndìran of the University of North Carolina, Charlotte, and native of Ìbàdàn city, opens his comments in language that recalls Professor Àlàó's terms about Fálolá's prodigiousness: "It is not difficult to find superlatives to describe Professor Toyin Falola. He is after all the author and editor of record shattering 120+ books making him the most published academic historian in the world. He is also the most decorated Africanist scholar ever, and one of the most prominent sons of Ibadan. Professor Falola is known for writing big books. *Ibadan: Foundation, Growth and Change, 1830–1960* may be his most audacious and biggest single-authored book so far!" ("Book Review," 71). Regarding the book, Professor Ògúndìran declares that Fálolá "has written the most definitive and comprehensive history of Ibadan from its evolution as a fledgling military camp to its stabilization as the largest indigenous city in nineteenth-century West Africa; and from its incorporation into the colonial Nigeria to its status today as the center of the modern Yorùbá world, and the bellwether of postcolonial Nigeria" (71).

I want to shift attention to other occurrences relevant to the book launch at the fifth Adegoke Adelabu Lecture, which, to reiterate, was also the occasion for presenting Fálolá's *Ìbàdàn: Foundation, Growth, and Change, 1830–1960*. I consider it effective to start by listing the names of those announced over the public address system as being in attendance. The book launch, it seems, has to be perceived as commanding the presence of as many high-achieving men and women as possible. At the lecture were Professor Akínwùmí Ìsòlá; Bánkólé Oláyebí (publisher of Fálolá's book and of many other eminent Nigerians, including Wole Soyinka); His Highness, Adédòkun Omoniyì Abólárìn (Oba of Òkè Ìlá); Dr. Lékan

Àrẹ (patron of the Ìbàdàn Foundation); Engineer Lérè Àdìgún (president of the Ìbàdàn Foundation); Professor Afọlábí Ọládàpọ̀; Mrs. Abímbọ́lá Ọlátúnjí Daniel, Registrar of the Ọ̀yọ́ State High Court (to represent the state chief judge); Chief Báyọ̀ Òyéró (president of the Ìbàdàn Council of Indigenes); Suliat Adépéjú (the eldest daughter of the late Chief Adégòkè Adélabú, the person for whom the lecture was named); Ambassador Olúṣọlá Ṣàánú; and Chief Àlàmú Múdà Ayẹni (the Ìbàdàn Foundation's planning committee chair). Also present was Chief Lékan Àlàbí (a high chief), who represented the chief launcher, Alhaji, Chief, Àlàó Azeez Aríṣekọ́lá (the Àrẹ Mùsùlùmí of Yorùbáland [the supreme leader of all Muslims in Yorùbá-land]). Ọ̀yọ́ Palace sent a representative and a retinue of chiefs complemented by the king's beaded staff of office. The aged king of Ìbàdàn, the Olúbàdàn, also sent a representative, who arrived with the royal trumpeter blasting out one praise line after another.

The master of ceremonies announced the presence of these important personalities, and I have listed them here because their presence in noticeable numbers is crucial to the projection and maintenance of eminence and prestige that the lecture, the book launch, the eminent speaker, the sponsoring foundation, the city, and Fálọlá's voluminous book about the city are meant to serve. The intended impression is unmistakable: Ìbàdàn is so great a city that all the announced important people could come together to honor it at a lecture endowed by a civic group devoted to the city's uplift. The eminent, universally acclaimed professor of history giving the lecture was born and raised in the city and had written an important book for the occasion. Eminence, as it were, begets eminence. The heightened pomp leaves little doubt that neither formal, academic, and policy talk, nor nuances of history writing, will be the focal point of the event. It is quite unlikely that the quality of Fálọlá's disquisitions will be the center of the reports that the Ọ̀yọ́ and Ìbàdàn palace representatives will give when they return home. Perhaps sensing this to be case, Professor Fálọlá did not deliver a formal talk but instead rendered a matter-of-fact summary of the prepared text, which had been published in advance under the imprint of the prestigious University Press, formerly the Nigerian affiliate of Oxford University Press. Although the audience had no chance to enjoy Professor Fálọlá's erudition live, those who were interested in the intellectual content of the occasion and were prepared to pay for the text had reference material to consult. It should not be left unnoticed, nonetheless, that the published text would be recited at the next event as further evidence of Fálọlá's eminence.

The Ọ̀yọ́ State governor, Abíọ́lá Ajímọ̀bi, himself an eminent Ìbàdàn citizen, arrived shortly after the beginning of the formal book launch, which Alhaji Aríṣekọ́lá, through his representative, had already declared open with a gift of one million naira. The governor gave a speech and, claiming to be a well-brought-up Yorùbá man who, for cultural propriety, will not outdo the chief launcher, whom he called his older sibling (ẹ̀gbọ́n), announced a launching donation of ₦999,000 and left. These two announced large donations, both massively acclaimed by the audience, constitute the main acts of the book launch.

The presiding personality at the book launch is always a wealthy individual, who is not expected to do much beyond proclaiming verbally, in imitation of the way the oldest person at a Yorùbá child-outing ceremony calls out a newborn's name to the gathered family, that the book is launched with a large amount of money. He or she also usually urges fellow wealthy people present to buy the book and recommends that public school officials adopt the book for educational purposes. Before the launch amount is announced, every large donor (or "launcher," as they are called) makes a short speech to recognize and acknowledge his or her connection to the author or to the subject of the book, or to both. At the launch of Fálọlá's book, the king of Òkè-Ìlá disclosed that he was Fálọlá's former student at the University of Ife (now Obafemi Awolowo University), Ilé-Ifẹ̀, acknowledged the author's enduring influence on him, and gave ₦50,000. Fálọlá's friend and colleague, Professor Jídé Owóẹ̀yẹ, founder of Lead City University, who was to host TOFAC 2013, donated ₦200,000 and declared that his gift was to honor the fraternity of teachers ("àwa olùkọ́"). Mr. Débọ́lá Ọ̀sínúbi, managing director of the Punch newspaper group, a publishing conglomerate founded by an Ìbàdàn-born financier, announced that he was giving one million naira for the edification of the city. Probably because the sums donated were not large enough or because the individuals were modest, many of the announced givers had no amounts attached to their names. Meanwhile, as the moneyed announcements continued, individuals were urged to go up to the book stand in the front of the hall to buy their copies at ₦5,000 each. Not many people went up. By my reckoning, the announced donations totaled ₦3,576,000, far more than half of which was given by the three largest donors—the chief launcher, the state governor, and the director of the Punch newspaper group. If all the gifts were collected in full, recovering the publisher's cost of production—an unadvertised purpose of the book launch—would have been realized.

Birthdays Are for Books: Alhaji Kọ́lá Anímáṣaun

It is unlikely that critical cultural inquiry was the main reason senators, state governors, bankers, traditional chiefs and rulers, and other people who ordinarily have nothing to do with newspaper opinion writing, gathered at the Nigerian Institute for International Affairs on a July weekday afternoon in Lagos to launch Alhaji Kọ́lá Anímáṣaun's memoir and anthology of newspaper columns. A more likely reason is that the pleasure of the gathering for these individuals was to reiterate their own eminent social status as they celebrated the author, a fellow eminent person. As it was at TOFAC 2012 in Lagos and at the fifth Adegoke Adelabu Lecture in Ìbàdàn, the roll call began with those deserving of places on the podium table at which sat Anímáṣaun and his spouse. First to be announced was the occasion chair, Aṣíwájú Bọ́lá Tinúbú, the former governor of Lagos State, who was "unavoidably" absent but who sent Chief Akínyẹ̀lúrẹ̀ to represent him and acknowledge the high esteem in which he held Anímáṣaun. Also called up was Àrẹ̀mọ Ṣẹ́gun Ọ̀ṣọbà, former governor of Ògùn State.[8] The Sultan of Sokoto, from the far northwestern part of Nigeria, was represented by former diplomat and wali of Sokoto, Alhaji Amzat Ahmadu. Others whose presence was announced but who had no place on the small stage included Chief Alex Nwokedi, a retired newspaper executive; Chief Bọ́lá Ajíbọ́lá, former attorney general of Nigeria; Alhaji Àlàdé Ọdúnewu, doyen of post-independence Nigerian journalism; Káyọ̀dé Akínmádé, representative of the governor of Ondo State; Tajudeen Ọláńrewájú, a retired general; and Alhaji Lai Mohammed, a preeminent politician in southwestern Nigeria. Other important presences "recognized" with announcements included Fọlá Adéọlá, eminent banker and onetime candidate for the office of the country's vice president, and Chief Bísí Àkàndé, onetime governor of Ọ̀ṣun State. Also recognized were Ṣẹ́gun Babátọ́pẹ́, Ayọ̀ Adébánjọ, Ẹniọlá Bello (managing director of *This Day* newspaper), Senator Gàníyù Ọláńrewájú Solomon (Senate Minority Whip at the National Assembly), and Yétúndé Aróbíẹkẹ (representing Senator Rẹ̀mí Tinúbú, Aṣíwájú Bọ́lá Tinúbú's spouse). Seats were found on the crowded stage for Sam Amuka Pemu, founder and owner of *Vanguard* and the celebrant's former employer, and the two reviewers, Sam Omatseye (a popular editor and columnist) and Steve Àyọ̀rìndé. Governor Ajímọbi of Ọ̀yọ́ state, keynote speaker at the Adelabu Lecture two days earlier, served as the "host governor." As it had been in Ìbàdàn, all the named eminent personalities were called and each of them announced large amounts of money to launch the book. As in Ìbàdàn, not many people were seen buying the books that occasioned the gathering. As it was in Ìbàdàn, the books cost ₦5,000.

Coda

How can a practice like the book launch be tagged Yorùbá? It may also be asked: Does the appearance of the Esama of Benin Kingdom, Chief Osawaru Igbinedion, in *Ovation* make him a Yorùbá? Does General Buba Marwa's adopting a "Yorùbá" pose in his official portrait after receiving a chieftaincy title from an Igbo community make him Yorùbá? The questions, were they to be posed by earnest readers of this book, would be signs of an unfortunate misreading because they would privilege inscription over commentary in cultural construction. The book launch, for instance, has developed into a new system of inscription spectacle out of the naming ceremony and the panegyric performance. *Ovation* is a new system of inscription that grew out of many such systems, among which the system of praise poems of the eminent (oríkì bòròkìnní) is the most influential. In each instance, the new formation does not name the primary cultural identity of its users. Quoting a Yorùbá proverb does not make a self-identifying Zulu culturally inauthentic. Igbinedion, Marwa, and Kòseemánìí—in the radio program about proverb usage—and Ìsòlá—in the several incarnations of his tragedy about Efúnsetán—are all authoring commentaries with systems of inscription that I have demonstrated derive from Yorùbá historical provenance. It is impossible to construe, for instance, how the peculiar conventions of the two events convened in Professor Fálolá's name in July 2012 could be digested intellectually without considering as critical factors the Yorùbá cultural gestures they quoted and paraphrased repeatedly. But individuals who do not identify as Yorùbá filled both events as participants and watchers. In this book's underlying conception of cultural formation, one need not speak Yorùbá or act as Yorùbá in everyday circumstances, all the time, in order to participate in the institution of Yorùbá-derived ways of being in the world.

Today at wedding ceremonies all over the globe, when either the groom or the bride self-identifies as Yorùbá, many times it is the extended family that so identifies, not the primary characters. A "traditional" Yorùbá engagement drama is usually staged one day before the "nontraditional" event, either at a church service, at a *nikah* led by an imam in a mosque, or at a civil ceremony led by a justice of the peace. At the "engagement," which actually revolves around the formal, public introduction of the two families to one another and the presentation of gifts and a symbolic trousseau from the groom, the Yorùbá group, whether of the groom or of the bride, almost always suits everybody up in the fabric or color, or both, they have selected for the day. This is done without regard for race, color, ethnicity, or tribe. I have witnessed families of Yorùbá brides deck out their non-Yorùbá son-in-law and their families in Yorùbá outfits for the engagement. I have also seen families of Yorùbá grooms do the same to the families of their daughter-in-law. Many times, the concerned party in the marrying couple identifies as Yorùbá only in his or her last names. It is not uncommon that the scripted exchanges during the formal introductions are conducted entirely in English, even within Yorùbá sections of Nigeria. Both the non-Yorùbá who play along and the English-speaking Yorùbá who supervises the exchange recognize the fleeting and contingent nature of the cultural affirmations they are staging. Both groups will inhabit their non-Yorùbá cultural being as the occasion requires. Three elements are involved here in the engagement: play (eré), orderly intricacies (ètò), and timeliness (àsìkò). However, none of these principles is exclusively Yorùbá. What the production affirms as such are the time-based (occasion-based) deployments of diverse inscription systems of fashion, language, familial relations, socioeconomic status, and municipal laws.

Many self-identifying Yorùbá to whom authentic cultural being encompasses only premodern, ostensibly pristine sensibilities might argue that the practices I have grouped together as Yorùbá in the last four chapters of this book, as well as the approach adopted for analyzing the truly Yorùbá forms in the divination and proverb usage chapters, are no more than contemporary deviations (àṣà ìwòyí) that are insufficiently Yorùbá. In this book, I have presented evidence and arguments to the effect that the allegedly authentic forms—newborn naming ceremonies, highbrow panegyrics, divination inscriptions and narratives, and wise sayings—that anthropology and ethnography invoke to demarcate Yorùbá being ought to be read as instituted, commentary making, culture forming, inscriptions. As I noted in chapter 1, Ọ̀rúnmìlà—the first Ifá divination priest—told his community, when he disappeared into a palm tree and occulted the wisdom of his divination writing system into palm nuts, that "Ẹni tẹ́ ẹ bá rí lẹ ẹ́ ma pè ní baba" (Whosoever you see is the one you refer to as father). In other words, even the titular figure in traditionalist constructions of being Yorùbá instructed his followers to notch being onto contingent, creative interpretations of the inscription before them. He also admonished those mourning his physical disappearance to not fall into melancholia, or unresolved mourning, because, as I have argued, cultural being subsists on subjecting inscriptions to the interest of commentary. The entity or practice that attains cultural prominence (àṣà) is that which has withstood the test of interest-driven intertextual machinations.

Notes

1. For patterns in Yorùbá naming traditions, see Adeoye, *Orúkọ Yorùbá*. For naming ceremonies, see Ilesanmi, "Naming Ceremony among the Yorùbá," and Akinyemi, "Integrating Culture and Second Language Teaching."

2. Examples include Wale Ademoyega's *Why We Struck*, Alexander Madiebo's *Nigerian Revolution and the Biafran War*, Benjamin Adekunle's *Nigeria Biafra War Letters*, and James Oluleye's *Military Leadership in Nigeria*. Elected leaders who preceded the soldiers in power—Nnamdi Azikiwe (*My Odyssey*), Obafemi Awolowo (*Awo*), and Ahmadu Bello (*My Life*)—also wrote about their rise to prominence.

3. Monumental self-praise in contemporary southwestern Nigeria attained epic dimensions at the launching of Olusegun Obasanjo's presidential library in May 2005. In October 2008, Kúnlé Ajíbádé, executive editor of the *News*, a prominent weekly news magazine in Lagos, filed a lawsuit demanding that the library be declared public property and not a private venture, because Nigerian laws prevent incumbent office holders from using public funds, under the guise of philanthropic donations, for private gain.

4. Announcements of the third meeting left out the full reference of the acronym.

5. The heated controversy generated by presentations made at the launch of Olusegun Obasanjo's *My Command* in 1980 shows that book-centered events in southwestern Nigeria used not to be the placid affairs they are now. It is difficult to imagine how the contemporary

form can generate the testy, but very productive, debates that occurred at the public forum on Oyin Ogunba's book on Wole Soyinka's theater, *Movement of Transition*, at the University of Ìbàdàn in 1978. For Obasanjo, see Abolaji, "An Appraisal of Readers' Comments"; for the Ogunba controversy, see Osofisan, "For Oyin Ogunba."

6. For canonical accounts of beliefs about orí, see Abimbola, *Ifá: An Exposition of Ifá Literary Corpus*, 113–149.

7. I was the featured reviewer at the launch of a two-disc set of Yorùbá songs, "Odù Orin Fún Ọmọlúàbí tí ó Tún Ara Rẹ̀ Bí," in Lagos on April 24, 2014.

8. Given the subject of this conclusion, it ought to be remarked that "Aṣíwájú" (literally, "Vanguard" or "Standard Bearer") and "Àrẹ̀mọ" ("First Son") are descriptive honorary chieftaincy titles which, through constant usage, have gained descriptive first-name and earned praise-name status in public references to these former governors in Yorùbá-speaking regions of Nigeria.

Bibliography

Abimbola, Wande. *Ifá: An Exposition of Ifá Literary Corpus*. Ibadan: Oxford University Press, 1976.

———. *Ifá Divination Poetry*. New York: Nok, 1977.

———. *Ìjìnlẹ̀ Ohùn Ẹnu Ifá: Apá Kinní*. Glasgow: William Collins, 1968.

———. *Ìjìnlẹ̀ Ohùn Ẹnu Ifá, Apá Kejì: Àwọn Ifá Ńláńlà*. Glasgow: William Collins, 1969.

Abiodun, Rowland. "Understanding Yoruba Art and Aesthetics." *African Arts* 27, no. 3 (1994): 68–78, 102.

———. "Woman in Yoruba Religious Images." *African Languages and Cultures* 2, no. 1 (1989): 1–18.

Abolaji, Joshua A. "An Appraisal of Readers' Comments on Olusegun Obasanjo's *My Command: An Account of the Nigerian Civil War, 1967–1970*." *Journal of Research in Peace, Gender and Development* 1, no. 9 (October 2011): 242–248.

Abraham, R. C. *Dictionary of Modern Yoruba*. London: University of London Press, 1958.

Addison, Graeme. "Drum Beat: An Examination of *Drum*." *Creative Camera* 235–236 (July–August 1984): 1462–1465.

Adebajo, Sola. "The First Yoruba Novel: Segilola . . . Analysis of Content and Form." *Savanna* 13 (June 1992): 39–46.

Adéẹ̀kọ́, Adélékè. *Proverbs, Textuality, and Nativism in African Literature*. Gainesville: University Press of Florida, 1998.

———. Review of "Odù Orin Fún Ọmọlúàbí tí ó Tún Ara Rẹ̀ Bí." Naijatowncrier, May 22, 2014. http://naijatowncrier.com/odu-orin-fun-o%CC%A3mo%CC%A3luabi-ati -o%CC%A3mo%CC%A3-ti-o-tun-ara-re%CC%A3-bi-adeleke-adee%CC%A3ko% CC%A3/.

———. *The Slave's Rebellion: Fiction, History, Orature*. Bloomington: Indiana University Press, 2005.

Adeoye, C. L. *Orúkọ Yorùbá*. Ibadan: Oxford University Press, 1972.

Adeyemi, Lere. "Representation of Gender in Fiction: A Reading of the Novels of Fagunwa." *US-China Foreign Language* 8 (November 2010): 97–106.

Akinnaso, F. Niyi. "On the Similarities between Spoken and Written Language." *Language and Speech* 28, no. 4 (1985): 323–359.

Akinyele, I. B. *Iwe Itan Ibadan ati Die Ninu Awon Ilu Agbegbe Re bi Iwo, Oshogbo, ati Ikirun*. 3rd ed. Exeter: James Townsend & Sons, 1951.

Akinyemi, Akintunde. "Integrating Culture and Second Language Teaching through Yorùbá Personal Names." *Modern Language Journal* 89, no. 1 (2005): 115–126.

Alao, Akin. "Professor Toyin Omoyeni Falola." In *2012: Adegoke Adelabu Memorial Lecture, Education for Self-Employment*, 7–14. Ibadan: University Press, 2012.

Animasaun, Kola Muslim. *1 Thousand 9Hundred and Thirty9: An Autobiography*. Lagos: Telletes Consulting, 2012.

———. *The Voice of Reason 2, the Obasanjo Years: The Best of His Journalism.* Lagos: Telletes Consulting, 2012.

Anonymous. *Flash Afrique: Photography from West Africa.* Zurich: Steidl, 2002.

Apter, Andrew. "On Imperial Spectacle: The Dialectics of Seeing in Colonial Nigeria." *Comparative Studies in Society and History* 44, no. 3 (2002): 564–596.

———. "Yoruba Ethnogenesis from Within." *Comparative Studies in Society and History* 55, no. 2 (2013): 356–387.

Arewa, E. Ojo, and Alan Dundes. "Proverbs and the Ethnography of Speaking Folklore." *American Anthropologist* 66, no. 2, pt. 2 (December 1964): 70–85.

Austin, Hal. "The Launch of *Root.*" *Creative Camera* 235–236 (July–August 1984): 1473–1475.

Austin, J. L. *How to Do Things with Words.* Ed. J. O. Urmson and Marian Sbisà. Cambridge, MA: Harvard University Press, 1962.

Awe, Bolanle. "Iyalode Efunsetan Aniwura (Owner of Gold)." In *Nigerian Women in Historical Perspective*, ed. Bolanle Awe, 55–71. Ibadan: Sankore & Bookcraft, 1992.

———. "The Iyalode in the Traditional Yoruba Political System." In *Sexual Stratification: A Cross-Cultural View*, ed. Alice Schlegel, 144–160. New York: Columbia University Press, 1977.

Babalọlá, Adébóyè. *Àwọn Oríkì Bọ̀rọ̀kìnní.* London: Hodder & Stoughton, 1975.

Bakare, Kunle. "At Home in London with Ovation's Publisher Dele Momodu." *Encomium Special*, December 2002: 60–64.

Bal, Mieke. "The Narrating and the Focalizing: A Theory of the Agents in Narrative." *Style* 17, no. 2 (Spring 1983): 234–269.

———. *Narratology: Introduction to the Theory of Narrative.* 2nd ed. Toronto: University of Toronto Press, 1997.

Bámgbóṣé, Ayọ̀. *The Novels of D. O. Fagunwa.* Benin City: Ethiope, 1974.

———, ed. *Yorùbá Metalanguage (Èdè Ìperí Yorùbá).* Ibadan: University Press, 1992.

Barber, Karin. "Discursive Strategies in the Texts of Ifá and in the 'Holy Book of Odù' of the African Church of Ọ̀rúnmìlà." In *Self Assertion and Brokerage: Early Cultural Nationalism in West Africa*, ed. P. F. De Moraes and Karin Barber, 196–224. Birmingham: Center for West African Studies, University of Birmingham, 1990.

———. *Print Culture and the First Yoruba Novel: I. B. Thomas's "Life Story of Me, Ṣẹgilọla" and Other Texts.* Boston: Brill, 2012.

———. "Quotation in the Constitution of Yorùbá Oral Texts." *Research in African Literatures* 30, no. 2 (Summer 1999): 17–41.

———. "Yoruba Oríkì and Deconstructive Criticism." *Research in African Literatures* 15, no. 4 (1984): 497–518.

Barthes, Roland. *Camera Lucida: Reflections on Photography.* Trans. Richard Howard. New York: Hill and Wang, 1980.

Bascom, William. *Ifa Divination: Communication between Gods and Men in West Africa.* Bloomington: Indiana University Press, 1969.

———. "Odu Ifa: The Order of the Figures of Ifa." *Bulletin de l'Institut Français d'Afrique Noire* 23, no. 3/4 (1961): 676–682.

Batchen, Geoffrey. *Burning with Desire: The Conception of Photography.* Cambridge, MA: MIT Press, 1997.

Belting, Hans. "Image, Medium, Body: A New Approach to Iconology." *Critical Inquiry* 31 (2005): 302–319.

Boadi, L. A. "The Abstractness of Formulaic Expressions in Traditional Oral Poetry." *Paideuma* 36 (1990): 5–11.

Boadi, Lawrence A. "The Language of the Proverb in Akan." In *African Folklore*, ed. Richard Dorson, 183–191. Bloomington: Indiana University Press, 1972.

Bowen, T. J. *Central Africa: Adventures and Missionary Labors in Several Countries in the Interior of Africa from 1849 to 1856*. Charleston, SC: Southern Baptist Publication Society, 1857.

Chief Commander Ebenezer Obey and His International Brothers. "Ko Sogbon Te Le Da." In *The Horse, the Man and His Son* (WAPS 98). Lagos: Decca Records, 1973.

Church Missionary Society. *Dictionary of the Yoruba Language*. Lagos: Church Missionary Society, 1913.

Delano, Oloye Isaac O. *Atúmọ̀ Èdè Yorùbá*. London: Oxford University Press, 1958.

Denzer, Laray. *The Iyalode in Ibadan Politics and Society, c. 1850–1997*. Ibadan: Humanities Research Center, 1998.

Derrida, Jacques. "Limited Inc abc . . ." *Glyph* 2 (1977): 162–254.

——. *Of Grammatology*. Trans. Gayatri Chakravorty Spivak. Baltimore, MD: Johns Hopkins University Press, 1976.

——. "Signature Event Context." In *Margins of Philosophy*, trans. Alan Bass, 307–330. Chicago: University of Chicago Press, 1982.

——. *Specters of Marx: The State of the Debt, the Work of Mourning, and the New International*. Trans. Peggy Kamuf. New York: Routledge, 1994.

Diawara, Manthia. "The Sixties in Bamako: Malick Sidibé and James Brown." In *Malick Sidibé: Photographs*, ed. André Magnin, 8–22. Gothenburg: Hasselblad Center, 2004.

——. "The Song of the Griot." *Transition* 74 (1997): 16–30.

——. "Talk of the Town." *Artforum* 36, no. 6 (February 1998): 64–71.

Drewal, Henry John H. "Pageantry and Power in Yoruba Costuming." In *The Fabrics of Culture: The Anthropology of Clothing and Adornment*, ed. Justine M. Cordwell and Ronald R. Schwarz, 189–230. The Hague: Mouton, 1979.

Drewal, Margaret T. *Yoruba Ritual: Performers, Play, Agency*. Indianapolis: Indiana University Press, 1992.

Eades, J. S. *The Yoruba Today*. Cambridge: Cambridge University Press, 1980.

Ellis, A.B. *The Yoruba-Speaking Peoples of the Slave Coast of West Africa*. London: Chapman & Hall, 1894.

Enwezor, Okwui. "A Critical Presence: *Drum* Magazine in Context." In *In/Sight: African Photographers, 1940 to the Present*, ed. Clare Bell, Okwui Enwezor, Danielle Tilkin, and Octavio Zaya, 179–191. New York: Guggenheim Museum, 1996.

Enwezor, Okwui, and Octavio Zaya. "Colonial Imaginary,Tropes of Disruption: History, Culture, and Representation in the Works of African Photographers." In *In/Sight: African Photographers, 1940 to the Present*, ed. Clare Bell, Okwui Enwezor, Danielle Tilkin, and Octavio Zaya, 17–47. New York: Guggenheim Museum, 1996.

Epega, Afolabi A. *Ifa: The Ancient Wisdom*. New York: Imole Oluwa Institute, 1987.

Epega, Afolabi A., and Philip J. Neimark. *The Sacred Ifa Oracle*. San Francisco: HarperSanFrancisco, 1995.

Fágúnwà, D. O. *Adiitu Olodumare*. Edinburgh: Thomas Nelson, 1961.

——. *An Expedition to the Mountain of Thought*. Trans. Dapo Adeniyi. Ile-Ife: Obafemi Awolowo University Press, 1994.

——. *The Forest of a Thousand Daemons*. Trans. Wole Soyinka. Edinburgh: Thomas Nelson, 1968.

——. *Igbo Olodumare*. Edinburgh: Thomas Nelson, 1949.

——. *In the Forest of Olodumare*. Trans. Wole Soyinka. Ibadan: Nelson, 2010.

——. *Ireke Onibudo*. Edinburgh: Thomas Nelson, 1949.

——. *Irinkerindo Ninu Igbo Elegbeje*. Edinburgh: Thomas Nelson, 1954.

——. *The Mysteries of God*. Trans. Olu Obafemi. Ibadan: Nelson, 2012.

——. *Ògbójú Ọdẹ Nínú Igbó Irúnmalẹ̀*. Edinburgh: Thomas Nelson, 1939.

Fálẹ́yẹ, Adéọlá. "Ìbàdàn Ọmọ Ajòrosùn." Audio CD, 2012.

Falola, Toyin. "Education for Self-Employment." *In 2012: Adegoke Adelabu Memorial Lecture, Education for Self-Employment*, 19–69. Ibadan: University Press, 2012.

——. *Ìbàdàn: Foundation, Growth, and Change, 1830–1930*. Ibadan: Bookcraft, 2012.

Fleming, Tyler, and Toyin Falola. "Africa's Media Empire: *Drum*'s Expansion to Nigeria." *History in Africa* 32 (2005): 133–164.

Foucault, Michel. "What Is an Author?" In *Textual Strategies: Perspectives in Poststructuralist Criticism*, ed. Josué V. Harari, 141–160. Ithaca, NY: Cornell University Press, 1979.

Fried, Michael. "Barthes's Punctum." *Critical Inquiry* 31 (2005): 539–574.

George, Olakunle. *Relocating Agency: Modernity and African Letters*. Albany: State University of New York Press, 2003.

Gisters. "Dele Momodu (Bob Dee)." Gisters.com. Lagos. Retrieved July 11, 2004.

Goody, Jack. *The Domestication of the Savage Mind*. Cambridge: Cambridge University Press, 1977.

Goody, Jack, and Ian Watt. "The Consequences of Literacy." *Comparative Studies in Society and History* 5, no. 3 (April 1963): 304–345.

Gusdorf, Georges. "Conditions and Limits of Autobiography." In *Autobiography: Essays Theoretical and Critical*, ed. James Olney, 28–48. Princeton, NJ: Princeton University Press, 1980.

Hallen, Barry. *African Philosophy: Analytical Approach*. Trenton, NJ: Africa World Press, 2006.

——. *The Good, the Bad, and the Beautiful: Discourse about Values in Yoruba Culture*. Bloomington: Indiana University Press, 2000.

Hallen, Barry, and J. O. Sodipo. *Knowledge, Belief, and Witchcraft*. London: Ethnografika, 1986.

Hinderer, Anna. *Seventeen Years in the Yoruba Country: Memorials of Anna Hinderer*. 3rd ed. London: Seeley, Jackson, and Halliday, 1873.

Ibadan Foundation. *2012 Adegoke Adelabu Memorial Lecture: Education for Self-Employment*. Ibadan: University Press, 2012.

Ilesanmi, T. M. "Naming Ceremony among the Yorùbá." *Oríta: Ibadan Journal of Religious Studies* 14, no. 2 (1982): 108–119.

——. *Yorùbá Orature and Literature: A Cultural Analysis*. Ile-Ife: Obafemi Awolowo University Press, 2004.

Irele, Abiola. "The African Imagination." *Research in African Literatures* 21, no. 1 (Spring 1990): 49–67.

———. "Tradition and the Yoruba Writer: D. O. Fagunwa, Amos Tutuola and Wole Soyinka." *Odu*, n.s., 11 (January 1975): 75–100.

Isola, Akinwumi. "The African Writer's Tongue." *Research in African Literatures* 23, no. 1 (Spring 1992): 17–26.

———. *Ẹfúnṣetán Aníwúrà: Iyálódé Ìbàdàn*. Ibadan: Oxford University Press, 1970.

———. *Efunsetan Aniwura*. DVD. Directed by Akínwùmí Isola and Kelani Tunde. Ibadan: Golden Link Productions & Communications, 2005.

———. *Ẹfúnṣetán Aníwúrà, Ìyálóde Ìbàdàn and Tinúubú, Ìyálóde Ẹ̀gbá: Two Yorùbá Historical Dramas*. Trans. Pamela J. Olubunmi Smith. Trenton, NJ: Africa World Press, 2005.

———. *Two Contemporary African Plays*. Trans. Niyi Oladeji. Dubuque, IA: Kendall/Hunt, 1991.

———. *Une Sombre Destinée*. Trans. Michka Sachnine. Paris: Éditions Karhala, 2003.

Jeyifo, Biodun. *The Yoruba Popular Travelling Theatre of Nigeria*. Lagos: Nigeria Magazine, 1984.

Johnson, James. *Yoruba Heathenism*. Exeter: James Townsend and Son, 1899.

Johnson, Rev. Samuel. *The History of the Yorùbás*. 1921. Reprint, Lagos: CMS Bookshops, 1997.

Julien, Eileen. *African Novels and the Question of Orality*. Bloomington: Indiana University Press, 1992.

King Sunny Ade and His African Beats. "Funfun Niyi Eyin," In *E je N Logba Ara Mi* (SALPS 23). Lagos: Sunny Alade Records, 1983.

Kòṣémánìí, Ṣùpọ̀, Alàgbà. *Òwe àti Àṣàyàn Ọ̀rọ̀ Yorùbá*. Ibadan: Vantage, 1987.

Lamunierè, Michelle, ed. *You Look Beautiful Like That: The Portrait Photographs of Seydou Keita and Malick Sidibé*. Cambridge, MA: Harvard University Museums, 2001.

LaPin, Deirdre A. "Story, Medium and Masque: The Idea and Art of Yorùbá Storytelling." PhD diss., University of Wisconsin–Madison, 1977.

Law, Robin. "A West African Cavalry State: The Kingdom of Oyo." *Journal of African History* 16, no. 1 (1975): 1–15.

Lawal, Babatunde. "Àwòrán: Representing the Self and Its Metaphysical Other in Yorùbá Art." *Art Bulletin* 83, no. 3 (2001): 498–526.

Lijadu, E. M. *Ifá: Imọlẹ Rẹ ti i Ṣe Ipilẹ Isin ni Ilẹ Yoruba*. 1898. Reprint, Ado-Ekiti: Omolayo Standard Press, 1972.

———. *Ọrûnmla Nipa*. 1908. Reprint, Ado-Ekiti: Omolayo Standard Press, 1972.

Lindfors, Bernth. "Form, Theme, and Style in the Narratives of D. O. Fagunwa." *International Fiction Review* 6, no. 1 (1979): 11–16.

Lindfors, Bernth, and Oyekan Owomoyela. *Yorùbá Proverbs: Translation and Annotation*. Athens: Center for International Studies, Ohio University, 1973.

Magnin, André. "Introduction." In *Seydou Keita: Texts by André Magnin and Youssouf Tata Cissé*, ed. André Magnin, 7–17. Zurich: Scalo, 1997.

Magnin, André, and Malick Sidibé. "In My Life, as in Photography, I Have Told the Truth and I Have Given My All." In *Malick Sidibé—Photographs*, ed. André Magnin, 75–81. Gothenburg: Hasselblad Center, 2004.

Miller, Christopher. "Orality through Literacy: Mande Verbal Art after the Letter." *Southern Review* 23, no. 1 (January 1987): 84–105.

Miller, J. Hillis. *Speech Acts in Literature*. Stanford, CA: Stanford University Press, 2001.

Norrick, Neal R. *How Proverbs Mean: Semantic Studies in English Proverbs*. Berlin: Mouton, 1985.

Nzegwu, Nkiru Uwechia. *Family Matters: Feminist Concepts in African Philosophy of Culture*. Albany: State University of New York Press, 2006.

Obiechina, Emmanuel. *Language and Theme: Essays on African Literature*. Washington, DC: Howard University Press, 1990.

Odhiambo, Tom. "Inventing Africa in the Twentieth Century: Cultural Imagination, Politics and Transnationalism in *Drum* Magazine." *African Studies* 65, no. 2 (2006): 157–174.

Odumosu, Ajayi. *Iwe Egbogi Iwosan Fun Gbogbo Arun*. n.d.

Oguibe, Olu. "Photography and the Substance of the Image." In *In/sight: African Photographers, 1940 to the Present*, ed. Clare Bell, Okwui Enwezor, Danielle Tilkin, and Octavio Zaya, 231–250. New York: Guggenheim Museum, 1996.

Ogunba, Oyin. *The Movement of Transition: A Study of the Plays of Wole Soyinka*. Ibadan: Ibadan University Press, 1975.

Ogundipe-Leslie, Omolara. "The Poetics of Fiction by Yoruba Writers: The Case of *Ogboju Ode Ninu Igbo Irunmale* by D. O. Fagunwa." *Odu* 16 (July 1977): 85–96.

Ogundiran, Akin. "Book Review: Toyin Falola, Ibadan: Foundation, Growth, and Change, 1830–1960" In *2012: Adegoke Adelabu Memorial Lecture, Education for Self-Employment*, 71–77. Ibadan: University Press, 2012.

Ogunleye, Foluke. "A Male-Centric Modification of History: *Efunsetan Aniwura* Revisited." *History in Africa* 31 (2004): 303–318.

Ogunsina, Bisi. *The Development of the Yoruba Novel*. Ibadan: Gospel Faith Mission Press, 1992.

Ojeikhere, J. D. 'Okhai. *Photographs*. Zurich: Scalo, 2000.

Ojoade, J. O. "African Proverbs on Proverbs." *Folklore Forum* 10, no. 3 (1977): 20–23.

———. "African Sexual Proverbs: Some Yorùbá Examples." *Folklore* 94, no. 2 (1983): 201–213.

———. "Proverbial Evidences of African Legal Customs." *International Folklore Review* 6 (1988): 26–38.

Okediji, Moyo. "Semioptics of Anamnesia: Yoruba Images in the Works of Jeff Donaldson, Howardena Pindell, and Muneer Bahauddeen." PhD diss., University of Wisconsin–Madison, 1995.

Òkédìjí, Oladejo. *Ṛẹ́rẹ́ún*. Ibadan: Onibonoje Press, 1973.

Okpewho, Isidore. *Myth in Africa*. Cambridge: Cambridge University Press, 1983.

Olabimtan, Afolabi. "Religion as Theme in Fagunwa's Novels." *Odu*, n.s., 11 (January 1975): 101–114.

Olajubu, Oyeronke. "Seeing through a Woman's Eye: Yorùbá Religious Tradition and Gender Relations." *Journal of Feminist Studies in Religion* 20, no. 1 (Spring 2004): 41–60.

Ọlatunji, Ọlatunde. *Features of Yorùbá Oral Poetry*. Ibadan: University Press, 1984.

Oliver de Coque and His Expo 76 Ogene Super Sound of Africa. "People's Club of Nigeria." In *I Salute Africa* (ORPS 126). Lagos: Olumo Records, 1982.

Ologbondiyan, Kola. "Momodu's Loud Ovation in Ghana." http://www.thisdayonline .com/archive/2003/11/29/20031129plu02.htm. Accessed June 1, 2005.

Olupona, Jacob K. *City of 201 Gods: Ile-Ife in Time, Space, and the Imagination.* Berkeley: University of California Press, 2011.

Ong, Walter J. *Orality and Literacy: The Technologizing of the Word.* London: Methuen, 1982.

Osman, Colin. "*Drum*: An Introduction." *Creative Camera* 235–236 (July–August 1984): 1438–1441.

Osofisan, Femi. "For Oyin Ogunba: An Incantation." In *Ìbà: Essays on African Literature in Honour of Oyin Ogunba*, ed. Wole Ogundele and Gbemisola Adeoti, 1–7. Ilé-Ifè: Obafemi Awolowo University Press, 2003.

Owomoyela, Oyekan. *The African Difference: Discourses on Africanity and the Relativity of Cultures.* Johannesburg: University of Witwatersrand Press, 1996.

———. *A Kii: Yorùbá Proscriptive and Prescriptive Proverbs.* Lanham, MD: University Press of America, 1988.

———. "Proverbs: Exploration of an African Philosophy of Social Communication." *Ba Shiru* 2, no. 1 (1984): 3–16.

———. "The Sociology of Sex and Crudity in Yorùbá Proverbs." *Proverbium* 20 (1972): 751–758.

———. *Yoruba Proverbs.* Lincoln: University of Nebraska Press, 2005.

———. *Yoruba Trickster Tales.* Lincoln: University of Nebraska Press, 1997.

Oyètádé, Akíntúndé B. "Body Beautification." In *Understanding Yoruba Life and Culture*, ed. Nike S. Lawal, Matthew N. O. Sadiku, and P. Ade Dopamu, 389–308. Trenton, NJ: Africa World Press, 2004.

Oyěwùmí, Oyèrónkẹ́. *The Invention of Women: Making an African Sense of Western Gender Discourses.* Minneapolis: University of Minnesota Press, 1997.

Pankhurst, Richard. "The Political Image: The Impact of the Camera in an Ancient Independent African State." In *Anthropology and Photography*, ed. Elizabeth Edwards, 234–241. New Haven, CT: Yale University Press, 1992.

Peel, J. D. Y. *Ijeshas and Nigerians: The Incorporation of a Yoruba Kingdom, 1890s–1970s.* Cambridge: Cambridge University Press, 1983.

———. "*Olaju*, A Yoruba Concept of Development." *Journal of Development Studies* 14, no. 2 (1978): 139–165.

———. "The Past in the Ijesha Present." *Man*, n.s., 19, no. 1 (March 1984): 111–132.

———. "The Pastor and the Babalawo: The Interaction of Religions in Nineteenth Century Yorubaland." *Africa* 60, no. 3 (1990): 338–369.

———. *Religious Encounter and the Making of the Yoruba.* Bloomington: Indiana University Press, 2002.

Pinney, Christopher. "Notes from the Surface of the Image: Photography, Postcolonialism, and Vernacular Modernism." In *Photography's Other Histories*, ed. Christopher Pinney and Nicholas Peterson, 202–220. Durham, NC: Duke University Press, 2003.

Quayson, Ato. *Strategic Transformations in Nigerian Writing: Rev Samuel Johnson, Amos Tutuola, Wole Soyinka, Ben Okri.* Oxford: James Currey, 1997.

Raji-Oyelade, Aderemi. "Postproverbials in Yorùbá Culture: A Playful Blasphemy." *Research in African Literatures* 30, no. 1 (Spring 1999): 74–82.

Roach, Mary Ellen, and Joanne Bubolz Eicher. "The Language of Personal Adornment." In *The Fabrics of Culture: The Anthropology of Clothing and Adornment*, ed. Justine M. Cordwell and Ronald R. Schwarz, 7–21. The Hague: Mouton, 1979.

Rowlands, E. C. "The Illustration of a Yorùbá Proverb." *Folklore Institute Journal* 4, nos. 2–3 (June/December 1967): 250–264.

Samuel, Adekunle Ayeni. "At Home with Dele Momodu." http://www.hiphopworld magazine.com/features.php?detail+53. Accessed June 8, 2005.

Sanborn, Herbert C. "The Function of Clothing and of Bodily Adornment." *American Journal of Psychology* 38, no. 1 (1927): 1–20.

Saro-Wiwa, Zina. "Hello Nigeria! Notes from Director Zina Saro-Wiwa." http:// africanfilmny.org/network/news/Isarowiwa.html. Accessed September 23, 2004.

———. "Nigeria's New Celebrity Class." http://news.bbc.co.uk/go/pr/fr/-/hi/africa /4119365.stm. Accessed June 1, 2005.

Scheub, Harold. "A Review of African Oral Traditions and Literature." *African Studies Review* 28, nos. 2–3 (June/September 1985): 1–72.

Schipper, Mineke. *Beyond the Boundaries: African Literature and Literary Theory.* London: Allison and Busby, 1989.

———. *Never Marry a Woman with Big Feet: Women in Proverbs from around the World.* New Haven, CT: Yale University Press, 2003.

———. *Source of All Evil: African Proverbs and Sayings on Women.* London: Allison and Busby, 1991.

Searle, John R. *Expression and Meaning: Studies in the Theory of Speech Acts.* Cambridge: Cambridge University Press, 1979.

———. "Reiterating the Differences: A Reply to Derrida." *Glyph* 1 (1977): 198–208.

Seitel, Peter. *The Powers of Genre: Interpreting Haya Oral Literature.* New York: Oxford University Press, 1999.

Smith, Pamela J. Olubunmi. "D. O. Fagunwa: The Art of Fabulation and Writing Orality." *Literary Griot* 3, no. 2 (Fall 1991): 1–16.

Sontag, Susan. *On Photography.* New York: Farrar, Straus, and Giroux, 1977.

Soyinka, Wole. *Myth, Literature and the African World.* Cambridge: Cambridge University Press, 1976.

———. *You Must Set Forth at Dawn.* New York: Random House, 2007.

Sprague, Stephen F. "How I See the Yoruba See Themselves." *Studies in the Anthropology of Visual Communication* 5, no. 1 (1978): 9–28.

———. "Yoruba Photography: How the Yoruba See Themselves." *African Arts* 12, no. 1 (1978): 52–59, 107.

Storr, Robert. "Bamako: Full Dress Parade." *Parkett* 49 (1997): 24–32.

Street, Brian V. *Literacy in Theory and Practice.* Cambridge: Cambridge University Press, 1984.

Tagg, John. *The Burden of Representation: Essays on Photographies and Histories.* Minneapolis: University of Minnesota Press, 1993.

Táíwò, Olúfẹ́mi. *How Colonialism Preempted Modernity in Africa.* Bloomington, Indiana University Press, 2010.

Tempels, Placide. *Bantu Philosophy.* Trans. Colin King. Paris: Presence Africaine, 1959.

Trachtenberg, Alan. "Brady's Portraits." *Yale Review* 73, no. 2 (1984): 230–253.

———, ed. *Classic Essays on Photography.* New Haven, CT: Leete's Island Books, 1980.

Ulmer, Gregory. "The Puncept in Grammatology." In *On Puns: the Foundation of Letters*, ed. Jonathan Culler, 164–189. Oxford: Blackwell, 1988.

University Press. *A Dictionary of the Yoruba Language.* Ibadan: University Press, 2001.

Viditz-Ward, Vera. "Alphonso Lisk-Carew: Creole Photographer." *African Arts* 19, no. 1 (1989): 46–51, 88.

———. "Photography in Sierra Leone, 1850–1918." *Africa* 57, no. 4 (1987): 510–518.

Warhol, Robyn R. "How Narration Produces Gender: Femininity as Affect and Effect in Alice Walker's 'The Color Purple.'" *Narrative* 9, no. 2 (May 2001): 182–187.

Wilkinson, Jane. "Between Orality and Writing: *The Forest of a Thousand Daemons* as a Self-Reflexive Text." *Commonwealth* 9, no. 2 (Spring 1987): 41–51.

Yai, Olabiyi. "In Praise of Metonymy: The Concepts of 'Tradition' and 'Creativity' in the Transmission of Yoruba Artistry over Time and Space." *Research in African Literatures* 24, no. 4 (Winter 1993): 29–37.

———. "On Omoralara Ogundipe-Leslie's 'The Poetics of Fiction by Yoruba Writers: The Case of *Ogboju Ode Ninu Igbo Irunmale.*'" *Odu* 18 (July 1978): 120–122.

———. "Wútùwútù Yáákí." *Yoruba: Journal of the Yoruba Studies Association of Nigeria* 2 (1976): 43–58.

Yankah, Kwesi. "Do Proverbs Contradict?" *Folklore Forum* 17, no. 1 (1984): 2–19.

———. "Toward a Performance-Centered Theory of the Proverb." *Critical Arts* 3, no. 1 (1983): 29–43.

Yusuf, Yisa Kehinde. "Countering Misogyny in English Proverbs." *Language, Gender and Sexism* 7, no. 2 (1997): 63–79.

———. "English Imposed Sexism in Yorùbá Language: The Case of 'Baby' and 'Aya.'" *Women and Language* 12, no. 2 (1989): 27–30.

———. "A Semantics Classroom Connection of Connotations, Stereotypes and Misogynous Proverbs." *Proverbium* 18 (2001): 365–374.

Yusuf, Yisa Kehinde, and Joyce T. Methangwane. "The Ethical Value of Women's Speech in Yorùbá Proverbs." *Proverbium* 11 (1994): 283–291.

———. "Proverbs and HIV/AIDS." *Proverbium* 20 (2003): 407–422.

Index

ADÉLÉKÈ ADÉÈKÓ is Humanities Distinguished Professor in the Department of English and the Department of African American and African Studies at The Ohio State University. He is author of *Proverbs, Textuality, and Nativism in African Literature* and *The Slave's Rebellion: Literature, History, Orature* (Indiana University Press).

Lightning Source UK Ltd.
Milton Keynes UK
UKHW021830031020
370837UK00024B/718